WHALE COAST

Jim Dykes

Acknowledgements

I wish to acknowledge the assistance of Dr Helen Hogan and
Dr Harry Evison in some matters Maori, and the staff of
Quoin Press, particularly Susan Young, for much work on the
original manuscript.

Thanks to my wife, Jean and the family for so cheerfully putting up
with me during the researching and writing of this book.

First published 1997
Copyright © 1997 Jim Dykes

ISBN 1-877163-06-6

Published by Quoin Press
P.O. Box 2151, Christchurch, New Zealand
Production and design by Orca Publishing Services Ltd

Printed in Malaysia

CONTENTS

❖ ❖ ❖

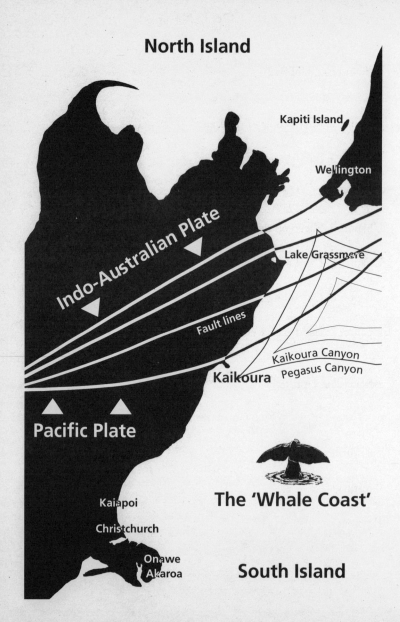

North Island

Kapiti Island

Wellington

Indo-Australian Plate

Lake Grassmere

Fault lines

Kaikoura Canyon

Pegasus Canyon

Kaikoura

Pacific Plate

The 'Whale Coast'

Kaiapoi

Christchurch

Onawe
Akaroa

South Island

Before
Land Uplifted

The wave crouches and hurls itself against the dark crags of the almost submerged reef. From the impact, the white sea spray blots out the coastal hills and mountains.

Along the Whale Coast land and sea have always been in conflict. From at least 150 million years ago, when the flinty sandstones first raised themselves to create land, the sea had been envious, and had attacked the emerging mountains.

When the younger limestones and softer mudstones had emerged, a mere 150 thousand years ago, as the result of successive earthquakes, to form headlands and rounded hills, they also had been savaged by the sea.

In this almost timeless contest, the sea seemed to have the advantage, as the great ocean deeps, in which marine dinosaurs once swam and in which today the sperm whale dives to hunt giant squid, could easily, at any time, have swallowed the land.

But the land continued to emerge – and endured.

There was one positive outcome of this two-way struggle between the land and the Maori sea god, Tangaroa, along this south-east coast of Aotearoa: it provided the energy to sustain abundant sea life, from microscopic plankton to the mighty sperm whale.

The arrival along this coast of humankind, introduced a third protagonist into the coastal conflict.

Chapter 1
First People of the Land

The steep, forested hills immediately behind the Kaikoura coast provided only meagre supplies of food to the early Maori settlers. They had arrived there after being driven to the southern island of Te Wai Pounamu by the more aggressive tribes of the northern island, about the time that Shakespeare was writing. Although bird life was abundant in the bush-covered hills and the big fat kereru and ducks were snared and highly prized as food, it was to the coast and the sea that the Kati Kuru subtribe of Ngai Tahu turned for most of their food. Tribal legend told of hunting the giant moa in the days of the ancestors but except for a few foot-long eggs and some moa bone ornaments, preserved as treasures of the tribe, nothing remained of the moa age, which had reached back another five hundred years before the arrival of the Ngai Tahu. Small birds now provided the flesh for which the tribe hungered. If they were lucky, a captured sea lion pup or a stranded small whale or dolphin would provide real meat, but the staple of their diet was fish. All the Kati Kuri men were expert fishermen who had a great knowledge of the sea and the coast and were cunning in the ways of catching the fish that were so abundant.

Moki had fished all his life. He still remembered the rock pool where, as a very small child, his father showed him the wealth of pool life – opening and closing anemones, limpets that never moved, and slowly crawling snails. Learning their names and habits were his earliest lessons. He could still remember the sunrise-sunset, fish-scale shining colours of the inside of the first paua shell he had seen, which his father had revealed after cutting out the snail. That was the first time he had chewed its black, tough flesh. He remembered how his father had laughed at his blackened lips and his sooty face.

Moki stood now, at nearly low water, with bare toes gripping a ridged band of sandstone on the rock shelf that he had been able to reach by walking waist-deep through the writhing bull kelp.

The sun had only just gone down behind the bush-covered coastal hills at his back and long shadows reached out across the sea which a few minutes before had sparkled under the clearest of blue skies. The blueness was highlighted by the glistening white of the limestone peninsula on which were located the tribe's two pa. In these troubled times of skirmishes between the tribes, when war parties could suddenly appear, Moki preferred to fish within sight of the peninsula and its pa. He shivered as the warm sun no longer penetrated below the surface, which now appeared cold and menacing. The butterfish he had seen, as the kelp drifted apart, lazily flicking their tails as they fed on the barnacles attached to the underside of the kelp, were now lost in darkness. Moki chuckled, 'Well, my friends, if I cannot see you, perhaps you cannot see me.'

However, good as the koeaea was to eat, wrapped in seaweed and cooked under hot coals, he was not after butterfish today. He was brought back to the evening's task by the savage tug on his line.

A big one, for sure, but watch your footing, Moki. The gentle swell, dying waves from a storm in the southern ocean, caused occasional rushes of water and white spume across the rock on which he was standing, but as long as he kept clear of the slippery kelp, which streamed over the jagged rock and back into the cleft into which his line disappeared, he was safe. The kelp reminded Moki of his mother, whose hair would stream behind her as she swam in the sheltered bay below their pa. He thought how remarkably fit she was for her age. She must have come into this world almost forty seasons ago, which made her old, since many in the tribe died before thirty. She was still adept at catching koura in shallow water by feeling for them with her feet and then ducking under water to seize them by their spiny backs, or by diving for them in deeper water. Women had tougher feet anyway, thought Moki. The koura the women caught were cooked in the umu and then the flesh was taken out of the red shell, flattened and, after sun-drying, stored in flax baskets as winter food. The koura Moki was catching, mainly for sport, using the same sort of bob as he used for fresh-water eels, he would eat fresh for his evening meal. He normally shared the fish he caught with his family but tonight this koura was just for him.

Another tug, more insistent this time, brought him back to the task in hand. Give the red one more time to grip the bait, he reminded himself. He had a good hold on the plaited flax line, as thick as his thumb, and its roughness gave it little chance of slipping. Once the bait had been well taken he began to edge the line in slowly. He was using a forked stick, an old friend, as a rod, and drew the line gently through the fork. He knew that the koura seizing the bait of paua (the thick, black foot-part prised out of the single back-shell) would entangle its spiny claws in the scraped flax in which the bait had been wrapped.

As he pulled gently but firmly the crayfish responded by trying to pull backwards into the crevice in which it had lurked ready to seize unwary shellfish from the rocks or floating food on the outgoing tide. Crayfish, as Moki knew, crawled forward slowly but with a flick of their thick tails could shoot backwards, the forward-pointing spines providing streamlining and the claws trailing behind. This one is truly big, thought Moki as he used both hands to coax the crayfish slowly forward. The line was only about five metres long, and as he had won back all but about two metres of it, he reached down to release from under his left foot the flax-rope hand net. If the sun had been on the water the koura would have released the bait and dropped back into the darker water beneath the rock and kelp, but now it resolutely held on to the chance of a meal of paua.

Moki now had to co-ordinate his movements to make sure of his catch. He held the fork of his rod-stick close to the water and, as he raised it gently and sighted a blur of subdued orange and purple in the darkened water that indicated the koura was still greedily hanging on, he slipped the pole-net under it. In one sweeping motion of rod-stick and pole-net the violently flapping koura was lifted from the water. The tail that now clap-clapped so frantically had been the koura's downfall because as it had sighted the light of the early evening sky and Moki's silhouette it had flipped backwards – into the net. Moki looked up towards the stars of the Southern Cross and said his prayer of thanks to ocean-god, Tangaroa.

The tide was now noticeably on the turn and the rock platform on which Moki stood was submerged, and the higher seventh wave was coming up to his knees. He shook the big crayfish into his flax basket, hung it round his neck and backed carefully off the rock into the bull kelp, which writhed uncomfortably around his chest, and pushed through it to the clearer shallow water of the stony beach.

He bent to retrieve his flax and feather cloak which he had shed before fishing, but in the half-dark he grasped a bunch of slithery seaweed. 'Ugh,' he grunted, 'that might have been Maui himself,' as he flung it back on the stones and the kelp flies settled back. Moki mused: this might have been the very beach on which Maui's exploits began. (Maui, aborted by his earth mother and cast into the sea, had been washed up, entangled in seaweed and left to the flies and gulls before Rangi had reached down and taken him up into the sky where he was nursed back to life.)

As Moki trudged along the beach towards the barely discernable limestone cliffs of the peninsula and the warmth of the family's whare he remembered the many times he had heard his father reciting the stories of Maui, as they sat around the hot stones. The last glowing coals of the manuka branches lit up the old man's face and the blue-black spirals of his moko, as he told of Maui having to use his own blood to bait his magic hook. Well, thought Moki, it must have been true because Maui stood here to fish up Te Ika a Maui, the North Island.

By some trick of light, possibly the sun shining through a gap in the inland mountains, the limestone glowed more brightly gold than a newly opened kowhai flower. Moki stopped in his climb up the steep cliff leading to the pa, raised his arms above his head and addressed the peninsula on which stood his pa, 'You, Te Ahi Kaikoura, are not afraid to stand against Tangaroa and you had the mana and strength to support Maui when he pulled Te Ika a Maui out of the ocean – continue to protect my people while I am away.'

The next morning he would leave in his canoe for the south on an urgent and special mission to the pa tuwatawata at Kaiapoi of the paramount chief Te Mai to whom his local chief of Kaikoura owed allegiance.

Moki reached the village gates just as they were being closed by the night sentry. The sentry's call from the lookout tower echoed off the cliffs across the bay at the foot of the peninsula and into the night:

Tenei te pa   This is the fort
A, tenei te pa   Yes, this is the fort!

Tenei te pa tuwatawata	This is the fort with the high palisades
Te aka i houhia	Bound with the forest vines
O ko roto, ko au e…	And here within am I…

The long drawn-out 'e' hung in the air and then slowly merged with the sound of the waves on the beach below.

The next morning, well before sunrise, Moki and five other warriors strode out of the main gate. The night sentry farewelled them with a plea to Tangaroa to protect them, and they descended the cliff track to their fishing canoe. It was a puny craft compared to the great war canoes drawn up on the beach, which needed sixty to eighty warriors to paddle them.

Moki's subtribe possessed a number of fishing canoes like this one, but only three war waka. Two were very old but the third he, as a boy, had seen constructed. Moki remembered well the upset it had caused in their family life during its three years of construction. As the fishing canoe was pushed down the beach into a still sea and as they jumped on board and began to paddle out from the shore, Moki recalled the far-off happy days of his boyhood when the canoe had been built. He remembered having to be particularly careful as all manner of new restrictions applied during the building of the great waka. The totara tree from which the canoe would be fashioned had been selected by Moki's great-grandfather three generations before as being straight and large enough and worthy of becoming a waka taua. The felling of the tree had been a happy time in Moki's boyhood, if somewhat of a strain on his mother, camping out from the pa.

As he struck his paddle into the gentle swell from the south and their canoe rose and thrust forward, Moki could see the palisades and high food-houses of the pa above the white cliffs of Kaikoura peninsula. Paddling with a powerful rhythm that they could keep up all day, they would soon be at the great trading pa of Kaiapoi but they would pull in to shore and camp the first night of the two-day journey. None of them was happy to be paddling in the dark. After a short canoe chant to set up their rhythm to adapt to the changed set of the sea on the southern side of the peninsula, they paddled on in silence and as their main pa on the top of the peninsula dropped out of sight, Moki's thoughts once again turned to the time of the making of the great war canoe.

 No doubt their chief would have been guided by the advice of the tohunga that the auspices were right for the building of a mighty war canoe, and this was clearly demonstrated by the abundance of food, but there was always the fear that war parties would come raiding from the north. Te Wai Pounamu was so much richer than the North Island and the treasures of pounamu that had given the South Island its name were known by the envious chiefs of the north to be richly abundant in pa such as Kaikoura and particularly Kaiapoi, which was the largest trading village in New Zealand for greenstone. It had regular contacts with the West Coast tribes where the stone was found in their swift-flowing rivers. Moki was leading a trading party with offers of food to the Kaiapoi subtribes of Ngai Tahu in exchange for greenstone but, more importantly, and unknown to the warrior crew of the canoe, he had been secretly charged by his chief to take particular note of the much-admired defences of the Kaiapoi pa, which had recently been further strengthened to withstand musket attack. The earth walls that enclosed the cliff-top pa of Niho Niho at Kaikoura had been recently added to on their inner side to withstand musket fire but Rerewhaka, chief of Moki's subtribe, thought further improvements could be made. Some slaves who had escaped from Rauparaha's Ngati Toa tribe, which had moved south to Kapiti Island and launched attacks from there on tribes in the northern part of the South Island, had been afforded refuge at Kaikoura. They had described, in wide-eyed terror, the muskets that the fighting chief of the Ngati Toa used to defeat all who opposed him. Trickery was also an important part of Te Rauparaha's strategy.

As Moki and his fellow warriors paddled south on their peaceful mission, to the north, at the Wairau River, only a day's paddling by war canoe from Moki's village, Te Rauparaha had landed with a strong war party. He said he had come to assist the local tribe against Moki's Kaikoura people, as he had received secret information that their chief, Rerewhaka, was planning an attack. Rauparaha's war party were received as allies and under Rauparaha's direction the local warriors turned out with their ko to strengthen their defensive trenches in expectation of an attack from the Kaikoura tribe. When these were deemed deep enough by Rauparaha, who was supervising the strengthening work, he gave his men the signal and they quickly dispatched the digging warriors, clubbing them to fall into the trenches they had just dug. Those remaining in the pa paid the price of the gullibility of their chiefs, with either their lives or the loss of their freedom.

On hearing of Te Rauparaha's treachery, Rerewhaka had become very angry. It was not until some years later that Moki learned the full story from his wife, Moana, who recalled that night in the chief's house vividly. Rerewhaka was related to the Wairau chief and had been sitting around the central fire chatting with his family when one of the warrior sentries had dragged in a Wairau survivor. Although he had had an ear ripped off by a glancing blow from a patu, he had been able to run off in the uproar, slide one of the small fishing boats into the water and make his escape. After hearing his account, Rerewhaka sprang to his feet in a terrible rage. Grasping his patu and striking it into his palm, he began to call down a terrible curse on Te Rauparaha. He promised Te Rauparaha that if he ventured further south he would rip open his stomach with a barracouta's tooth aha and proceeded to demonstrate this with his patu. Moana thought that if she had been chief, rather than just a woman, she too would want to strengthen the pa's defences, but the magical and terrifying 'fire-spears' perhaps could be best combated by the special powers of the tohunga, for mortal man with traditional weapons could not stop Te Rauparaha's raiding parties. As the Kaikoura men paddled south they had no idea that he, with one of his war parties, was so close.

Moki certainly had fears concerning the ambitions of Te Rauparaha but he was lulled into a pleasant feeling of contentment by the cadence of the dipping paddles and his thoughts again turned to his boyhood and the building of the big war canoe. It was a time of peace with only vague rumours of battles in the far north, so they were building it mainly to add to the mana of their chief and the tribe.

Food had been plentiful at that time. Crayfish practically caught themselves. Each evening Moki would toss several basket traps, baited with fish heads and paua and weighted with stones, into the deep pools behind the rock stacks. He would retrieve them in the early morning and be rewarded with an entertainment that caused him to shout in glee as he dragged up the baskets and red, flapping tails and silver droplets of sea water glistened in the sun rising out of the sea.

The felling of the great totara provided entertainment on a grander scale. Moki used to watch the tohunga going out from the village most days to supervise the work because Tu, the god of war, would exact a terrible price if the tapu relating to things of war was not respected. He made sure that the workers were given their food away from the canoe tree, that the tapu women were cooking it correctly, that wood chips were left where they fell and not used in the cooking fires, and so on. To Moki it had all been a great and frightening mystery although later his grandfather had explained what was happening at the tree site. The tohunga would also bless the adzes, some of which had been in the tribe for generations, so they did not break or lose their edge. On the day the leader of the tree-fellers judged the tree to be ready to fall, the tohunga was again present. Moki should not have been there but, hidden in the ferns, making sure he was on the opposite side to the scarf so the tree would fall away from him, he was lucky enough to see the giant tree slowly lean forward, like a wounded warrior, as the final axe cuts were made. The men, uphill from Moki's hiding place, pulled on the ropes attached to the upper branches. With slow dignity, the giant tree crashed through the undergrowth. Moki remembered birds flapping away in all directions, and the tree finally settling with a 'thump' that shook the ground under Moki's feet and the tree fern he was embracing.

E! kua hinga a Tane   O! Tane, God of the Forest, has fallen

The tohunga was again present when the first boat builder climbed on top and started to chip with his adze. Moki had not seen this but his father had told him and kept the family informed of progress on the canoe. His father, Moki knew, was more a fisherman – although primarily a warrior – but in this time of comparative peace, when the decision had been made to construct the war canoe he had been asked to assist as he had had experience in making smaller fishing boats. He certainly wasn't entitled to wear the beautiful moko of the chief boat builder. The graceful swirls on forehead and chin, which Moki so much admired, proclaimed to those able to read the moko that he was a master carver and, moreover, from the lines above the signature of his nose pattern, that he was also a commander of the tribal warriors.

As Moki paddled steadily the sun rose burning gold and long

reflections were cast across the crests of the gentle swell. The paddlers welcomed the warmth which took the chill off the early morning air. Meanwhile, only seventy-five kilometres north of Moki's pa, Te Rauparaha was preparing his warriors for the attack south. Moki, unsuspecting and untroubled in his thoughts, continued paddling and returned to the recollections of his boyhood.

He remembered that it had been many moons later that the village men and boys again assembled in the valley to drag the canoe to the beach. Moki had not been one of the many hundred men and older boys who had helped pull on the ropes as he and his father had the important task of picking up the slippery skid logs that the canoe-tree travelled along, after the major obstructions from the valley floor had been cleared, down to the beach. The skid logs emerged from the rear as the canoe-tree was inched down the valley, and Moki would seize one and stumble with it down to the front end to be relaid. In overall control of the operation was the most senior tohunga, his long white hair contrasting starkly with his face almost totally blackened by the intricate spirals of his face moko. Moki's father had explained to him that the tohunga's moko, among other things, indicated that he had first been a carving tohunga. He had been stark naked except for a small apron of fresh leaves and Moki remembered being most impressed, and frightened, by the way he leaped about emphasising his directions by flourishing his greenstone mere, one of the great treasures of the tribe.

At the steepest parts of the valley, one, or both, of the stern ropes would be taken back and passed around a tree and used to ease the canoe down the difficult part. Moki soon picked up the words of the canoe-hauling chant and as the leader sang: 'Ka tangi te kiwi,' he joined in the chorus, 'kiwi'. And so on through the forest birds – moho, tieke – with the leader at regular intervals coming in with injunctions to keep the ropes tight.

It was not until the winter of the third year after the great totara had been felled that it reached the sea. There was no hurry as the wood was allowed to dry out slowly and mature. This made it easier to hollow out by adze and fire. Moki's father was often away in the bush at this time as the waka was shaped. On another memorable day, with every canoe assembled, the waka, now recognisably a canoe but without raoa, stern decorations or figurehead, was towed across the wide bay to the sheltered waters of the beach beneath the cliffs

Thinking of the past, thought Moki, helps break the monotony of paddling a canoe over a long distance but it doesn't do much for my aching muscles – and we've hardly started. Meanwhile, to the north, the high stern posts of Te Rauparaha's war canoes had already been decorated with the heads of the senior chiefs of Wairau and food had been loaded on the accompanying fishing canoes. Te Rauparaha joked with his nephew Te Rangihaeata that they should not need food for their warriors as Kaikoura was famed for its crayfish and a surprise attack on the Ngai Tahu pa would assuredly be successful so that they would soon also be feasting on human flesh.

 Moki, without checking his paddle stroke, looked shoreward. This part of the coast had seen many bloody conflicts between his people and earlier Ngati Mamoe inhabitants. Moki recalled the story of his great ancestor Rakai who had tricked the Ngati Mamoe. The remains of their hill pa with its broken palisades and trenches, could be discerned through the early morning mist rising above the bounding river. Moki chuckled as he noticed the seals, which had been catching some of the early morning sun on the rocks, slide into the water as their canoe approached, and roll with flippers waving in the surging kelp. They reminded him of the ruse his great ancestor had used to lure his enemies out of their hill pa. Before first light he had put on two feather cloaks and, concealing his patu beneath them, went to the shingle beach below the hill pa and threw himself into the waves to be rolled back and forth. The sentinels at the hill pa, as the sun rose further, soon noticed this object and the cry went up, 'He ika moana'. They believed it to be a stranded seal or small whale. The gates were opened and the people poured down to the beach. The first warrior to arrive and stoop over Rakai died instantly from a patu blow to the temple, but before the besieging forces could cross the river and profit from this surprise, the defenders quickly rallied and counter-attacked so fiercely that Rakai and his warriors had to flee down the beach towards the safety of their own pa at Kaikoura. But just before they reached it, Rakai rallied his men, turned and killed a leading chief of the Ngati Mamoe. His people halted and, after a brief hand-to-hand encounter and being forced back into the Kowhai river, retreated, never

to bother Moki's people again.

The shingle beach where all this had taken place had now slipped past them as they continued to paddle steadily south. It gave way to the rocky coast so beloved of the seals and crayfish. There would be few safe landing places along this rugged coast until they reached the flatter land where the mighty fortress of Kaiapoi had been built, sited near a swamp to provide additional protection from attack.

Soon they would take advantage of a break in the rocky coastline to stop at the friendly pa at Omihi. As they rose and fell on the gentle north-east swell the promontory just ahead seemed also to be water-borne. Moki signalled the steerer to bring them into the gap where the Omihi stream entered the sea. Legend had it that the valley of this stream had been formed from the blood of ancient warring tribes. As they drew closer Moki could see people scampering for safety into the pa and hear a wooden warning trumpet being sounded. They had obviously had some news of the troubles to the north. As the canoe turned towards the shore, Moki stood up in the bow and waved his paddle in a friendly gesture. His tribe was on good terms with the Omihi people mainly as a result of intermarriage which linked the tribes. Moki, as a boy, had had a minor run-in with local warrior fishermen when he was thought to be pulling up some of their crayfish pots. Moki said he was just interested to see if they had caught anything but this did not impress them and he received a beating and a dunking but was allowed to escape home in his one-man canoe. His chief did not go along with Moki's pleas that an immediate retaliatory war party raid was required to restore his wounded pride.

Riding a wave, they shot into shore through a narrow gap in the rocks and crunched on to the small, stony beach. Moki had been recognised by the sentries and a small group of warriors, fully armed, came out of the main gate. Moki and his crew had already stepped out of the canoe and stood without their weapons and waited nervously for them to challenge and advance. With threat of war in the air, no one took any risks. The tension was broken by a chief of the advancing group calling out to Moki, 'You've come for some of our crayfish, I suppose?' Moki recognised him and replied, 'Not this time, Hiku, but I wouldn't mind some of your dried whitebait.'

As this was just an informal visit there would be no large-scale welcome on the marae but they were taken there when Moki explained he had urgent news to impart to the principal chief concerning Te Rauparaha's northern raids.

The sea mist had dispersed and the morning was now pleasantly warm as they squatted on the marae outside the chief's house. Soon he, the tribe elders and the tohunga had all assembled. With a nod from the chief, one of the women who were permitted to enter the chief's storehouse hurried off and returned with the finest of dried crayfish and whitebait in bark containers that, with another glance from the chief, she placed before Moki and his men. Moki had on previous visits admired the chief's food store. Like theirs at Kaikoura, it was elevated on stilts, but it differed in that the frontal carvings of ancestors were much more elaborate and fine. He particularly liked the whale theme which reached right across the bargeboard and linked the carvings on each side. The woman served Moki some dried crayfish on plaited flax and as he lifted some to his mouth he could not help grinning at Hiku who, as a warrior chief, had joined the group. Moki noted the pattern of his moko change shape as Hiku smiled back.

The chief of Omihi introduced Moki to a young chief about his own age whose moko told him he was the first-born of chiefly rank, his father having been a principal chief, and that he came from the Ngati Ira tribe who occupied the Sounds area in the north of the South Island. His name was Kekerengu and, like so many others in the north, his tribe had been attacked by Te Rauparaha and his father and most of his tribe killed.

After Moki had given the Omihi chiefs the latest news from the north and warned them of how close Te Rauparaha had come, the talk became more general. Moki asked Kekerengu how he had escaped alive from the disaster that had overtaken his tribe as he was seeking all the information he could concerning Te Rauparaha's war strategies.

Unknown to Moki, horror of the most dreadful kind had already been moving to overtake his village. At the very time he had been pushing off from the beach below the pa at Kaikoura, at Wairau to the north Te Rauparaha's war party had set off, in a fleet of nearly thirty canoes.

In response to Moki's question, Kekerengu replied, 'Well, to understand how I came to be in Te Rauparaha's pa on Kapiti Island I need to explain that my mother was a high-born woman of the Ngati Kuia hapu of Pelorus Sound and she married the principal chief of the Ngati Ira who lived on the shores of Raukawa.' As he explained this to Moki his fingers traced on his face the moko pattern that recorded his family history and indicated his rank.

'Now,' Kekerengu continued, 'the wily old dog Te Rauparaha knew that much of the valuable pounamu trade moving from the South Island to the North Island passed through our village and he greatly desired more greenstone. It was easy for him to find a pretext for attacking us. The one he used went back to an incident in which some of his fishermen had approached one of our own fishing parties too closely and words had been exchanged. Because some of them displayed red ochre faces, our people compared them to kumukumu. Since this is not a very good fish for eating, Rauparaha seized on the incident and said they had been insulted and therefore he as paramount chief had cause to exact revenge to restore his mana. It was just an excuse to attack us to secure slaves and greenstone.'

Moki realised that Kekerengu was having difficulty continuing his account, so great was his rage and so deep his grief.

'We had no warning of the attack. A great fleet of twenty or thirty canoes, including some full-sized war canoes that he had captured, you remember, from the unsuccessful combined tribes attack on his stronghold at Kapiti Island, just appeared round the point in the early morning mist. They were on us before we could get the gates closed. There must have been three hundred warriors. I actually saw Rauparaha, that little potiki, wrapped in his war cloak standing near the centre of one of the big war canoes and directing the attack from there. We had no chance as they had many fire-spears and we had only the two that the pakeha who hunt whales had given us. We warriors had only our taiaha and patu. My father was blown apart by the fire-spears, as many of the enemy had pointed their fire-sticks at him as our leader and chief. There would have been little of him left when later they lit the fires of their ovens. For the rest of us, if we had not withdrawn into the pa, we too would have been knocked down by the fire-spears. We fell back to the marae after killing some of the enemy whilst they were feeding their fire-spears. One I killed attempted to use his empty fire-spear like a pouwhenua but against my taiaha he was too slow. It was small utu for the death of my father. We attempted to shield our women and children. I stood beside my mother and younger brother and sister. We were surrounded by Ngati Toa with fire-spears, who goaded us but did not cause their fire-spears to make the deafening noise that caused the terrible wounds. What was the point, they could kill us in their own time.'

Kekerengu was breathing heavily as he continued, 'Then that mad dog Rauparaha pushed through the encircling warriors and stared at us. This was the end; one slight movement of his greenstone mere and we would be dead. My mother, knowing our end was near, had sunk to her knees and was chanting her farewell to the land and sea which had nurtured us so well. At that moment one of Rauparaha's principal chiefs alongside him said something and his mere hand did not move. I learnt later that this chief was Rauparaha's lieutenant, Te Rangihaeata, son of his sister, Waitohi, and one of the fiercest of Rauparaha's fighting chiefs. They spoke together, with Rangihaeata seeming to point at me, but only later did I realise that it was my mother they were speaking about. Then Rauparaha gave the signal, but not for our death. We were pushed against the inside of the palisade and told to sit down. Our hands were then tied behind our backs and like that we spent the night. More than enough of our tribe had been slaughtered in the battle to fill the ovens that had now been lit up. I could only wish I too had been killed rather than being captured to become a slave, or food at some later time. It was not until the next morning, quite late, when Rangi-haeata himself came to inspect his captives and spoke almost kindly to my mother that I began to supect why we had been spared. He said that he had been touched by her lament and had prevailed on Rauparaha to allow him to claim her as a wife. I learned later when I was taken back to their pa at Kapiti that he had done the same thing for a chieftainess of the Ngati Apa tribe on a previous raiding party. He explained to my mother that she would not be a slave as Rauparaha had assumed the powers of the chief of the defeated tribe. He further tried to console her by saying as a chieftainess she would be tapu until after a period of mourning for my father. He then had my mother and some of the other women released so they could obtain water for us as we'd had neither food nor drink since before the battle of the previous day. He must have seen the fury in my eyes. Although I had no weapon I would still have thrown myself at him. They did not untie the warriors.'

Moki was interested in Te Rauparaha's stronghold fortifications on Kapiti Island. Not that it was likely they would be able to attack it as its island location gave it an initial advantage, but who better than Te Rauparaha to devise defences against the new fire-spears that he had been able to obtain so readily from the pakeha traders for flax and potatoes. Moki was interested to hear Kekerengu's explanation of the complex earth works capable of giving protection from musket fire that had recently been constructed round Te Rauparaha's main fortress on Kapiti. Kekerengu was able to describe them in detail because as a slave he had dug and carried the baskets of earth for their construction.

Daily fearful of his life, and of being consigned to the ovens, Kekerengu after several weeks realised that through his mother's 'marriage' he was now related to Te Rangihaeata whose mana protected him. In fact, after the dreadful return journey to Kapiti lying trussed on the woven floor of one of the larger war canoes, unfed and in great discomfort, life had become almost worth living, although the shame of being a slave was still with him. He had joined Te Rangihaeata's extended family group, including three other wives and their progeny. This had been his downfall because Kekerengu had been attracted to the chief's youngest wife. Whether or not they had shared 'the food of the night' Moki, from Kekerengu's undoubtedly biased account, was unsure. But Kekerengu was particularly handsome, with his hair tied in a tikitiki decorated with feathers, although he would not have been permitted to wear these in captivity, as they indicated his chiefly lineage. The elegantly carved wooden comb thrust into his hair was further indication to Moki that he was something of a dandy. With his impressive facial moko and his one long greenstone ear pendant, Moki thought to himself that few women could resist him, particularly the young junior wife of a chief who spent most of his time away from Kapiti leading Te Rauparaha's war parties. Kekerengu continued with the account of his misfortunes, 'Te Rangihaeata's senior wife took bad stories to him about me and Hine. She accused me of playing my flute to her and using love charms to persuade her to be unfaithful to Rangihaeata.'

'It just wasn't true,' insisted Kekerengu. 'Lies, lies, lies.' The way he tossed his head and smiled caused Moki to believe the account of the senior wife rather than Kekerengu's protestations of innocence. The upshot had been that Kekerengu, rightly fearful for his life and possible discomforts before he died, had, with two other captives, stolen a fishing canoe and headed south to seek refuge with a tribe that would not hand him back to Rangihaeata.

It now occurred to Moki that Kekerengu's inside knowledge of

Rauparaha's plans and strategies would be useful to the Ngai Tahu hapu at Kaiapoi, whom he hoped to reach in a day or two, and his suggestion that Kekerengu accompany him was endorsed by the chief of Omihi. Although invited to stay overnight, and sorely tempted by the thought of further dried crayfish and whitebait, they made their excuses to the Omihi chief and went down to the small beach to launch their canoe. Moki was pleased to see one of the women had placed bark containers of dried food on the floor of their canoe, which would be useful if they encountered head winds and took two days. It was quite proper for them to carry food as this was not a war canoe. If Te Rauparaha was about to go on the rampage again they had little enough time to reach Kaiapoi, warn them and perhaps enlist help.

How little time Moki and his crew had, they did not realise. By the time they paddled out from the beach and headed into the wind which, unfortunately, was blowing up from the south and was already ruffling the sea into whitecaps, Te Rauparaha's fleet of war canoes was coming from the north and before nightfall would land and camp close enough to the Kaikoura pa to reach it for an attack at dawn. No one at Kaikoura believed that Te Rauparaha would have the temerity to venture further south than Wairau.

There was no hope. The last musket had been discharged. Hand-to-hand fighting was no doubt still going on but the beach had become a killing field. Moana had escaped the horror of the beach after she had scrambled up the secret path to the top of the limestone cliffs. She heard the shouts of the warriors. The screams of the women and the crying of the children, people of her iwi, rose like a lament above the regular cadence of the surf and the sounds of death on the beach. Indeed a song of mourning for my people, she thought as, oblivious to the sharp flakes of limestone under her bare feet, she ascended the little-used track and emerged on the flat top of the peninsula. She skirted the palisades of the pa and entered through the small back gate.

The women had already started the welcome and the first of the large waka had swept towards the beach before Moana had realised this was a war party. For the welcomers in the water it had already been too late. Unarmed, they had been easy targets. A warrior chief, Te Rauparaha himself, armed with his favourite taiaha had sprung from the leading canoe and with left and right strokes killed four people. They had been the 'first fish' and her people fled like herrings before a barracouta.

The other waka had swept in and turned side-on to the beach and the rowers had reached for the muskets that had been concealed on the woven floor gratings. They had raised them over their heads, stocks uppermost, like two-handed clubs, shook them and, uttering a blood-freezing shout, they had turned their muskets on the Kaikoura welcoming party. Moana had escaped from the mêlée on the beach, having recognised from their moko, particularly the pattern of the black lines of tattooing on either side of their noses, that these were Ngati Toa – foes not friends.

Moana had already turned towards the safety offered by the cliffs and fortified pa before the clap of thunder of over a hundred muskets slaughtered the welcomers on the beach. Those who had gone out into the water to welcome the visitors were dead before they heard the shots that struck them. Most of those nearest the beach, warriors, women and children, were knocked back as if struck by a great wind, and either lay dead where they had fallen in the gentle surf or, rose on their knees only to be given the death blow from musket butt or axe, as the enemy warriors, shouting fiercely, splashed to the shore. The sea changed colour as it does when the tiny red crayfish-like whale-feed abundant along the coast endeavour to climb over each other's backs to leave the sea to escape the fierce predators attacking them from the depths. Like them, the Kaikoura people further up the beach turned, stumbled into each other and fled for their lives, for they knew Te Rauparaha and his war party would spare none of them. The few unwounded Kaikoura warriors ran for their weapons.

When the flotilla of canoes had first been sighted, just offshore in the morning mist, by early risers from the pa, the cry had gone up, 'they are here', as the tribe was expecting a related tribal group from the south. Moana had placed her best cape around her shoulders, not because it was cold but in respect for their guests, as she would be leading the women in the welcoming songs. Hone, when he heard the visitors had arrived, wanted to go down to the beach but Moana had sent him with a message to the slave women who would be preparing food for the guests. The standing of a tribe and its chief rested very much on its ability to provide generously for visitors.

As Moana fled from the carnage through the small side gate she looked past the huts in the centre of the pa across to the main entrance. The main gates were open and undefended. It seemed no time, yet also an age, since she had left the protection of the palisades earlier in the morning. Sun and tide had barely had time to move since they had issued out of the pa to greet the visitors from the north and her people's songs of welcome became their cries of death. The undefended gates and fighting platforms, which would have allowed the warriors to have withstood a siege of months, were now grim monuments to the terrible fate her tribe would suffer. Warriors with hastily snatched weapons were rushing through the gates, too late to close them now with half the tribe on the beach. Among the warriors rushing headlong was Hone, warrior-naked and clasping his father's old taiaha in one hand and a bone patu in the other, having guessed, from the progression of the sounds, the nature of the tragedy being enacted on the beach. Moana knew that her people had little hope. She had heard of the terrible power of the muskets, the 'fire-spears', and the fighting power of Te Rauparaha's war parties. The entire pa possessed but two ancient flintlock muskets. Her men would fight bravely but some of their best warriors, including her husband, had gone south with the trading party. The others would have little chance with their taiaha and patu against the muskets of the raiders.

'Quick, come with me,' she gasped as she took the patu from Hone. The admonition that children do not touch their father's weapons died unspoken on her lips. She thrust him towards the largest house of the pa, that of her father, the chief, with its richly carved face-boards of ancestors. The beautiful red-painted bargeboards, ending in three fingers, which seemed to enfold and protect the outside porch, glowed as if on fire as they faced the rising sun. Would they see another sunrise, or would the sacred carvings this night be put to fire and light up the sky, she thought. She drew in her breath, and the bright morning light caused her to screw up her eyes as she paused, raised her head, and looked up to Rangi in the sky and prayed for her husband and her son. She ducked her head under the carvings and slid open the small wooden door. They stepped into the sunless interior.

Moana steadied herself against the central post in the meeting house, carved to honour her most illustrious ancestor, Te Rakai, and felt her heart pounding. Not for much longer, she thought. She looked up past the curving tongue and shining eyes of the carved figure and could just discern the ridge-pole of the house. Her eyes followed down the line of the rafters. These are the backbone and ribs of my ancestor and I am in his bosom; surely he will protect my son.

After the terror of the beach she was now thinking clearly and calmly. The meeting house will provide no hiding place or safety from those Ngati Toa dogs, they will not respect this place, they will defile it and destroy it. But by the time they come to unleash their devastation on the pa their frenzy of killing may have cooled and my son is young enough perhaps to be spared.

For herself, her fate was sealed: at the least, rape and slavery then, possibly sooner rather than later, the cooking ovens. She would make sure that she did not suffer the earlier indignities, as she was a woman of considerable rank, but over the latter final indignity she had no control. But Hone might be spared, he was young enough. She grasped the patu and was strengthened in her resolve by the smoothness and weight of the whalebone club. She would fight, and to accompany the thought she slipped off her cloak, and placed it round the shoulders of her son. He slipped from under it, tightened his grip of his father's taiaha, brought it into the 'ready' position and through clenched teeth, in true warrior fashion, hissed, 'I will fight with you'.

Moana intended to die as quickly as possible. After all, one patu blow to the side of the head and her soul would leap from Cape Reinga into the afterworld. Let the boy fight with you, she thought. It will be better for him to accompany me. Moki on his return will seek utu for us both. These Ngati Toa will then be food for dogs.

Turning to Hone she said, 'You are as brave as your father, the most courageous of the Ngai Tahu, and we will take some of the Ngati Toa with us. We will show Te Rauparaha how we can fight.' Grasping the patu in her right hand, she started to beat it against her left palm, and as the tempo grew her right heel took up the beat and as she thought of suitable words of hate she started to hum part of the welcoming song with which they were preparing to welcome the visitors:

He tewakawaka ahau na Maui   I am a fantail of Maui

and began to flutter her left hand and raise her patu as she launched
full-throated into a haka of hate:

E hiakai atu ana	How I long to sink my teeth into
ki Rauparaha, ki Nohorua	Rauparaha and Nohoru
Ki te okiokinga o	Dwelling place of those bastards,
te upokokohua nei, o Te Kapiti	Kapiti Island

Hone, by this time, had picked up the rhythm of the haka and his small
foot raised the dust on the meeting house floor as he swept the taiaha
in threatening fashion, point just above the floor, before engaging in
some of the twirls, blocks and sideways sweeps he, with the other boys,
had practised with sticks. As his mother ended the haka with a cry more
of anguish than hate, Hone drove the point of his taiaha under the chin
of his imaginary foe.

But unlike when he had played with the sons of other warriors, the
foes outside were no longer imaginary. The noises of the conflict outside
were coming closer. The occasional musket shot indicated that some
of the Ngati Toa were having time to reload. Moana thought, we might
not die like warriors but be struck down at a distance by magic from
the fire-spears.

Moana motioned to Hone to take up station with his back against
the centre roof pole. She took her stand, patu across her breasts, with
her back to him. Between them and rising to the roof, stood their
ancestor, his patu clasped in his three fingers and looking, as Moana
was, with his unblinking paua eyes at the door through which their
enemies would enter.

Hone looked dismally at the blackened embers and grey ash of last
night's fire and looked longingly upward at the shaft of light that
pierced the roof where a wisp of smoke spiralled out. How he hated
the dark and loved the light. How good it was to leave the dark places
of the forest or the caves where taniwha lurked and emerge into the
sunlight above the bush line. The worst was when the light went out,
when the night fire burned away and the conversation suddenly stopped
because the family could no longer see each other's faces. Would he be
able to tell of his deeds of bravery as his grandfather did when they sat
around the cheerful fire, or would the darkness claim him?

 Moki realised from what Kekerengu had told him that they needed to enlist assistance from their southern Ngai Tahu kinsmen against the threatened invasion by Te Rauparaha as soon as possible. They paddled hard and fast, digging into the rising seas deeply. But the wind from the south-west was increasing by the minute and dark storm clouds were building up in the south. Petrels and other sea birds were flying across their bow seeking shelter on land. Moki did not want to waste precious time by pulling in and seeking shelter on shore. In any case the sea had already been whipped up into white caps as the wind veered further to the south. It would now be almost impossible to make a safe landing along this rocky section of the coast. He decided that they would ride out the storm and he had the anchor stone paid out from the stern by the steersman as the paddlers continued to keep the canoe headed into the storm. Waves were breaking over the bow and some of the paddlers were bailing. Under Moki's direction the crew carefully eased further to the stern. This move and the effect of the sea anchor brought the bow high out of the water. Seas were no longer breaking over the bow. The steersman kept a grip on the heavy four-sided rope to prevent the stone anchor settling on any shallow shelf, but this was hardly necessary here in the hunting ground of the great sperm whales where they dived to black, immeasurable depths seeking their prey.

Moki had many times experienced this sort of storm, to which the coast was very exposed, when he had been far out to sea fishing, particularly for giant hapuku which shared the deepest water with the sperm whales. He knew the storm would quickly blow through to the north. So it proved. Within the hour they had pulled up the sea anchor and were underway again.

The light was starting to fail and although Moki had hoped they might have reached Kaiapoi by nightfall, Kekerengu pointed out that if they arrived after dark the great pa would have all gates secured. If their Kaiapoi kinsmen had heard anything of Te Rauparaha's northern raid they would be unlikely to admit any visitors until morning. They decided therefore to pull in to shore at Motunau where at high tide they could follow a stream inland to a small fishing village of Ngai Tahu kinsmen and sleep overnight. There, they were well looked after and the meal provided for the guests included dried tuna caught locally, which was another favourite of Moki's.

The black shags were still on their branches and the mist on the river when Moki's canoe pulled away the next morning. Little did he realise that at the same time, further north at Kaikoura, the fate of his wife, and his son, had already been decided.

 The small sliding door of the meeting house in which Moana and Hone were now standing back to back against the carved centre post was thrust back with a thud. Screams of agony and grief could now be clearly heard from the marae but from the porch immediately outside the sliding door was silence. Slowly but with great menace, which caused Hone's heart to skip a beat as he looked back over his shoulder at the doorway, the barrels of muskets and the feathered heads of taiaha filled the doorway through which the morning sun shone. Shielded by these weapons, an almost naked figure leaped from the light into the gloom of the meeting house. Others followed as they realised they were not going to be struck down as they entered, and stood silhouetted against the morning light.

The lack of light and the mana of the meeting house caused them to pause but, almost in unison, they sucked in their breath and advanced on the woman proudly holding a whale bone patu and the small boy grasping his father's taiaha. They circled them and with threatening grunts thrust forward musket barrel and taiaha. The woman ignored their feints and continued to hold her patu across her breasts but the boy responded with wild flourishes of his taiaha without moving away from the carving of his ancestor who protected his back. Those of the enemy with muskets seemed loath to use them within the confines of the meeting house or perhaps they had not had time to reload. Perhaps the woman and the boy reminded them of their own families awaiting their return to Kapiti. The futile show of courage merely delayed their deaths. The warriors circled the pair and taunted them as Moana prepared to sell her life as dearly as possible; all she could hope for Hone was that his end would come quickly and before hers. For a moment the morning light streaming through the low and narrow doorway into the room was dimmed as another figure squeezed through, with great difficulty because of his heavy war cloak. The circling warriors froze in their tracks. Te Rauparaha was accompanied by his lieutenant, Te Rangihaeata, and another chief, who scrambled through the doorway, and stood beside him. Te Rauparaha was apparently unarmed but would undoubtedly be grasping his greenstone mere in the hand concealed beneath his cloak. Moana looked straight at him with unflinching eyes. She was a chieftainess, daughter of an ariki and he, Rauparaha, was only a kaitahutahu arikinui. Te Rauparaha shifted his gaze to her son and as he looked back over his shoulder Hone caught the flash of the white feathers Te Rauparaha wore from one ear.

Moana waited for the signal that would send them both to join their ancestors. She saw Te Rauparaha's arm begin to move and he drew out his mere from under his war cloak. Hone could just make out the gleam of the highly polished surface as it caught the glimmer of light coming through the roof hole. Brave as he tried to be, he held his breath as the mere was slowly extended and directed at him. Te Rauparaha spat out an order to the waiting warriors. Hone was too frightened to take it all in, but he heard the words tui, undoubtedly referring to him, and hopu. One of the warriors armed with a taiaha leaped forward, arms extended and the spear along the right arm. With the blade behind his back he advanced with a series of staccato grunts and short, mincing steps. Hone responded, as he had been taught by the toa, with the popotahi, which was the orthodox guard position, with the taiaha held vertically in front of the body. He began to rock right and left and moved his taiaha across his body accordingly, remembering his teacher's instruction to watch his opponent's toes as well as his taiaha. As his opponent also brought his taiaha forward Hone had time to notice that the tongue blade was beautifully carved but was no better than his weapon, which might have been old but was his father's favourite. Moki had taken a club with him but left the taiaha behind since the journey to Kaiapoi was expected to be a friendly visit. The enemy warrior was causing the pigeon feathers tied just below the tongue-blade of his spear to tremble as a distraction. Moana remained as still as a second carving, with her back against the centre post. The slightest movement could distract Hone. He disregarded some minor feints. He knew the first real blow would come when his opponent bunched his toes, which would give away his intention, so that the blow could be parried. Suddenly, it all happened, just as in practice and, almost without thinking, Hone parried the overhead blow. But his opponent was much too shrewd and the survivor of a great many hand-to-hand struggles. Just as Hone was congratulating himself on blocking the stroke his opponent allowed his own taiaha to be knocked from his hands which, with the speed of a barracouta, seized Hone's taiaha. The boy was no match for the strength of the man and his taiaha was ripped out of his hands. Assisted now by his fellows, who had set down their muskets, the warrior held Hone fast. Hone was more angry now than frightened and attempted to bite his captors but with arms pinned behind his back he had little chance and in this position was thrust forward to kneel at the feet of Te Rauparaha. Surely a taniwha has captured me, thought Hone as he looked at Te Rauparaha's left foot and its six toes.

Hone was also ashamed at putting up such a poor fight and now understood Te Rauparaha's words, 'catch the tui' as he himself had many times caught tui by hand early on winter mornings when they were practically frozen on the branches.

Te Rauparaha pulled him up by the hair, a further terrible insult to Hone's already hurt pride, and at the same time raised his mere to strike and looked full at Moana.

'Drop your patu, woman.' The way he said it and the gleam in his eyes gave no cause to misunderstand the alternative. Moana realised that though she might be killed her son might be young enough to be spared. Drawing herself up to her full height, and realising, with the little pleasure her predicament allowed, that she was at least a hand's span taller than Te Rauparaha, she threw her patu down and prepared for death.

It did not come immediately. Te Rauparaha spoke to his lieutenant and departed. Moana closed her eyes but made no futile plea for mercy. She was seized but held only until one of the warriors returned with flax rope to bind their arms behind their backs. They were left alone in the meeting house and, although Moana would have preferred a quick death for herself, she looked up to the paua shell eyes of the carved centre post and gave thanks to her ancestor for protecting her son. The sound of strife outside had ceased except for the occasional outcry of lamentation, sometimes taken up by a number of women, sometimes a single wavering voice, dying away. The horror of what had happened seemed even more monstrous in that it had taken place in full light of day. She recalled that the day had begun beautifully with the sun climbing out of a flat blue sea and only gentle waves breaking over the limestone rock shelves extending from the peninsula. The height of the peninsula should have provided them with protection from that taniwha, that monster, that had arisen out of the ocean to devour them.

Much later, with approaching evening, she heard the cry of 'light up'. The manuka wood had already been stacked in the oven pits and the stones piled above them, and soon she smelled the wonderful aroma of the smoke seeping through the thatched walls. Moana knew from the change in the smell what had followed the stones into the oven pits. As a woman she was forbidden to eat human flesh but she knew its smell. She tried to reassure Hone that they would be safe and that his father would already be returning from the south with kinsmen who would exact utu for what had happened.

In truth she did not believe they would last another day and Te Rauparaha would leave as quickly as he had arrived, richer in food, slaves and greenstone, long before their cousins further south could organise a counter-attack.

 Moki's thoughts at that time were totally focused, not on his home and family, but on the prospect that he was about to enter the great stronghold of his paramount chief at Kaiapoi. Moki had visited the Kaiapoi pa on several earlier occasions on trading ventures for the greenstone, the pounamu, for which the South Island was renowned, but had previously come overland. The sea entrance to the pa, however, was easy to locate as it was quite close to one of the largest rivers that crossed the plain from the main mountain divide. Crossing the bar at low tide was not easy and the paddlers had to use all their skills to counter the current of the great river and the outgoing tide but finally they reached the slower waters of a tributary creek. This led only a little way through a deep swamp to a landing place at the pa itself.

On his first visit here as a boy with his father he had been overawed by the size and strength of the mighty stronghold. According to Ngai

31

Tahu folklore, even Tu could not have scaled the cliffs of its palisades. These comprised a double row, three times the height of a tall man with cross ties of aka. Supporting the walls at intervals were taller totara posts. These were magnificently decorated with carvings of ancestors, painted in red ochre and decorated with paua shell. Since his last visit Moki noticed that the space between the two rows of palisades had been filled with a mixture of sand and flax capable of absorbing musket fire. A trench behind the palisade provided additional cover for the defenders.

This pa, thought Moki, could withstand a siege of months. The swamp, which gave some protection to the pa on three sides, would also provide the defenders with both food and water. There were a great number of food stores throughout the pa, identified by their raised platforms. On one side a gate gave access to a bridge across the swamp. This was guarded by a tall tower from which marksmen could bring down defensive fire.

Moki noticed all these features as their group came through the main gate and he resolved to take this knowledge back to Kaikoura to strengthen their own pa to withstand what he was later to hear the Kaiapoi people refer to as 'pu'. This was a new term to him for the fire-spears and he presumed that they thought that fire-spears looked and sounded like a trumpet. It was in this very pa that, on his second visit, as a young warrior, he had seen a demonstration by the present para-mount chief, Te Mai, of the terrible power of the first fire-spear that had come into the possession of the Ngai Tahu tribe. A subtribe with a fishing village on the deep water harbour of Akaroa had acquired it by trading food with a whaler who had come in for water and shelter. Moki would never forget the demonstration, nor did he ever wish to be near one again when it was discharged. The musket was loaded for the chief by the warrior who had charge of it, who also explained about pointing and firing it. The chief summoned an unsuspecting slave to little more than arm's length away and blew his head off. Moki had been astounded but no more than was Te Mai who stood transfixed, not believing the power he had unleashed. Both realised that it meant the end of the way they, and their ancestors before them, had fought with traditional weapons of bone, stone and wood.

Their reception on the marae on this occasion was not formal as their group was small and Moki was of no great rank. However Te Mai, and most of the fighting chiefs were present as they were eager to hear any fresh news of Te Rauparaha's advance south. Also present was the venerable figure of Te Auta, the high priest of the tribe. When Moki, as a boy, had first seen him he had been absolutely terrified by his imposing appearance and straggling white beard and hair and had hidden behind his father's cloak. That cloak, fine though he had thought it, could not have compared with the one worn today by Te Mai. It was a kahu kura, covered completely with the red feathers from beneath the wings of the kaka parrot. His kuru and the ceremonial mere he carried so proudly were, as was to be expected here, made of pounamu of the first grade.

As they stood with heads bowed, Kekerengu looked sideways, and Moki saw that he was impressed by the mana of the paramount chief. Moki was asked by Te Mai what news he had of Te Rauparaha and Moki explained that Kekerengu had for some time been at Te Rauparaha's stronghold on Kapiti Island. It was while Kekerengu was repeating the information that he had given the Omihi chief that there was a commotion at the side gate and the sentries came running in, half carrying, half dragging a warrior whom Moki instantly recognised as from his own pa. He was in a bad way, his head was gashed, dried blood had closed one eye and he could barely stand.

'Te Rauparaha is at Kaikoura,' was all he was able to get out before he collapsed at Te Mai's feet. Two of his warriors dragged the Kaikoura man to his feet, none too gently.

Te Mai demanded, 'Speak!'

The wounded warrior lifted his head and rolled his eyes. Obviously in great pain, he drew in a laboured breath.

'He has defeated us. All are either dead or captured. Our chief was killed by Te Rauparaha himself. He has 300 warriors with him, slaves to carry food and a fleet of war canoes. He caught us by surprise and many were dead before we could take up our weapons.' And so he continued with the details of the attack. He and two others had only escaped because the day before the attack they had been collecting sea-bird eggs from nests on the cliff face on the east side of the peninsula and, as night had come on, they had left the ropes they were using in place. The next day when the slaughter started they raced from the back gate of the pa to the ropes and let themselves down. They ran headlong, fearing instant pursuit, to a small fishing hamlet where they were able to warn the inhabitants and find a fishing canoe in which they had paddled south. Their terror of what was behind them had overcome their fears of travelling at night and whereas Moki had stopped they had continued and arrived not long after him.

 Meanwhile at Kaikoura, Te Rauparaha, in consultation with his two principal chiefs, Te Peehi and Rangihaeata, decided his war party would march overland to Kaiapoi. The decision was made mainly because although they had captured some large canoes, including the Kaikoura waka, they did not have sufficient canoes to transport the warriors as well as their hundred slaves. Some canoes had also been used to transport captives back to Kapiti. It was some 200 kilometres to Kaiapoi but by forced marching and using the slaves to carry food they could cover the distance in two or three days.

In the cold light of morning Moana and Hone were herded with the rest of the prisoners down to the beach. Moana did not lift her eyes but she heard the crackle of burning thatch and wood and felt the sea breeze blowing towards the flames as she passed through the gate in the palisades. These would be too difficult to burn but the rest of the pa would be razed. Their own mighty waka, which her husband Moki had helped build, and which had featured in so many of the stories told round the meeting house fire, had been pushed out into the sheltered bay and was riding easily in the gentle swell. Moana bit her lip as she saw it now manned by Ngati Toa warriors. Food would not be taken on the war canoes as these were tapu but supplies were being loaded on the other fishing canoes. Moana and Hone, prodded on by taiaha-carrying warriors, waded out waist-deep and were pulled roughly aboard the waka that had been the greatest treasure of their tribe.

Moana was pulled over the side by her hair and this insult was just too much and she kicked at and spat on the warrior endeavouring to push her down on to the matting deck of the canoe. He drew his pakeha steel axe and would have removed her head then and there if a chief from the centre of the boat had not shouted a command that stayed his hand. Moana sank to her knees and moaned her grief and her shoulders shook as she spread her arms to cover Hone. Above her the paddlers were taking up their positions on the cross thwarts, one on each side. Eighty of the Kaikoura men had been needed to man the war waka but now a skeleton crew of Ngati Toa warriors took up the paddles for the long two or three-day open-sea journey back to Kapiti Island. The prisoners lay huddled on the decking along the centre of the boat.

Moana, when she finally raised her head, found they were well underway and the paddlers, after starting with a canoe chant, settled into a silent steady rhythm. She could see down the centre of the canoe and her spirits rose a little when she saw that there were other survivors. As she looked at the sides of the canoe about half a metre above her head she remembered how she had helped her mother and the other women to make the three-plait flax cord with which the top strake had been lashed. Boat building was men's work and for a war canoe there was little that women could be allowed to do without incurring the wrath of Tu. The cord she had helped weave, seemingly so very long ago, had been used by the men to lash on the great carved stern post, standing more than twice the height of a man, and also the shorter but still intricately carved prow. The waka had never sailed in war. Moana remembered it sailing fully manned with paddlers, chiefs, time givers and steersmen, almost a hundred men, across the blue of the bay, the canoe chant echoing from the limestone cliffs below their pa. She reflected on the terrible events of the previous day and thought of the old saying:

Ko Tu ki te awatea,   War in the daylight,
ko tahu ki te po   fire in the evening.

The fighting that Tu had seen the previous day, thought Moana, had taken place in daylight and even on the marae where previously they had welcomed so many in friendship. But she and Hone had been saved in the darkness of the meeting house where even the lighted fire had been out. Their pa would now be ashes. From the happy times of girlhood and marriage, her time of light, she had now entered her time of night. She sobbed and all manner of random thoughts crowded her mind. What had she, or her family, or the tribe, done to have brought the scourge of Te Rauparaha upon them?

The three-day journey was agony for Moana and the other prisoners.

In the calmer seas along the east coast it was bad enough as they were constantly buffeted but across Raukawa strait the paddlers battled steep seas and each wave sent shock waves of pain through Moana. She was desperately seasick but could only dry retch as food had been denied them. At the Wairau River, where they had pulled ashore and camped overnight, the captives, still with hands bound, had been permitted to throw themselves into the river to drink. There two of the few surviving younger warrior captives had made an ineffectual attempt to escape into the kowhai and manuka scrub along the river bank but had been easily captured and lashed to the prow of the war canoe. The next morning Moana and Hone and most of the other prisoners were again hauled aboard the canoe. The two young escapees were left hanging by their wrists from the prow. As heavier seas were encountered the rhythm of the paddling warriors hardly changed but the bow dipped more deeply, spray came over the top strakes, and the cries of the two prisoners dangling from the bow faltered and finally died. Moana had known them both well from boyhood and, as she could no longer hear them, presumed them dead and grieved for them.

Moana never discovered the reason, but most of the paddlers had been blindfolded with leaves of the karaka tree before they had set out to cross Raukawa. They had been assisted out to the canoe by others who had presumably made the crossing before and did not need to wear the blindfold. In spite of her predicament Moana found the sight of grown men groping their way out to the canoe rather ridiculous. The rite was no doubt intended to pacify Tangaroa but Moana thought to herself that they had been singularly unsuccessful, for the waka pitched and yawed in the waves that seemed to come from every direction. The paddler sitting above Moana set down his paddle and once again drew his axe. Moana had not previously seen one as close as this before, as there had been none like it at Kaikoura, but the shape was enough like a stone adze for her to recognise its deadly purpose. Axes were, however, readily available to Te Rauparaha's men from the whalers and trade ships which now called regularly at Kapiti Island. She was so seasick that the axe would have been a merciful release. But the warrior used the blade, which must have been very sharp, to cut her bonds and he kicked her and pointed to the wooden bailer and the gap in the floor matting and told her to bail for all their lives. Moana would have preferred to drown and collapsed on to the deck matting which by this time was awash with sea water. Hone who, except for constant hunger pangs, had suffered little from the journey, since he accompanied his father fishing and was quite at home on the sea, bent forward and thrust his hands backwards to have his bonds cut, shouting through the rising wind, 'I'll bail'. He and many of the others who were fit enough were cut free and bailed furiously until they passed from the south-west storm which was funnelled through Raukawa to the somewhat calmer sea of the west coast of the North Island off which lay their destination, Kapiti Island.

Moana realised that not all of Te Rauparaha's considerable flotilla of war canoes had returned with them to his stronghold. What she did not learn until later was that he had left sixty of his warriors at Kaikoura to guard four hundred captives who would later be brought back to Kapiti as slaves. She had had no idea how much Te Rauparaha was dependent on slave labour at Kapiti until she had been put to work herself as a slave. His own personal household employed over two hundred slaves. To obtain the muskets he so dearly wanted from the whalers and traders, hundreds of other slaves had been put to work scraping flax for fibre and growing potatoes and pigs for the pakeha. Te Rauparaha, Moana was to discover during her captivity on Kapiti, was fast becoming a considerable trader.

What she also did not know was that the main body of his force was carrying on south to 'visit' the main Ngai Tahu fortified pa at Kaiapoi and the paramount chief there. Moki had also set out for Kaiapoi. Had she known of Te Rauparaha's intended 'visit' she would have been most concerned for Moki's safety as Te Rauparaha had been disappointed at how little of the precious greenstone he had found in the Kaikoura pa and was covetous of the great stocks of the precious stone he knew to be held in Kaiapoi, which was the main trading centre for Te Wai Pounamu. If he could not obtain what he wanted by trade then he would undoubtedly resort to trickery and war.

On his approach to the Kaiapoi pa Te Rauparaha realised that the small kainga were all deserted, but it was a normal precaution for the inhabitants to seek refuge in the main pa when a war party was moving through their area. Anyone crossing the path of a war party would be killed as a matter of course. Te Rauparaha did not believe that the Ngai Tahu at Kaiapoi could have been informed yet of the defeat of their

kinsmen at Kaikoura. He pressed on to the main pa. He assumed that the gates would be secured as a normal precaution, and as they approached the pa he saw sentries on the towers. Te Rauparaha signalled for his warriors to sit and in no way to make a warlike display. At the same time Te Peehi, a senior chief, went forward, unarmed, as spokesman. He knew the Ngai Tahu paramount chief very well and his intentions were genuinely peaceful as he had suggested to Te Rauparaha that, as they had plenty of muskets, they could trade them for pounamu. He also knew that they could never take Kaiapoi by force and certainly not in the limited time they had before the local Ngai Tahu learned of the fate of their kinsmen to the north. He called greetings to Te Mai and suggested he might wish to discuss the possibilities of trade with them. Te Rauparaha realised that normally Te Mai would not have ventured from the security of his pa but the possibility of acquiring muskets might tempt him to take a risk. But he certainly would not admit Te Rauparaha and his party into the pa. Te Rauparaha would not even have attempted this sort of approach if he had not been sure that Te Mai's Ngai Tahu had not yet learned of his attack at Kaikoura. Te Rauparaha's generalship had been so successful because he always made sure he acquired full information about his enemy and the terrain they would be fighting on before he launched an attack. At Kaiapoi, being unaware that his potential enemy already knew that he had attacked and defeated their northern kinsmen was to cost him and his war party most dearly.

Te Mai and his chiefs planned to lure Te Rauparaha into a position of false security by agreeing to come out from the pa and discuss trade with him. Te Mai, wearing his magnificent red parrot-feathered cloak, came out through the main gate with an escort of some hundred warriors. One of these was Moki who had begged to be allowed to join the heavily armed escort, as he was hoping for a chance to take utu on Te Rauparaha for what he had done to his people. Those who had escaped had been unable to tell Moki how his immediate family had fared but had seen their chief Rerewhaka struck down by Te Rauparaha just before they had made their escape. Kekerengu wanted to join the bodyguard for the same reason but he might have been recognised and

Te Rauparaha would know that the Kaiapoi tribe had already learned of his treachery towards their northern cousins.

Te Rauparaha had retired his warriors well beyond musket range so that Te Mai and his chiefs would not feel threatened. He with Te Peehi and his nephew Rangihaeata and three other senior chiefs, all unarmed, went forward to greet Te Mai. Te Peehi took the leading role in making the introductions and Moki, who had remained further back with the warrior escort, realised when they squatted down and began to talk, that there would be no fighting that day. Te Mai spoke directly to Te Rauparaha. 'Which way did you travel from the north?' Te Peehi glanced at Te Rauparaha who replied, 'We left our canoes at Wairau pa and came inland.' Te Peehi added, 'We thought the weather might change and it is not a good time of the year to follow the coast.'

Te Mai replied, 'The weather can change very quickly at this time of the year but it is a pity you decided not to travel by canoe as my people at Kaikoura and Omihi would have been honoured to have provided food for you and your party.' His smile twisted as he thought yes, my people there have already provided your warriors with their own kikokiko tangata but you will now pay for this.

Moki had moved far enough forward to have picked up the last exchange and knew that both chiefs were lying but Te Rauparaha was disadvantaged by not knowing that the Ngai Tahu chief knew he lied and so, thought Moki, like a fat pigeon he was about to walk right into a trap.

Te Mai baited his trap by bringing the talk round to pounamu and noted with satisfaction that Te Rauparaha's eyes lit up in his wizened face as he replied, 'Yes, we have come for pounamu and have muskets and powder and shot we will trade for it. We know you have much pounamu but we would be interested only in stone of the highest quality. If we could see some of your best pieces then we could make a generous offer of muskets.' Te Mai seemed to be pondering this suggestion but Moki knew he already had his own plans. Te Mai spoke, 'Why don't you and some of your chiefs come into the pa to inspect our best pieces?'

Oh, no, thought Moki, Te Rauparaha is too wily an old bird to be trapped as easily as that. The poa has been dangled in front of him too obviously. Te Rauparaha hesitated in his refusal of the offer and Te Peehi, who was most anxious that they should trade for pounamu, broke in, 'I could lead a small group, say ten of our chiefs, who could inspect the pounamu and I, who know both the value of the stone and of muskets, could arrange a trade.' This was not the bird that Te Mai was hoping to catch but the fowler cannot always chose which bird will put its head in the noose.

It was soon arranged that Te Peehi would lead a group of senior chiefs, including Te Aratangata, Te Rauparaha's half brother, into the pa the following morning. Te Mai and his escort returned to the pa, Moki fuming that a fight had not started and that Te Rauparaha might escape their utu. Although not informed of Te Mai's intentions, Moki hoped that he would in some way exact payment for Te Rauparaha's treatment of his people at Kaikoura.

At Kaiapoi the next morning, Te Peehi's group entered by the Kaitangata gate. Moki watched them enter the trap with considerable relish. This gate was aptly named 'the eating man', but a tohunga had once told Moki that it referred to the tight way the cat's-eye shellfish sealed its shell.

Whichever the meaning, thought Moki, they will not come out alive! In the open space just inside the gates were the houses of a number of the principal chiefs. These were larger than the simple shelters of the commoners which were located further away and nearer the kitchen shelters. But the structure that held Te Peehi's attention was a larger building, beautifully decorated with red-painted carved facing boards much like a food storehouse but larger and not on stilts. Te Peehi knew it was here that the large blocks of pounamu, brought with great hardship through alpine passes from the far West Coast were stored. Some of the greenstone blocks had been in the possession of the Kaiapoi pa for generations and had gained mystical properties. Some pieces were even known by name.

Chief Te Mai himself met the Ngati Toa delegation and gestured to the greenstone storehouse as they approached it. 'Inspect our treasures. Some we do not wish to trade but for some smaller pieces we would be pleased to hear your offer of muskets.' A Ngai Tahu chief slid across the wooden door and Te Peehi stooped and entered first, followed by his trading party in order of seniority. By the light from the doorway they were able to make out the greenstone arranged on patterned flax mats. Some pieces would have taken a strong man to lift, let alone carry on the many-days' journey from the Arahura river area where it was found, back through the mountains to the east coast.

However most of the treasure was in the form of finished or semi-finished pieces: mere, tiki breast decorations and ear pendants. Te Peehi picked up an adze head piece. As it was of the finest quality, it was obviously intended for a toki pou tangata. He would trade a musket for that piece. A large, partially cut piece of wonderful colour, almost translucent, caught his eye. Te Peehi and his fellow chiefs were so eager to view the pounamu that none of them had noticed that the Ngai Tahu had not followed them into the treasure house.

Moki had not been party to what act of revenge chief Te Mai was planning until he summoned Moki and Kekerengu forward and, gesturing with his mere towards the treasure house, hissed at them, his eyes now blazing with hate, 'The fish are in the trap. You who have lost your families can take the first of them.'

Te Peehi took little interest in Moki as he straightened after coming through the doorway but immediately recognised Kekerengu. Their purpose was not left in any doubt when Moki, bringing his taiaha to his front, proclaimed, 'I am of the hapu of Kaikoura.' Te Peehi immediately realised that Te Rauparaha had miscalculated and their chances of escape were slight.

'Put it down,' ordered Moki. He referred to the block of greenstone, which was known to the local people as 'Kaoreore'. 'That should not be touched by a Ngati Toa dog.'

'A person as badly tattooed as you should not question what I do,' shouted Te Peehi angrily, but at the same time he dropped the greenstone and drew his mere. Kekerengu felled the chief nearest to him with a sideways stroke to the head and Moki struck at Te Peehi who countered with his mere. Moki pulled back and struck upwards with the point of his taiaha under the chest of the chief standing on the other side of the doorway. Kekerengu had already dived back out through the doorway and Moki quickly followed him.

Te Mai appeared leading his warriors, who had been concealed in the sleeping huts, and were now assembling fully armed, and began to stamp a haka of hate:

Kai tataia ki runga ki
te turuturu poto
Kai titiro iho ki te hoa o te kai,
ki a Kaiapoi

Oh that from the short poles on
which they are displayed
They might gaze down on the
ceremonial feast of Kaiapoi.

Te Peehi, hearing these threats, was in no doubt as to their fate. Te Aratangata, who was armed with Te Rauparaha's own mere, which had been thrust on him by Te Rauparaha as they had left to enter the pa, almost as if he had realised treachery was planned, stepped forward. There was little point in their remaining in the greenstone treasure house to be butchered one by one.

'I shall go out first. Follow close behind and make for the nearer gate.'

Shedding his cloak, he dived through the doorway and rolled to avoid the warriors who stood either side of the doorway ready to strike. He sprang to his feet and charged, uttering a war cry, not so much to cow his attackers but in the hope that his Ngati Toa kinsmen outside the walls would hear the commotion and come to their assistance. His surprise attack had allowed him to get close enough to the enemy warriors to be able to jab and parry with his mere without their being able to counter effectively with their taiaha. As he was almost surrounded by his attackers, those with muskets dared not fire. He broke out of the ring of some twenty warriors attacking him and tried to force his way to the gate, but he was struck by at least three spears which slowed his progress. The Ngai Tahu warriors then fell back to clear a field of fire for those with muskets. A ragged volley passed mainly over his head but one shot struck his mere, shattering it so that he was left with only the butt in his hand. He was now defenceless and, as he turned to try to climb over the gate, he was sprung on from behind and another warrior struck him again and again on the head and neck with a long-handled tomahawk.

Moki had a special score to settle with Te Peehi and attempted to engage him but now muskets were being discharged in all directions and those of the pa killed and wounded in the skirmish were victims of the erratic fire of their fellow tribesmen. Before Moki could reach Te Peehi he and the others of his party had been shot down or toma-hawked.

Te Peehi's head was claimed by one warrior. Swinging it above his head by the hair and spraying those about him with gouts of blood, he clambered up on to the fighting platform above the gate and held his bloody trophy high above his head for the Ngati Toa below to see.

Te Rauparaha himself came forward but not close enough to be within easy musket range and shouted, 'Cherish your children now because they will certainly die in the future.'

He quickly withdrew and signalled his chiefs. The one hundred Ngai Tahu captives were without mercy put to the club. This was immediate utu for the death of his senior lieutenant and friend, Te Peehi, and his half-brother and the other chiefs. But Te Rauparaha would not now rest until fuller and more terrible utu had been claimed.

His force immediately set out on the long and hungry march back to their canoes at Kaikoura. On arrival there Te Rauparaha and Rangi-haeata debated long into the night whether the Ngai Tahu captives remaining at Kaikoura should also be killed as further utu for the death of Te Peehi and the other chiefs but Te Rauparaha was finally persuaded by Rangihaeata that they should be spared, not out of any sort of kindness but because they would be more valuable alive as slaves back at Kapiti Island growing potatoes, rearing pigs and preparing flax which could be used to buy even more muskets, which in turn could be used in exacting full utu, payment for the deaths of Te Peehi and the others. Thoughts of revenge were to dominate Te Rauparaha's actions for the next two years and saved the lives of Moana and the other Ngai Tahu captives: they were better left alive to increase Te Rauparaha's stock of muskets to enable him to bring down ultimate vengeance on Te Mai.

As she lay on the woven decking, wet, cold and now hungry as she recovered from the sea-sickness, Moana felt Hone squeeze her hand. She opened her salt-sore eyes and heard Hone whisper, 'We are there.' More used to the motion of a canoe, he had realised that they had reached calmer waters as the canoe had moved into the shelter from the westerly swell provided by Kapiti Island. This had been confirmed when the canoe swung at right angles, probably heading into a beach. Moana remembered the stories she had heard of Te Rauparaha's main pa on Kapiti from those who had been brave, or foolhardy, enough to take greenstone to the north to trade. She knew the island was just off the west coast of Te Ika a Maui and was only a half-day canoe journey from Arapoa in the South Island. This was where, in ancient times, Kupe had slain the giant octopus that had led him on his journey to discover Aotearoa, and where Te Rauparaha's war party and their captives had camped on the second night of their return journey. Moana was reminded of the ancient song that spoke of Kupe having severed the land so that Arapoa and Kapiti islands stood apart from the mainland. They had come the same way back to Kapiti as Kupe in the mists of time.

The two paddlers on the thwart above Moana started to stamp their feet on the floor-deck matting as they took up the words of the haka with which they answered the women who Moana knew would be welcoming them home:

Ka mate, Ka mate!   I die, I die!
Ka ora, Ka ora!   I live, I live!

It was only after she had been living at Kapiti for some time and came to know Te Rauparaha's sister, Waitohi, that she learned that this haka had been composed by Te Rauparaha himself. As they drew even closer to Kapiti the chant changed again.

'E kura wawa wai… i.' The paddles were held just out of the water as the paddlers above her ceased paddling. Moana felt that they must be very close to the landing beach and dreaded the moment she would change from captive to slave. There was some honour in the former, nothing worth living for in the latter. She resolved to seek her death.

'Toro patu tute tata.' The paddles were brought on board and held vertically with a butt just above Moana's face. As she looked along the centre of the boat she could see the blades pointed skyward. She remembered a similar manoeuvre by her own men in this same canoe. They were about to come ashore.

'Taakarara! Taakarara! Taakarara!' The paddlers tapped their paddles three times, once for each word.

As all this was happening Moana realised that the steersman had brought the canoe about so that they would now be stern towards the beach. All she could see was legs stamping in unison with a wild piioi but as she looked through the legs she could see the chiefs standing up near the stern post swinging severed heads. More shouts came from the prow end and she saw some of the warriors there hack off and brandish the heads of her two kinsmen who had been lashed there.

Moana sucked in her breath and thought, better dead than a slave. She, the daughter of a principal chief, and wife of a chief, would now be expected to perform the most menial of tasks; she would now count for less than a commoner.

Along the centre of the canoe there were other captives, mainly women and children, and Moana was glad some had survived Te Rauparaha's onslaught. Moki, her husband, was also still alive, and she knew that he would seek utu for what they, his people, had suffered. She could now do no more for Hone and she must face the long darkness. Remaining in this world was too shameful. Above her on the cross-thwart were the elaborately tattooed buttocks of the Ngati Toa paddler but she chose the nearer target and sank her teeth into the warrior's calf. His cry was louder than the haka he had been chanting. His response as a warrior was, as Moana had hoped, immediate and deadly. He brought the butt-end of his paddle into the side of her face and, as she fell back, reversed the paddle to strike her on the side of the head. She fell on to the deck matting and did not move. The warrior had just bent to inspect the wound in his calf when Hone hit him a glancing blow on the head with the shovel-like wooden bailer. At the same time the canoe came to an abrupt stop as it rode up on to the beach sand. Hone, who had been about to swing the heavy bailer again was caught off balance and landed in a heap across his mother's body. He too would have been dispatched with the canoe paddle but one of the chiefs in the bow had seen the commotion and issued an order that stayed the paddle in full swing. Hone could see the blood oozing from his mother's mouth and trickling through the opening left for bailing into the bilge-water. But, more importantly, he could feel through his body that his mother was still breathing. The warrior paddlers had by now leapt over the side and would no doubt be greeting their families. Hone picked up the bailer again and scooped seawater out of the bilge on to his mother's head. The skin was torn a finger-length and swollen where the paddle had struck. Whether in anger or kindness the blow had been delivered with the flat of the blade and, for whatever reason, this had saved his mother's life. As he poured more sea water on to the wound her eyes opened and she grimaced and slowly attempted to sit up.

They and the other captives were seized and bundled over the side into ankle-deep water where Moana could still have drowned had Hone not picked her up and supported her as they were herded up the beach. As their group stood wet and shivering on the beach they were taunted, reviled and spat upon by the Ngati Toa women. Moana had by now recovered sufficiently to realise where they were and could not stop herself thinking, what have we done to you to deserve this? These women may have lost their men in other encounters but my Ngai Tahu had not fought against them and killed them. That she was wrong in this she did not discover until Te Rauparaha's sister, Waitohi, explained many things about her brother. Apparently shortly after Te Rauparaha had brought his people to Kapiti Island they had been attacked by a combined force of a thousand warriors in a great flotilla of canoes. Some of this confederation had been Ngai Tahu and now they would be made to pay for this. Utu was everything to Te Rauparaha.

They were herded up to the pa and through the narrow winding gate section through a double palisade, something Moana had not seen before, and pushed through the metre-high doorway of a large whare that Moana, even in her shocked state, was surprised to note was on the side wall. Otherwise the hut was much like the sleeping whare of the common people at Kaikoura. She realised with a pang that only the burnt stumps of the walls of her home would now remain. They were crowded inside and they could stand only along the centre in line with the ridge pole. Along the low side walls, fresh bracken fern stalks had been piled for bedding. Moana was able to make out, as her eyes became accustomed to the gloom, that raupo stalks had been used to thatch the roof and fern tree slabs formed the outer walls with earth piled high to keep out the wind and the cold. Moana sank exhausted on to the bracken fern which was at least soft, after the canoe floor anyway, and still springy, and held Hone in her arms, partly for warmth, partly for solace. She began to murmur words of comfort to him and the words became a waiata tangi in which the other women joined, softly, but with great intensity. The singing with its sliding notes and the catches in the voices of the women as they remembered their loved ones, most of whom had perished, would have plucked at any heart. One who heard it was Titimoko, mother of Kekerengu, who had been brought back to Kapiti pa by Te Rangihaeata after her husband had been killed at the sacking of their pa at Pelorus Sound. She shared the grief of the survivors of Kaikoura; none could appreciate their terrible grief more than she. But she too was not much better than a slave and powerless to help. If Te Rauparaha required further utu and decided to send them to the ovens then her influence counted for nothing and even Te Rangihaeata, highly regarded as Te Rauparaha's lieutenant and body guard in battle, could not save them. But one who could also heard the plaintive song of the Kaikoura women. She was Waitohi, Te Rauparaha's elder sister and mother of Te Rangihaeata.

Waitohi resolved to have the women and their children captured in the Kaikoura raid spared. Late in the day, she had come to their hut and stared at the Ngai Tahu captives. She could explain to Te Rauparaha that their pa needed more slaves particularly as so many of the men were away with war parties. But she did nothing to help the captured warriors. They were enemies, had been defeated, and must pay the price. Rerewhaka, chief of Kaikoura had already joined his ancestors. Te Rauparaha himself had, with much relish, told his sister how the Kaikoura chief had died.

Moana and the other captive women were set to work the following morning. Waitohi's intervention with her brother the previous evening had saved their lives.

After being given some fern root to chew and fresh water, Moana and Hone and the other women and children captives set out to dig fern root under the watchful eye of a young warrior armed with one of the new pakeha axes for which he had made a long carved handle. Hone had not thought much of the roasted fern root. He was still chewing it and spitting out the coarse outer skin. To him, it was slaves' food and he complained to his mother that his stomach was still empty. She suggested he help himself from the gourds to more water.

They made several trips for fern root which they dug with a pointed stick. Moana had seen the men of her tribe using the digging stick to plant kumara but it had not been women's work, except for some weeding. Her hands were quickly blistered by the unfamiliar work and were painful when she had to pack the thumb-sized roots into flax baskets. She was also required to plait the baskets, which was a great insult to her skills, as she was a weaver of the first rank and had created magnificent cloaks, some decorated with the green neck feathers of the wood pigeon.

The ferns were slightly different from those she had known in the Kaikoura area but the preparation was much the same. This was slaves' work and it was shameful for her to perform such tasks. The baskets were also heavy to carry although Hone helped her. He seemed to enjoy the work, although he continued to complain of hunger. The fern roots they had gathered were hung up in the food storage hut and they were told by one of the Ngati Toa women, who supervised their work, to bring out some of the already-dried bundles for preparation.

Moana was given the task of pounding the roots on stones then in a wooden bowl using a wooden beater, much like the warrior's patu with which she had defied Te Rauparaha. She gripped the beater and had no trouble conjuring up his wizened face with its moko in the swirling patterns of flour created with each angry blow. She would later make this flour into cakes that were cooked in hot ashes. She had done this before for her own family and she found some comfort in this simple task. The only difference was that this food was for chiefs, and they as slaves would have to make do with chewing on the roots. She did sneak some broken cakes to Hone and he smiled for the first time since that terrible morning when he had been asked to help the women provide food for the 'visitors'.

Visitors, indeed, thought Moana. I wish more of those Ngati Toa dogs had been killed. What chance did our warriors have? I don't think there were more than three muskets in the whole pa. Te Rauparaha boasts he now has over a hundred. At least Moki escaped the attack and might still be safe.

As she continued with her pounding, Moana turned over in her mind the thought of poisoning Te Rauparaha and his family. As a member of the household she had the opportunity. Moana continued pounding the roots in the bowl. I am perhaps lucky, she thought, that because of my rank I am given the easier tasks and am spared the back-breaking work other slaves have to do, such as flax and potato carrying. Some of the older slaves can barely straighten themselves at the end of the day. What has he done to my people? Te Rauparaha deserves to die. He is a monster.

Thump, thump, as she pounded his face. He was obsessed with the need to produce more flax and potatoes so that he could buy more and more muskets. Even a failed attempt at poisoning would earn her the death she preferred to slavery. If she did not soak the karaka fruit long enough, that would do it. Along the Kaikoura coast the karaka grew well and produced prolific crops of large fruit. She remembered how as a little girl she had helped in the preparation of the kernels. The ripe fruits were collected in flax baskets and trodden with bare feet to remove the fleshy outer part. The kernels were cooked in large earth ovens for more than a day and then placed in a stream in fenced enclosures where they were left for the poison to be washed out. If they were not washed would they be poisonous enough to kill? Even better for her purpose though would be the seeds of tutu. Back at Kaikoura they had used the fruit for flavouring but she remembered being warned by the tohunga that the seeds were deadly poisonous. She was interrupted in these thoughts by being summoned to help cook the main meal of the day.

The kitchens for Te Rauparaha's large household and related kinsmen were made of manuka logs and were much grander than the lean-to structures back at Kaikoura that gave only partial shelter to their cooking pits. As cooked food destroyed the tapu of man the kitchens were well away from the main sleeping houses. Moana was required to assist in the preparation of two meals a day, the main meal being in the evening. She had been able to order slaves and commoners to do her family's cooking at Kaikoura but now the roles were reversed. She knew the procedure well enough: branches were piled in the metre-diameter earth pit and special oven stones placed on top. As the wood burned, the stones became heated and sank into the pit. The embers were then raked aside and the stones levelled out. This was hot work in the middle of summer. In the height of winter she and Hone had slept in the cooking-house for warmth. How strange, Moana thought, as the daughter of a chief back at Kaikoura I would not have been permitted to do that, but now I am a slave I have no worth, am of no account, I cannot be touched by these things.

Te Rauparaha arrived unheralded back at Kapiti. Moana was now very much part of his household, but still a slave. She realised by his demeanour that Rauparaha had suffered some sort of reverse since his attack on her people at Kaikoura but it was not until some time later, after she had asked Waitohi, that she learned the full story and the extent of Raha's loss, of Te Peehi in particular, and his burning desire for revenge.

'Te Peehi was one of our greatest warriors,' Waitohi told her, 'and one of our wisest and most respected chiefs. Did you know that from this very beach he swam out to a pakeha ship?' Waitohi chuckled, 'And he would not leave it until they had taken him to the country of the pakeha. At first they treated him badly but during the voyage he saved the captain from drowning and became his friend. In the country of the pakeha he met many great pakeha chiefs who gave him many valuable presents, but not the muskets that he wanted. However he was very clever and after he was brought back here to Kapiti he sailed again to the pakeha settlement in Sydney and exchanged his presents and some tattooed heads for a great number of muskets.

'He had fought alongside Raha in many earlier battles in the north,' Waitohi smiled, 'but of course the muskets were the best gift he could have made to Raha. Now with his death, Raha has every slave that can be spared scraping flax so that he can trade this for even more muskets. When he is ready he will again lead a taua south to sack Kaiapoi pa and to deal with that treacherous dog, Te Mai. He is in no hurry but when his war party again crosses Raukawa and paddles south, your Ngai Tahu people will indeed have cause to mourn.'

Moana wondered whether Moki was still at Kaiapoi and whether he would survive a further attack from Raha when it came. Meanwhile she was kept working far too hard for her to have much time for thoughts of what had been back at her pa. She was fortunate to be under the protection of Waitohi. No attempt was made to give her as a wife to one of the Ngati Toa warriors. She was safe enough from Raha, she thought, as he had his hands more than full with seven wives and, according to Waitohi, could have done with fewer rather than more wives.

 Hone seemed quite at home on Kapiti. He had several friends of his own age among the other captives and wasn't bothered too much by being treated as a slave by the Ngati Toa boys and girls. For most of the time he assisted his mother in fuel and fern gathering and food preparation, His mother was quickly gaining a reputation for her weaving of cloaks but he kept out of the way of this as it was women's work. However there were other activities to interest him. He had always been fascinated by his father's and grandfather's moko and here at Kapiti was a tohunga who was a great expert in tattooing and whose services were much sought after by both warriors and young women. Hone wondered why Te Rauparaha had not had his fine face moko completed. Some of the cheek spirals seemed incomplete, probably, thought Hone, because he could not spare the time as the healing process was quite slow. Hone remembered the story told by his grandfather of the wily chief who sent his tattoo tohunga to visit a rival tribe

and made his services available, as a goodwill gesture, free of charge. This was most generous as payment could be as high as a greenstone mere or ear pendant or decorated spear. A large number of the young warriors availed themselves of this opportunity. Whilst most of them were still recovering from the very painful face wounds the generous donor of the tohunga's services attacked the tribe and inflicted a heavy defeat. Hone liked this story and thought it could well have been one of Te Rauparaha's tricks.

Hone spent much of the little spare time he had watching the tohunga ta moko create some beautiful moko. At Kaikoura it was not the custom for women to wear the lip and chin moko but here it was very popular. One of Te Rauparaha's female servants, a Ngati Toa of good birth, not a slave, had her lower lip blackened and some scrolls tattooed on her chin, a simple design but still very painful. Hone recalled the calming song her friends sang:

Takoto ra e Hine	Lie there, o girl.
Pirori e	Roll on.
kia taia o ngutu	to let your lips be tattooed.
Pirori e	Roll on.

The tohunga used different stone and bone chisels for each stage, Hone liked seeing the design being applied according to the person's rank, position, work, mana and so on. This was done with charcoal and was painless. But when the tohunga took up the chisel and mallet and started to open up the skin and the blood spurted, Hone often shut his eyes. Victims were not permitted to make a sound, though Hone could tell by the way they clenched their hands they were in great pain. Round the eyes on the upper cheek the tohunga put down the wide chisel and used a finer chisel for the tighter spirals, and the in-between decoration. Hone thought the cleverest part was the way the tohunga used tow and mallet in the one hand alternately to strike and mop up blood. The pigment was soot from burnt gum mixed with water in a carved wooden bowl. Between each tap of the mallet the chisel was dipped into the pigment. The serving girl Hone had seen tattooed had hers done in the one sitting, as the design was quite simple, but warriors would need to come back again and again, particularly if they were having buttocks and thighs done as well. Hone would have liked a tattoo but it was obviously very painful. Anyway he was a slave here. Perhaps when they were freed by his father and they returned to Kaikoura, since his father was a chief, he could be tattooed too. However, he thought, being a slave gives me a chance to see some things which would be tapu to a warrior.

There was another very good reason why Hone was not keen to be tattooed. Not only was Te Rauparaha trading flax tow for muskets with the pakeha traders who now called regularly at Kapiti but the traders were increasingly asking for dried heads as curios. Some of the few surviving warriors from his tribe had disappeared in recent weeks, and Hone knew that sometimes they went into the stone ovens but the other captives said that these men had very fine facial moko. Rumour had it that the tohunga was tattooing slaves with impressive but meaningless tattoos and then these heads were removed for trade. No doubt the original owners had not thought much of this idea and Hone also thought it wise to decline any tattooing, even if offered it free.

 The potato harvest was in at Kapiti and the potato pits and food storehouses were full. This was the time of the year, Waitohi told Moana, that the warriors became restless and eager to take part in a taua. The autumn evenings were still mild and Te Rauparaha's household usually remained outside after their evening meal. On one such balmy evening, a clear, dark blue sky, the bush-clad hills behind the pa black-green, the aromatic smoke of manuka wood from the ovens still in the air and only a whisper of waves from the beach, Moana might have been content. But her thoughts were still of Kaikoura and of how her husband fared. After almost two years she still did not know if he was alive or dead.

Just as they were preparing to move from the marae into the meeting house, Te Rauparaha emerged from it followed by his principal chiefs. He wore one of his finest kiwi-feather cloaks and drew it about him and signalled with his greenstone mere for his people to sit. The chiefs gathered behind him, Te Rangihaeata, at his side. Moana realised that he was going to say something of considerable importance.

He began by extolling the virtues of Te Peehi Tame, and reminding his people what a noble chief he had been, the bravest of warriors and how he had spoken to the pakeha on behalf of the tribe. The trade goods they now possessed they owed to him. Particularly muskets, Moana thought to herself. As he launched into his speech, he began to strut. He was so short, thought Moana. He reminded her of the male roosters the pakeha traders had brought. When he recounted the way Te Peehi 'had been foully murdered by that treacherous Ngai Tahu dog Te Mai,' his mere rose and fell as he chopped it into the palm of his other hand to emphasise what he intended would be the fate of Te Mai. Moana was appalled at the plan he outlined.

He proposed bribing one of the traders with a shipload of muka to take 200 warriors by ship to Akaroa. Moana knew the harbour well, it was a twin harbour to Whakaraupo (Lyttelton) with several Ngai Tahu pa and fishing villages around its shores. On arrival Te Rauparaha and his warriors would lie in wait for Te Mai. It was known that the considerable trade in flax fibre of the Kaiapoi tribe was centred on Akaroa and that Te Mai visited there quite regularly to supervise loading. If a trading ship sailed into the harbour he would be drawn there like a bird to the snare. My people there will suspect nothing, thought Moana, certainly not that a pakeha ship in their peaceful harbour conceals 200 enemy warriors. Moana's dismay at this plan was in contrast to the fervour of the Ngati Toa who greeted it with wild cries and quite spontaneously broke into Te Rauparaha's haka: 'Ka mate, ka mate.'

Additional slaves were set to work the next day scraping flax to produce fibre, and canoes were sent across to the coast opposite Kapiti to bring in loads of fresh flax and already scraped fibre. One ton of flax fibre bought one musket.

Moana learned from Waitohi, who may well have suggested the plan to Te Rauparaha, that several pakeha captains had been approached but none had been prepared to hand their ships over to 200 well-armed tribesmen, until Captain Stewart of the brig *Elizabeth*, perhaps not fully realising what he was undertaking or blinded by the gold he could get at Sydney for a shipful of flax, agreed to transport the war party.

It was not until the triumphant war party returned some weeks later that Moana learned of the horrors of the raid. The brig had arrived back off the beach at Kapiti and their victorious return was announced with a salute of cannons from the *Elizabeth* and wild musket fire from the warriors. After landing, a fierce haka was performed and then there was a procession to the place of offerings where some of the baskets containing the remains of her Ngai Tahu people, but the gods please, thought Moana, not Moki, were left to placate the spirit of Te Peehi and the other Ngati Toa killed at Kaiapoi. Moana wept and tore her hair as she saw the baskets of butchered bodies being unloaded from the brig. The warriors, still stark naked, again broke into a haka and circled the new captives who had come ashore from the brig. Practically all the capering warriors held a bayoneted musket, halfway up like a taiaha in one hand, in the other some held heads that they swung at the terrified captives. The warriors were so frenzied that Moana feared for the lives of her people. She had been fully occupied cooking, in the oven pits, nearly a hundred baskets of potatoes and green vegetables and she was relieved afterwards to learn that the captives had not been killed, no doubt on Te Rauparaha's orders, so that they could be used to produce flax fibre for even more muskets. Moana was sickened by the victory feast that followed. What made it so much worse was that the portions of human bodies had been hastily cooked after the massacre at Akaroa but during the return voyage had become putrid. Moana took several days to recover from this experience but she gained grim satisfaction from the large number of warriors who were ill for some time longer after the victory feast.

Waitohi thought that the revenge exacted on the Ngai Tahu chief and his people was fully justified by the treacherous death of Te Peehi. He had obviously been close to Waitohi and Moana wondered how close. Waitohi was rather amused that Moana should be so upset at the fate of her kinspeople. She took malicious pleasure in relating to Moana what had occured at Akaroa after the brig *Elizabeth* had arrived with its murderous crew. Moana was even more convinced that Waitohi herself had hatched the plan.

According to Waitohi, the *Elizabeth* was anchored just off the largest village in Akaroa harbour. A John Cowell who could speak Maori was sent ashore to try to lure chief Te Mai on board but he was not located in the village. On his return to the brig they were hailed by a canoe and John Cowell recognised one of the Maori, although he was well muffled up in a cloak, as Te Mai. He had a distinctive tiki-shaped pattern tattooed on his forehead that Cowell recognised. He told Te Mai his master wanted flax fibre and would pay in muskets and trade goods. Te Mai agreed to come on board. In telling this to Moana, Waitohi could not disguise her contempt for Te Mai in being so stupid, but she also could not conceal her obvious pride in the success of her plan. Te Mai was escorted to the captain's cabin by John Cowell and left there.

Waitohi clapped her hands as she came to this part of her account. 'Then Te Hiko (son of our noble Te Peehi) entered the cabin. He sat for half an hour staring at Te Mai, not saying a word. Then Te Hiko approached him and pulled down Te Mai's lower lip.' Waitohi, as she recounted this, pulled down her own heavily tattooed lower lip, baring her teeth. 'Then he said, "These are the teeth that ate my father."' Waitohi eye's glittered as much at Moana's discomfiture as at her story. She continued, gloating, 'Many of your Ngai Tahu were killed, all who were on the ship, and more when the three villages in the harbour were attacked. Our warriors ate well and brought much kaitangata back with them.' Waitohi did not spare Moana any of the details. Moana did not want to hear more but had to ask, 'What happened to our chief?' Waitohi smiled, 'Oh, he was brought back here alive. His wife Te Whe and his daughter were later enticed out to the big ship and so they were captured too. It was a pity they strangled their own daughter as she may have been spared for one of our chiefs.'

Moana knew the answer to her next question would horrify her but she had to know. 'What happened then?'

'Te Mai and Te Whe were shown to the people here. After what the women who had lost warriors did to her she died fairly quickly, she was lucky. He was taken across the water to Te Peehi's widow and family. They treated him well for almost half a month and then the grief of Te Peehi's widow became too great and she killed him quickly. He was fortunate.'

Moana's grief was great. She had asked Waitohi on many occasions if she had heard anything about Moki. At least, Moana thought, nothing bad has happened to Moki, or Waitohi, with her cruel nature, would have passed it on. The captives from Akaroa, when she was able to speak with them, had heard nothing of Moki either except that he was probably still at Kaiapoi where the pa, as all knew, was unassailable.

Moana wept that night and Hone could not console her. She did not want to upset him further and did not weep again, but something inside her had died. She would never see Moki again and the worst horror of all was that Te Rauparaha had still not exacted all the utu he required for Te Peehi's death. Was there no bottom to the well of his hatred? If he made yet another southern raid it would be against the only pa in the northern part of Te Wai Pounamu he had not sacked – Kaiapoi. And Moki, as far as she knew, if he was still alive, was at Kaiapoi.

Moana, although a slave, was increasingly being regarded as a member of Te Rauparaha's extended family. She had long since given up the idea of poisoning him, though she assuredly wished him dead. Too many others who ate the same food would also die. One would be Te Rauparaha's sister, Waitohi, with whom Moana had developed an understanding. Waitohi hated the Ngai Tahu and Moana despised the Ngati Toa but they nevertheless respected each other.

Moana had noticed that Te Rauparaha had taken to consulting his tohunga every day and together they sought from the atua a favourable time to resume his attack on the Ngai Tahu. Te Rauparaha was obsessed with exacting further utu and Moana knew that it was only a matter of time before some sort of sign would come from the gods for him to lead his taua south again.

It happened just as Moana had feared. One morning out from the beach thirty large war canoes, some with as many as eighty paddler-warriors suddenly appeared from the morning mist. By the time Moana came down to the beach the tohunga had made his invocations to Tu and the women had already sung their sad farewell. For such a large war party some must have come across from the adjacent coast. Before they had started the canoe chant and turned south Moana knew with dread in her heart where they were headed.

It was only later when she had been talking to Waitohi over a late breakfast of fern-root cakes (both Moana and particularly Hone, with a growing boy's appetite, were grateful they now received better than slaves' food) that the reason for the sudden departure of the war flotilla was revealed. Apparently some three nights previously Te Rauparaha had experienced a vision of a great fire and he was visited by the spirit of the dead Te Mai, and also a visible god whose predictions concluded with the words:

| Kia kite koe i | That you may see the fire |
| Ahi i Papa-kura ki Kaiaapohia | On the crimson flat of Kaiaapohia |

Waitohi explained this was too potent an omen to be ignored. Within a few days of the dream Te Rauparaha had gathered almost two thousand warriors, most armed with muskets. Within one day they were across Raukawa and within another were pulling their canoes up on to the beach at Wairau where, after the sacking, Te Rauparaha had set up a supply base. Ngai Tahu who had been spared, worked as slaves and under a small Ngati Toa garrison had built up food supplies for just such a war party stop-over as this.

'They continued south the next day,' Waitohi went on, 'and some canoes landed at Kaikoura to mop up any remnants of the Niho Manga battle, but the few of your Ngai Tahu who had crept back to the pa saw the flotilla of our canoes approaching from the north and fled like frightened pukeko into the flax of the swamp inland of the pa.' The Ngai Tahu at Omihi pa also had no trouble from their hill lookout in sighting the approaching Ngati Toa war party. The mistake they made was in deciding to stay and defend their pa rather than disappearing into the coastal forest.

The construction of their pa offered little protection from the fire-power of several hundred muskets. Amongst the many who died were Kekerengu, who had returned to the pa from Kaiapoi. Captives taken, who ultimately arrived back at Kapiti, told Moana they had fought to the best of their ability with taiaha and mere before being blown apart by the 'fire-spears'. The few survivors were forced to load their own canoes with food supplies and to accompany the main fleet south.

Some more Ngai Tahu were captured at Motunau, where Moki had so enjoyed the local eels, and the flotilla then paddled on until they came to the estuary of a large river where they could beach their craft. Leaving them under guard, they could reach the Kaiapoi pa overland within the hour.

Their landing point was the site of an undefended village from which the inhabitants had fled inland and south to the great fortress of Kaiapoi. Te Rauparaha's taua followed the well-trodden paths through the bush and across the shallow swampy areas until they shortly emerged on the open ground within sight of the Kaiapoi pa. Here they were greeted by a ragged volley of musket fire. Lead balls whistled over their heads and brought down a rain of leaves but caused no casualties. Te Rauparaha put down the poor marksmanship to the defenders not having possessed muskets until recently and probably not having fired them at an enemy before. What he did not know was that the main fighting force of Ngai Tahu at Kaiapoi was at a deep water harbour just to the south farewelling an important paramount chief and his escort, who had been visiting from their territory in the deep south of Te Wai Pounamu. The pa was defended by only old men and boys, which explained the randomness of the shooting. However, the natural defensive features of the pa with deep swamp on three sides and only a narrow neck of land on the side where Te Rauparaha's warriors had emerged, gave any defenders an advantage. This side was also protected by a double rank of tall palisades infilled with flax and earth capable of stopping musket fire. Some high towers, with protection for sharp shooters, gave Te Rauparaha further cause to pause. He was rather puzzled that the small group of a chief and six warriors he ordered forward to perform a haka challenge, mainly to determine the fire-power of the fort, were shot at but not with any great fire-power and with such inaccuracy that all returned. The only casualty was one of the defenders who fell from a tower after firing his musket. From the sound, Te Rauparaha recognised that a musket had exploded, probably from having been charged with too much powder. On Kapiti they had experienced this problem when the first pakeha traders had sold them old worn guns. If he could get close enough the defenders would be no match for his musket-experienced warriors.

Meanwhile, as his warriors had not eaten since early morning and the sun would in a few hours drop behind the mountains which backed the plain stretching inland from the pa, he led his war party back to their canoes on the river bank and there the slaves set about collecting stones and wood and preparing a meal.

Moana had later been able to fill out Waitohi's side of the story by accounts from Ngai Tahu captives. A runner had been dispatched immediately on the sighting of Te Rauparaha's taua to recall the force attending the farewell of Taiaroa. It took the messenger almost two hours to run along the hard sand of the beach and to climb the volcanic hills of the crater rim in which were enclosed the twin deep-water harbours of Whakaraupo and Akaroa. He had staggered down the steep inner wall of the crater harbour just as Taiaroa's warriors were pushing off from the beach. No time was wasted. The canoes were quickly pulled up above high water mark and the combined force of Taiaroa's escort of southern Maori and the main warrior force of the pa climbed the now darkening slopes of the crater wall. They came into the sun again as they reached the rim, took breath and, at a steady jog, headed down the valley leading to the sun-bathed plain. Beyond the sparkling waters of the mighty snow-fed Waimakariri they could see the smoke of cooking fires beyond the Kaiapoi pa and knew these to be those of Te Rauparaha's raiding party. Their chiefs needed to give no words of encouragement for them to begin the run north along the beach.

It was dark by the time they reached the outskirts of the pa. Te Rauparaha knew that none of the enemy in his right mind would leave the safety of such a well-defended pa and had not realised that a large reinforcing contingent would be entering it, and so had posted no lookouts. Taiaroa's southern Ngai Tahu and the Kaiapoi warriors silently circled the pa and used a bridge across the swamp, which was used to bring in water, to enter the pa. With such a defensive site, musket-proof walls, plenty of water and an abundance of food, they could withstand a siege from Te Rauparaha for months.

Certainly Moki, who had remained at the pa with the boys and old men when the farewell party had gone out, was most impressed with the pa's defences and all-round capability of withstanding a siege. During Te Rauparaha's first attack he had been amazed at the fire-power of the pa. Such muskets as the tribe possessed had been left behind by the warriors as traditional weapons would be used for the farewell to paramount chief Taiaroa. Fortunately some of the boys, although few of the old men, had taken an interest in their loading and firing. At the approach of Te Rauparaha's war party they had at least been able to discharge them in the right general direction. Reloading had presented problems.

Both sides settled down, prepared for a long siege. The time passed slowly for Moki and he thought often of Moana and the peaceful existence they had enjoyed at Kaikoura. Moki also missed his fishing and quite often he had slipped out, with the connivance of the night sentries, through the gate to the swamp where he was able to bob for eels, in much the way he had caught crayfish. The fresh eels were a welcome supplement to the pa's stock of preserved birds, dried fish and potatoes.

In the first few weeks of the siege Moki had been kept too busy to think about Moana although at night around the fire he would gaze into the embers and try to conjure up her image. But during the day he manned one of the towers and had been taught how to load and fire a musket. Te Rauparaha's warriors had started to build a zig-zag approach trench which was now close to the outer palisade wall. It cost the Ngati Toa dearly however as Moki and the other sharpshooters could see their every move, although the diggers obtained some protection from a roof of logs above the trench. Any warrior who exposed himself was shot at and, with practice, the defenders' fire became more accurate and the enemy casualties higher.

Early on in the siege Taiaroa led a night raid on the Ngati Toa. Moki, as a result of his eeling sorties, had a good knowledge of the swamp immediately ouside the pa and he was included in the raid. The aim was to sneak out of the water gate, choosing a dark night, move to the beach then head north to the mouth of the stream where Te Rauparaha's war canoes were beached and to set fire to them. The night was certainly dark enough and Moki joked with the Otago warriors that particularly large and hungry taniwha dwelt in the swamp. He was amused that they kept very close together as he led them through the shallower parts of the swamp. In parts it was chest-deep and some of the warriors went right under and needed considerable control to keep their muskets dry above water and to avoid spluttering when their heads surfaced again. All were naked and as rain set in Moki felt the cold settle on his bones. Another guide, who knew the tracks through the bush to the beach, took over from Moki. He bent and put his ear to the track to listen for any sounds of Ngati Toa scouts. Satisfied, he waved them on. Moki found it even colder when they reached the beach as the rain was driving in from the south-west. There was a brief delay while some untied, relieved themselves, and retied foreskins to thighs. If hand-to-hand fighting was called for a wiggling penis could result in a fatal lapse in concentration. They reassembled and headed north along the beach. At the stream's mouth they moved inland and crept forward to where spies had reported the enemy canoes. They were prepared to deal with guards but Te Rauparaha had not anticipated such an attack and none had been posted. A start was made immediately to use the fire-making materials they had brought in flax bags and small fires were eventually started on the wood sapling floors and against the walls of ten of the largest canoes. Mats placed over the top kept out the driving rain. The raiding party returned and sneaked back into the pa without challenge from the besiegers. It was only months afterwards that Moki learned that little damage had been done as the rain had put out the fires.

Taiaroa proposed another scheme. He and his Otago tribesmen

would steal out again on a moonless night and cause a diversion by attacking Te Rauparaha's force from the rear. The Kaiapoi defenders could then sally out for a frontal attack. Taiaroa's warriors in due course successfully got clear of the pa but Moki and the other defenders waited in vain for days for a diversion. Taiaroa and his warriors had instead made their way to their canoes and had paddled back to the far south.

Te Rauparaha now changed his tactics. He was still obsessed with his dream in which he saw Kaiapoi in flames. He ordered his men to drag manuka brush up through the sap they had dug nearly to the palisade walls and pile the dry brush against the palisades to await a favourable southerly wind before firing it. Moki added another element to his night excursions by taking out a small raiding party, without weapons, and dragging brush which had been added during the day back into the pa. Each day more would be added by the Ngati Toa but Moki with the other marksmen in the fighting towers made them pay with lives for every branch added. Te Rauparaha was obsessed with seeking revenge for Te Peehi's killing and pushed his men forward without regard for casualties. Minor wounds were treated with manuka leaves and manuka fire sticks were thrust into open bullet wounds to cauterise them to prevent infection but those with serious injuries were sent to their ancestors with a club blow.

In spite of the best efforts of Moki and his team, the pile of manuka brush was building up to alarming proportions. At a council of war on the marae, one of the senior chiefs, Pureko, advocated that they should chose a time when the wind was blowing from the north, away from the palisades, to fire the brush before Te Rauparaha did the same with the wind blowing the other way. None relished the thought of opposing Te Rauparaha's superior musket fire-power without the protection of the pa walls. The decision was made to fire the brush with the first favourable wind before Te Rauparaha was presented with an opportunity.

A few days later a red dawn presaged a warm day with the possibility of the required northerly wind. Sure enough the curling smoke of the dying morning cooking fires began to drift lazily seawards across the palisades towards and over the sap that the Ngati Toa had driven up to the wall. The chief Pureko consulted the tohunga and Moki could see from his firing platform that the priests were waving their hands towards the north-west. The sky was still clear, a burning blue, and Moki knew from his fishing expeditions off the Kaikoura coast that the big wind they wanted would not blow until it was able to come out of its cave, until the clouds formed a curved roof over the inland mountains, but Moki could smell the sea in the gentle easterly breeze wafting in from the coast. He was worried and climbed down from the firing platform to express his concerns. Pureko was making his way back after consulting the priests and Moki addressed him as befitted a senior chief, then expressed his doubts.

'Night is chased away by day, and then night steals up to capture day, one follows the other. We want the warm northerly wind but is it not, here, as out on the coast, followed by the cold south-west wind? The warm land wind would bring us joy but if it changed to the sea wind it would blow back in our face and out of the smoke would come Te Rauparaha.' Pureko was obviously set on putting his plan into effect and spoke bluntly to Moki.

'What you say may be true when you are out at sea but we are on land here,' and he stamped his foot in the dust.

'Furthermore, you will note though we have dug our potatoes, it is still not winter. You may be right in saying the wind often turns from land to sea but not at this time of the year. But what you and I think doesn't matter anyway as the priests have already determined we shall be successful and should fire the brush as soon as the white plumes of the toetoe bushes bend towards the sea. You can tell your warriors in the tower to provide us with covering fire when we go ouside the walls to fire the brush.'

He gestured angrily with his club for Moki to return to his post and turned on his heel to rejoin the small group of priests who continued to scan the northern sky. There was some desultory firing from the Ngati Toa trench ouside the walls and Moki and the other marksmen returned the fire without exposing themselves. Between flurries of firing, insults were exchanged, as the combatants were well within shouting distance. In discussing the sudden departure of Taiaroa and his southern Maori from the pa some of the defenders behind the palisade wall said that they had heard a Ngati Toa chief, who was later identified by another as Te Hiko, son of the murdered Te Peehi, telling the southern Maori that as they had not participated in the death of his father they would be allowed free passage from the pa. This may have influenced Taiaroa's decison to abandon, for a time at least, his northern cousins.

The hot afternoon dragged on and Moki could hardly keep himself awake, and in fact probably dozed off once or twice as he was conscious of being suddenly startled by volleys of musket fire. During the afternoon he had climbed down from the platform and obtained a gourd of water. The heat had become unbearable and the sea breeze remained light and fickle.

Suddenly the cry went up, 'It moves'. Moki shifted his gaze from the Ngati Toa trench below and looked back towards the swamp, and sure enough the white plumes of the toetoe were starting to dance in the wind. Wisps of cloud had already formed in the northern sky and were beginning to coalesce into a great arch from horizon to horizon. This was the cave of the wind from whence the great north-west wind issued to torment the plain. Fire-makers at the cooking kitchens had either made fresh fire remarkably quickly or, more likely, blown embers into life for, as Moki looked back over the pa, warriors seemed to appear from every part of it with raupo torches. Pureko signalled the warriors behind the palisades and on the firing plaforms to open up with covering fire so that the Kaitangata gate could be opened for the torch bearers. Moki was amused to see the musket firers reloading with stones and some not using shot at all as they opened a tremendous rolling fire at the Ngati Toa trench. The enemy quite naturally kept well out of sight beneath the covering logs.

Moki fired in the general direction of the Ngati Toa enemy, dropped the butt to the ground, letting the now warm barrel slide through his left hand and reached down with his right hand for his powder flask. He was still slower than some of the more experienced musket-armed warriors, but his weapon was truly ancient and slower to load. He still had difficulty handling the ramrod after he had loaded wadding and ball. He held his fire as the fire-lighters dashed out through the Kaitangata gate.

The brush was quickly fired and the dry manuka went up with a 'whoosh'. Even though the wind was carrying the sparks and smoke away from him, Moki could feel the intense heat. His worst fears were to be realised. He knew within his heart that they had left their fire lighting much too late. The wind was already gusting and the red shower of sparks and blue smoke were starting to swirl round like the water spouts he had sometimes seen at sea. The wind strengthened, perhaps partly in response to the extreme heat. The air moved towards the fire, as Moki thought, like the barracouta dashed in when sensing the slightest tremor of fish in difficulty. The setting sun flamed orange then red. Then Moki smelt the burning of his hair. He brushed it out of his eyes and the feathers in his hair came away stuck to his hand. The wind had turned. The defenders had been watching the northern sky but the wind had suddenly veered to a blustery southerly. The palisades, years old and tinder dry, were starting to burn. It would only be moments before the flames leapt across to the fighting platform. The warrior next to Moki suddenly disappeared in flames. He had been careless in loading his musket and the gunpowder on the mat floor had ignited. Moki could see nothing through the swirling cinders and smoke but could hear the screams from the tower and from the defenders behind the palisade wall. For Moki the most terrible sound was the war cries of the Ngati Toa enemy that he could now hear above the crackling of the fire. Moki up-ended the gourd of water over himself and dived in the direction of the ladder. There was less smoke near the floor and he went head first down the ladder and landed in a heap. He brushed off some glowing sparks and dragged himself to his feet. Nothing broken, he thought, but my musket is still up there.

His whalebone club had been tied round his waist and he now detached it and made sure the cord was securely fastened round his wrist. He had to withdraw further from the outer wall which was burning furiously. At least at the moment it would keep the Ngati Toa out. But once the fire burned down, what then?

Within the pa all was utter confusion. Sparks had set fire to a number of buildings including the main meeting house. Some of the priests were desperately trying to wrench off the carved face boards in an endeavour to save the ancestors from the flames. Te Auta, the old priest with the white beard, of whom Moki had been so terrified as a boy, was wandering about as if in a trance using his god stick to ward off the disaster which was about to overwhelm them. Moki was realist enough to know that incantations would not ward off the bullets of Te Rauparaha's muskets. In a hand-to-hand fight Moki knew they would hold their own but against hundreds of muskets they would have little chance.

And so it was to prove. The wind was now blowing a gale, as it turned to the south-west, usually a cold wind but now the air was as hot as a blast from a stone oven. Heavy blue-black smoke rolled over them and

Moki could hardly make out the warrior who stood next to him in their battle line. Moki looked down at his chest and arms which were blackened with wood ash. As he wiped his hand across his chest it left patterns much akin to his own face tattoo. The palisade wall had almost burned out. The Ngati Toa would be over the burning stumps as soon as the flames were low enough. Pureko rallied the fleeing warriors who still had their muskets and they advanced back to the wall to engage the enemy before they could cross the blackened stumps, or force a way through the palisade posts where the binding vines had been burned away. Moki grasped his club and moved forward in a second line with the warriors armed with more traditional clubs and spears.

At first the battle was fairly even and casualties were heavy on both sides as each shot at the other over the remains of the double palisade wall. Crouched down whilst reloading they were safe from enemy fire but once they stood to fire they were exposed. Warriors fell on both sides with terrible injuries but Moki could see that the fire-power of Te Rauparaha's warriors was too great.

Soon it was all over. Some of the enemy had gained the top of the wall and the Ngai Tahu had to flee, or die where they stood. Moki saw Pureko disembowelled by a musket shot at close range and then he found himself swept away in a mob running for their lives. The group he was with made for the gate at the rear of the pa which opened on to a deep part of the swamp. The hope was that here they might disappear into the dense rushes and flax of the swamp. Moki noticed some of the priests carrying the most precious of the carved face panels. They must have succeeded in wrenching some of them off before the panels were consumed in the flames. As they came to the swamp they waded in and the priests with words of farewell threw them into the swamp. As Moki waded and swam into the black water of the swamp he looked back. The priests were still desperately trying to conceal the carved panels by driving them into the black swamp mud before the Ngati Toa had finished their deadly work in the pa and started to pursue the survivors. Only a glimmer of sun rimmed the mountains to the west framed in the arch that had released the deceptive wind.

It was the cave wind, thought Moki, which tricked us and had brought the destruction of the pa, a stronghold my people had considered un-assailable. They said that not even Tu could scale its palisades. But fire had made it possible for even the Ngati Toa dogs to walk into the pa.

Moki remained under the brown swamp water with head tilted back and only eyes and nose above water. He could see the burning pa. The silhouette of what still stood was black. As black as Te Rauparaha's heart, thought Moki.

Those who had successfully escaped the slaughter like Moki, remained hidden amidst the tall flax and rushes of the surrounding swamp. Moki knew that within the pa the victors would be feasting. The survivors would be safe from pursuit until morning. After the south-west wind that had brought the pa's downfall the evening sky was overcast and rain was starting to fall. Moki and the other survivors took advantage of the dark to put as great a distance between themselves and their enemies as they could.

 The survivors scattered in all directions, like kahawai before a school of sharks. Most headed towards the sea coast and then south to the deep water harbour of Akaroa. Their destination was the Ngai Tahu pa on Onawe peninsula which jutted out into the head of Akaroa harbour and was connected to the hills at the head of the harbour by a narrow neck across which palisade fortifications had been erected. This location gave it great defensive advantages and it too was considered to be impregnable but as Moki jogged along the hard sand of the beach towards the harbour he thought that one short day ago they had said the same about Kaiapoi. Now it was a blackened ruin, its treasure of greenstone in the hands of the Ngati Toa, its people captured, eaten or fleeing for their lives.

Moki and the survivors heading for Onawe arrived there, exhausted, the following morning. The mournful wail of the shell trumpet echoed off the surrounding hills of the harbour calling the people of the fishing villages around the harbour into the pa. All was bustle in the pa as the women saw to food and water and the warriors checked the loadings for the few muskets they possessed. The short double palisade across the narrow neck of the peninsula would be easy to defend. Some warriors were running out long spears, like bird spears, through loopholes in the palisade, which could reach down into the dry moat on the outer side of the palisade. When every preparation had been made the pa settled down to await the enemy.

Te Rauparaha's chiefs wanted to return home. Winter was approaching and storms could blow up very quickly along this coast. If their canoe fleet was caught in one, particularly as they would be laden with captives and booty, it could turn a great victory into a disaster.

Te Rauparaha had told Waitohi on his return to Kapiti that he had had difficulty in persuading the chiefs to join him in an attack on Onawe. He had finally convinced them to take part by reminding them that their war tohunga had predicted the success at Kaiapoi and that they would return in triumph with many slaves and treasure of greenstone. But many Ngai Tahu had escaped and if they did not follow up their victory and kill or capture them now then they or their descendants would come north for utu. If they did not attack Onawe now, they, their wives and their children might in the future pay for their cowardice. Waitohi again seemed to gain some sort of strange satisfaction in relating this to Moana and was obviously proud of the way her brother had cast doubts on the bravery of his chiefs and thus gained their support. They had leapt forward as one to assure him they would go with him to attack Onawe. Te Rauparaha assured his chiefs he had a plan for the capture of Onawe which would be as successful as that employed against Kaiapoi. He explained it required the use of the captives from Kaiapoi and to move them and his attacking force to Akaroa harbour they would use the war canoes.

Fortunately the weather had settled after the gale of the previous day and by mid-morning they had beaten the captives with their taiaha, forcing them through the light surf and on to the war canoes. These were overladen by the time the warrior paddlers scrambled on board but with a chant they quickly settled to a rhythm which took them south towards Akaroa harbour and Onawe pa.

When Te Rauparaha's fleet came up the harbour the defenders thought that he might attack them from the sea but the war party and about the same number of captives disembarked at the head of the harbour and approached the pa gate at the narrow neck. Moki remembered the fate of the Ngai Tahu captives after the killing of Te Peehi at Kaiapoi pa and thought that Te Rauparaha was going to bargain with the captives' lives for the submission of the pa's defenders.

Moki watched through a loophole in the palisade as Te Rauparaha approached the gates of the pa. The defenders held their fire; they had few muskets and little powder and shot. Te Rauparaha said he was sending in their Ngai Tahu cousins from Kaiapoi to talk with them about his terms, which would be generous if they listened. If they preferred to fight, they would not be spared and none could stand against his muskets.

He and his chiefs withdrew and the captives surged forward, only too anxious to get out of club range of the Ngati Toa warriors who at the slightest whim of Te Rauparaha would have slaughtered them. Moki added his voice to those of the local chiefs and shouted, 'Don't let them in, it will be a trick.'

However, the main body of the Ngati Toa had withdrawn well out of musket range and too far away to be able to rush the gates if they were opened to admit the captives. The senior chief had consulted the tohunga and it was agreed that the lives of the captives might be spared, in the meantime anyway, if they were admitted to the pa.

Moki and the other Ngai Tahu warriors were unhappy at the decision but manned the fighting platforms as the gates were opened and quickly closed as the captives streamed in.

The majority were women and children and these were greeted warmly by their Ngai Tahu cousins. There was considerable celebration and Moki thought, as he looked back from his position on the fighting platform, from which the warriors kept a wary eye on Te Rauparaha's war party, you are not safe yet. Te Rauparaha is a wily fowler and may be setting a trap as we do for parrots: a slanting stick to make it easy for the prey to come within reach of the fowler and a decoy bird to start the parrot down the stick, then to be seized.

Moki could see, as he looked down, a heated altercation between one of the old men of the Kaiapoi pa, whom he recognised as a tohunga, not one of first rank but a fortune teller, and the rangitira of Onawe. Some of the words Moki could catch.

'He' (presumably Te Rauparaha), 'swore by the war-god Tu...' Moki lost the words momentarily because he was concentrating on watching for any signs of attack from the Ngati Toa, '...he said he would spare all but we must acknowledge him as our paramount chief now that Kaiapoi is no more.'

Out of the corner of his eye, Moki could see the rangitira of Onawe draw back his mere as if to strike the tohunga. 'We will fight. We are Ngai Tahu and will not become Te Rauparaha's slaves, better dead.'

'What of the women and children... kill them all... surrender... you will be just exchanging one paramount chief for another. If you survive, Taiaroa of the south will be here demanding your allegiance to him. Te Rauparaha has great mana and can protect us all.'

Moki heard only part of the chief's reply and what he heard was not flattering to the old tohunga's ancestry. Such sorcerers were not held in great regard anyway although sometimes women believed some of their stories of monsters. The old tohunga, with some of his cronies and older women of Kaiapoi, demanded to be let out of the gates to return to Te Rauparaha with the chief's reply. Some of Te Rauparaha's Kaiapoi captives outside the pa were crowding forward to meet their cousins as they demanded to be let back through the pa gates. Moki and the other warriors kept a careful eye on the war party. Many of the captives carried muskets as gun-bearers for Te Rauparaha's warriors. Compared with the few muskets of the Onawe defenders, their war party had more muskets than warriors.

All was confusion. Conflicting orders were given by the Onawe chiefs and the gates were opened. Some of the Kaiapoi captives dashed out as others came in and they all milled around. Suddenly Moki was aware that Ngati Toa warriors were also elbowing their way through the shouting and gesticulating crowd. Moki and the few Onawe defenders with muskets could not fire without risk of hitting their own tribesmen.

The Ngati Toa warriors rapidly appeared out of the jostling crowd and confronted the defending Ngai Tahu. Moki and the few others with muskets still could not fire. The crowd clustered about the gates had now become silent and parted to let the red-feather cloaked Ngati Toa war chiefs, including Te Rauparaha and his lieutenant Te Rangi-haeata, stride to the fore. Moki was tempted to fire at least one shot before he died but realised the ensuing slaughter would be very much one-sided. Undoubtedly Te Rauparaha had engineered this situation and now they were wholly at his mercy, an attribute in which he was singularly lacking, particularly since the murder of Te Peehi. Moki wondered if Te Rauparaha considered he had spilled enough Ngai Tahu blood as utu for that slaying. This question was to be answered by his nephew Te Rangihaeata, 'If you cease fighting and lay down your weapons there will be no further killing, this is the promise of our great paramount chief, Te Rauparaha.'

The Onawe defenders must have possessed, Moki thought, no more than four muskets all told, and these were antiquated models acquired from visiting whalers. He had been entrusted with one of them. The other proud owners of these weapons were very inexperienced in their use. Unfortunately they were also headstrong and were unable to perceive as Moki had that they were hopelessly outnumbered with at least a hundred muskets against them.

One of them aimed his musket at Te Rauparaha and fired. It was at point-blank range but Te Rangihaeata was standing so close that he was able to knock the barrel away and the shot missed. What followed was not a battle but a massacre.

Moki had known from the moment Te Rauparaha's warriors gained entry to the pa that the situation was hopeless. He made no attempt to join the defenders who were either being shot down or clubbed. He threw down his musket and joined his near cousins, the captives who were now huddled to one side, taking no part in the one-sided slaughter that had been unleashed. Moki to the end of his life held that the people of Onawe had brought their destruction down upon themselves and that it had not been his fight. The few Onawe survivors, three or four who fled the pa and swam to the far side of the harbour, held a different view.

Te Rauparaha's fighting chiefs were now anxious to return as quickly as possible to Kapiti Island before the winter storms blew up the east coast. With as many captives as they could cram into the war canoes and supporting boats, they immediately set out for Kaiapoi and then the following day for Kapiti. Te Rauparaha's fleet stopped at his Wairau pa supply base. Here Moki and a number of the captives were left to assist in food gathering whilst Te Rauparaha and his war party returned to Kapiti.

Perhaps it was for the best that Moana had known nothing of the further suffering that Te Rauparaha had inflicted on her southern kinsfolk and how close Moki had come to death. She had in her three years of captivity come largely to accept her role as a slave, but after her privileged life as the daughter of a chief at Kaikoura it was still not easy to have to perform the menial tasks of the household. She was still ashamed of her slave status but this was made more bearable by her being under the protection of Te Rauparaha's sister. Those of her own tribe still treated her with great respect and she, being a member of Te Rauparaha's household, was at least not abused openly by the pa women.

As for Hone, he played with the Ngati Toa children as one of them, although when the boys played at war and plucked raupo and toetoe stalks and threw them as spears, Hone was invariably 'the enemy'. But he enjoyed the battles nevertheless and when they fought with sticks, which they pretended were taiaha, the instruction he had received from the master of weapons back at Kaikoura stood him in good stead and he was more than able to hold his own. In most of these encounters it was the Ngati Toa boys who called it quits.

Hone had swum in the sea at Kaikoura from an early age, first in the rock pools where his father Moki used to call him a 'star gazer', a sluggish fish that prefers to lie on the bottom rather than swim. But within a year or two, Moki used to refer proudly to him as 'our kahawai', a sleek sea trout, particularly when he used to surf partly submerged in a wave.

On Kapiti Island there was plenty of opportunity for swimming. The beaches on the east coast facing the mainland opposite were sheltered from the great waves that pounded the exposed west coast. This had been one of the reasons Te Rauparaha had chosen Kapiti for his stronghold. Here, on the eastern side, was sheltered water which would lure the pakeha trading ships to load flax fibre for which they would pay in muskets.

One of the advantages of most of the able-bodied warriors being away from the pa on a war raid (Hone's mother had told him that it was again south to Te Wai Pounamu) was that the boys, supervised by the old men, did most of the fishing. This suited Hone fine. Fishing for kahawai was, Hone thought, the most exciting.

The small black and white terns would be seen from the beach circling and diving on a feeding shoal of kahawai. They were feeding on the sprats that the kahawai were forcing to the surface as they attacked them from below. A cry would go up and the boys would launch a number of the four- or five-man fishing canoes. It would be a race out to the feeding shoal. The spray flew off the paddles. The boys would race down the beach to get a front position in the canoe because here the paddler did not get as wet as those kneeling further back. The boys were most amused by the skiffs coming off the pakeha trading ships out in the bay because the pakeha rowers had their backs to the way they were going. They thought the pakeha were mad or had extra eyes in the backs of their heads. One friend of Hone suggested another location for the extra eyes which was much favoured by the other boys. Hone did not mind the spray coming back as the paddles lifted out and preferred to be at the stern because here he could control the fishing line. The fishing was much the same as he had known with his father and as he began to let the line out from the stern he wondered if he would see his home coast and father again.

Hone usually caught most fish and he knew that the reason for this was that he used lures he had made himself in the Kaikoura style. He kept them to himself and even after some bullying by the Ngati Toa boys would not show the hooks to them. He had made the body of the lure from rimu, which was just the right weight to skip over the water as it was trolled behind the canoe; the other boys had to keep rowing as the kahawai would take only a live bait. A piece of sharpened bone, one of the old men had told Hone that human bone was best, without a barb, was fastened at an angle through the rimu float. The Ngati Toa used paua shell to simulate the sparkle of scales, as Hone had been taught, but it was the small tuft of red parrot feathers that Hone added which gave his hook the advantage that told when the fish caught by each canoe were counted back on the beach. The actual catching took little skill but Hone enjoyed paying out the line and, whilst the fish were still feeding, every time the hook was thrown out there would be a strike and the fish would jump mightily as Hone pulled it in with great shouts. If the boys were lucky, greater fish would start to feed on the kahawai. Yellowtails and sharks would often snatch at kahawai that had already been hooked. A few weeks earlier Hone had hooked a mako shark which he brought up alongside their frail fishing canoe. The great scything tail had beaten against the side of the boys' craft but Hone, avoiding the array of long pointed teeth, smashed it senseless with a rain of blows from the heavy wooden bailer. They towed it in triumph to the beach. There, Moana was less excited with his catch, as she and the other slave women had the task of cutting up the larger fish and splitting the kahawai and putting the fillets on racks to dry. However, so long as Hone was happy she would not complain.

Hone regularly went inland with the other boys to a large swimming pool in a nearby stream and here they had set up a 'giant strides' with several flax ropes tied to the top of a stout pole. Several of the boys would take 'giant strides' and swing wildly out into the river and let go, dropping feet first into the water. A new boy had joined the group. The other boys were in awe of him, despite his being quite young, as he was the son of Rangihaeata, and grandson of Waitohi.

The newcomer watched the other more experienced boys taking a run and launching themselves on a rope far out into the river. He then insisted he be given a turn, and none of the boys dared deny the great-nephew of Te Rauparaha. They showed him where to start his run with the rope and he was away. He dropped short in the deep water not far from the higher launching bank. He rose once and then, with much ineffectual waving of arms, promptly sank. He could not swim. The other boys were frantic but did not quite know what to do. The boy must have breathed in water because he was now at the bottom of the pool and not moving. Hone swung in on one of the ropes, entered the water feet first, surfaced and then duck-dived to the bottom. He pushed back up to the surface holding the boy under the arms. He had been tempted to grab his hair but at the very moment of thinking it had also remembered that this was Te Rauparaha's great-nephew who had to be treated with the greatest of respect. However, as he towed him to the opposite shallow side of the pool he seemed dead. Hone dragged him out of the water and, remembering how he had seen an apparently drowned fisherman revived by being held upside down over smoke from a fire, he grasped the boy by the heels and held him upside down. Water gushed out of the boy's mouth but there still seemed no sign of life. Hone was really frightened now. This was the son of a principal chief. Hone, in desperation, still holding him upside down, shook him violently. This must have had the same effect as the smoke had in making the fisherman cough because the boy did just that and resumed breathing. Hone continued to hold him by the heels and to keep shaking him, until the boy shouted, 'Put me down, slave!' From this Hone gathered he had recovered.

They returned to the pa but Hone told his mother nothing of the incident as he feared he might have inadvertently weakened the mana of such an important person, or might in fact be blamed for breaking some tapu and bringing punishment on the group of boys. This punishment had nearly cost the life of Waitohi's grandson. He must keep this to himself.

When Hone and his mother were summoned before Waitohi he nearly died of fear. Slaves could be put to death on the merest whim of their masters. He should have told his mother but it was too late now. They had been taken to the meeting house, and this in itself Hone thought was ominous. He remembered their meeting house at Kaikoura where he had also been ready to die. This time he knew it was going to happen. But surely they could not blame his mother if he had inadvertently broken some tapu. They could not punish her too.

Hone cast his eyes to the ground as Waitohi entered the meeting house but out of the corner of his eye he could see she was accompanied. Hone saw enough to know who it was: long white hair and beard, the full striped flax cloak decorated with parrot feathers, no less than the high priest. Hone had seen him with Te Rauparaha when they had been consulting the gods, but only at a distance. Now this priest who could make the thunder roll and the lightning flash and raise storm over land and sea was about to use his supernatural powers on him.

Moana was at a loss to know why they had been summoned there. For the chief priest to be present it must be something serious and in some way concerned with the gods.

Waitohi addressed Moana and was brutally direct.

'Do you know what your son has done?'

Moana did not need to reply, her look of bewilderment was sufficient for Waitohi to continue.

'The son of my son, and great-nephew of our chief Te Rauparaha was nearly drowned. The other boys have told us that your son, as they followed the river to the swimming place, walked in the sacred water that had been sanctified by our chief priest. For this reason the gods brought misfortune on my grandson. Whilst his father and my son are on the war trail he is in my care and I have the right to claim utu. Turning to the tohunga she said, 'Deal with him.'

The tohunga approached Hone who still hung his head and looked at the ground. He almost expected to see the six toes he had seen when thrust before Te Rauparaha at the sack of Kaikoura all those years ago.

'Look at me, boy.'

Hone looked up and cringed as he came face to face with the god-stick thrust at arm's length at him by the tohunga. The carved head, of the short pointed stick, representing Tangaroa, the sea god, was decorated with red parrot feathers. Hone, in spite of his great fear, was reminded of his fish lures, perhaps appropriately enough as he was undoubtedly going to become 'the first fish', the first to die in this encounter.

'Did you touch the sacred water?' demanded the tohunga.

Hone was transfixed, the tohunga had entered his soul and words would not come out. He felt that he, too, was drowning. All he could manage was a slow shake of his head. The tohunga had taken total possession of his spirit.

The tohunga turned to Waitohi. 'This boy, though now a mere slave, is of chiefly blood and has not lied. He is a canoe of the god and was present by will of Tane to protect and save your grandson from death by drowning. Your grandson had already joined his ancestors but Tane, through this boy, snatched him back before the door closed. You and yours are in debt to Tane and this boy.'

Hone seemed still in a trance but it was all too much for Moana and she sank moaning at the feet of Waitohi begging for forgiveness for her son.

Waitohi was almost as much undone by the turn of events as Moana and immediately recognised her obligation under the code of honour to Moana and particularly Hone. He had recovered from the trance-like state and realised that again his life had been spared. He jumped with both feet off the ground and landed crouched, arms extended, in a haka position:

Ka ora, ka ora   I live, I live.

Waitohi could only smile at the cheek and courage of the boy using Te Rauparaha's own haka and a spark of amusement appeared fleetingly even in the stern eyes of the tohunga. Hone bent over his mother and drew her to her feet.

'I am sorry, mother, I didn't wish to bring further troubles to you.'

It was Waitohi who replied for Moana, who was still unable to gather her scattered thoughts.

'Your mother will have good cause to thank you for what you have done. When our noble ancestor Te Peehi rescued from drowning the pakeha captain of the ship on which he travelled to the other side of the earth he received great benefits from the pakeha and his tribe. I shall see that the Ngati Toa do no less for you and your mother. You may go with my blessing.'

One of the more important food-gathering tasks was the taking of moulting ducks from Lake Grassmere for preserving in fat, a most sustaining food for the tribe's war parties. Te Rauparaha often journeyed from Kapiti Island to take part himself in the duck hunt and the feasting.

At Te Rauparaha's supply base at Wairau, which was close to Lake Grassmere, although captives and slaves, Moki and the other Ngai Tahu warriors enjoyed considerable liberty. Moki, as a skilled fisherman, quite often went out of sight of the pa, although one or two Ngati Toa guards would accompany him. He would sometimes land for food at one of the small coastal fishing villages. It was not difficult to obtain news and pass on information. He learned that the new paramount chief of Ngai Tahu, Tuhawaiki, from the far south, had gathered together a strong force of warriors to seek utu from Te Rauparaha and was awaiting an opportunity to attack. On his next fishing trip Moki was able to pass on the information of when Te Rauparaha was expected at Wairau pa for the duck catching, and an ambush was planned.

According to Maori legend, Kupe, the navigator, had poured salt water on the cultivations known as Ka para te Hau (unpronounceable by the early whalers and rendered as 'Cobblers' Hole') and thus created Lake Grassmere. It was home to enormous flocks of ducks. The water was shallow and the moulting ducks could be rounded up and caught by hand. It was an annual outing that provided not only excellent food but a great deal of fun.

This is not quite what the waiting Ngai Tahu had in mind for the Ngati Toa as they lay in ambush, concealed in thick scrub on the southern side of the lake.

Te Rauparaha and his hunting expedition would come from Wairau pa to the north by sea and come ashore on the narrow spit separating the Grassmere lagoon from the sea. Moki was paddling in one of the canoes.

The wily Te Rauparaha was always on his guard and as they approached the spit he sent forward scouts to check on the landing place. They signalled all clear and the flotilla of assorted canoes each in turn picked up a wave and drove up on to the shingle beach.

The Ngati Toa warriors stripped off and formed a long line to herd the ducks. Most of the slaves, including Moki, remained back at the boats to gather and pack the birds as they were caught. Te Rauparaha and two other senior chiefs also stayed on the edge of the lagoon and urged the line on. The warriors laughed and shouted, splashed and often fell over. The ducks paddled furiously but were soon caught and their necks rung. Feathers floated in the air.

More than ten of the Ngati Toa fell in the first volley from the ambush. The Ngai Tahu leaped out of hiding with fearsome war cries and dashed into the shallow water to attack their enemies who, weaponless and as defenceless as the ducks, now became the quarry and could only endeavour to splash back to their canoes. Many were caught and clubbed. Tuhawaiki, leader of the southern war party, had a personal score to settle with Te Rauparaha and had marked him out from the first. Te Rauparaha was wearing a chief's fighting cloak, decorated with red parrot feathers, and heavier than usual. Its weaving had been supervised by Moana back at Kapiti Island and it had been a present to him from his sister, Waitohi, to celebrate his great victories in the recent campaign. It was thick enough to deflect a taiaha blow but not of course a musket bullet. However, it did save his life.

Tuhawaiki was anxious to take Te Rauparaha alive, since utu demanded he should suffer the pain he had inflicted on the chiefs of Kaikoura and of Kaiapoi before they died. Te Rauparaha fled through the shallow water at the edge of the lagoon, ran up the back slope of the shingle spit and down into the sea. The Ngati Toa warriors and slaves closest to the canoes when the first shots had been fired had already launched one of the large war canoes and were paddling into the surf. Moki had been forced aboard as one of the paddlers.

Tuhawaiki, with cries of 'Seize him' and 'I want him alive', rushed down the shingle slope into the sea and two of the leading warriors wrestled Te Rauparaha off his feet, with the assistance of a wave that crashed into them, and all three rolled in the surf. Te Rauparaha staggered to his feet and offered no more resistance, accepting his fate. Or so the two warriors who held his fighting cloak thought, for that was all they were left holding as Te Rauparaha slipped out of it and struck out for the one canoe that had been launched. It back-paddled and he was dragged over the side like a giant groper. To make room for him one of the slaves was flung overboard.

On shore, Tuhawaiki, with his blood lust up, and in a paroxysm of rage, ordered his men to open fire on the rapidly receding canoe. But their muskets were slow to load and several had wet pans after their owners had splashed through the lagoon after firing the first volley. The few who did get off shots had little chance of hitting a target that was going up and down with the waves, and at times disappearing from view altogether. Te Rauparaha had made his escape.

But Tangaroa, the sea god, was always even-handed in his distribution of justice. For as Te Rauparaha was rowed away to Kapiti Island, Moki, after having been thrown out of the canoe, swam the remaining distance and staggered up the shingle beach to collapse at Tuhawaiki's feet. He was too exhausted to speak but Tuhawaiki, although out to shed blood, realised from Moki's facial tattoo that he was Ngai Tahu and lowered his club.

If Moki had been taken back to Kapiti Island, he would have been reunited with Moana. As a captive at Wairau, he had had to content himself with having learned from a Ngati Toa chief that Moana and Hone were alive and slaves in Te Rauparaha's household, but he held little hope of seeing them again.

Alone, Moki returned with Tuhawaiki's force to Kaikoura to join the few survivors of the sacking of their pa. There he found that most of his whanau had been killed. An old friend, Chief Whakatau, told him how he had had to bury the remains of their tribe's people. Whakatau had survived because he had been supervising the cultivation of Kumara beds at Mikonui, a few miles south, when the pa had been sacked. Chief Whakatau had been greatly affected by the experience of having to bury so many of his people. As a chief he also bore the burden of not having been at Kaikoura to lead his warriors against Te Rauparaha's war party.

'If I had been there I could have rallied our warriors. That dog Te Rauparaha would never have set foot on our beach. That beach,' Whakatau pointed to it as he stood with Moki on the top of the peninsula, 'that beach was covered in our dead. There were dead all the way up to the pa here. We were not able to give them a proper burial.

Their wairua have not gone on their last journey, they are still with us, long after the three days permitted to them. Look, never have we seen so many butterflies at this time of the year. The spirit of our tohunga is just another of the shadows still on that beach. We must bring in another tohunga who will perform rituals to release the wairua so that the beach is no longer tapu.'

Not far from this beach, a year later, Moki joined a group who waited at Fyffe's Cove at the whaling station as a Sydney-based whaler coming from the north in full sail turned into Kaikoura Bay, dropped sails and anchored just out from the small wharf. All supplies for the small township that was growing up at Kaikoura came by sea, as well as news of the outside world. The traders and whalers had often stopped at Kapiti Island and from these ships Moki had learnt that Moana and Hone were probably still alive, but nothing more. He had told the Maori sailors on these ships that if they ever called back at Kapiti they should tell Moana he was still alive and was back at Kaikoura.

The whaler lowered boats and the crew seemed to be assisting or carrying down the rope ladders, frail-looking bodies, undoubtedly Maori. They have rescued a canoe that has been blown out to sea, thought Moki. He remembered his grandfather and stories of the Takitimu canoe of the great migration to New Zealand from Hawaiki and how their ancestors had come ashore just skin and bone after their long voyage. It was not until they were being assisted by the sailors up the steps on to the wharf that cries of recognition broke out from around Moki. Then he too recognised in these poor, twisted bodies, aged beyond their years, his own people, not of his whanau but undoubtedly from Kaikoura. These were survivors. Only then it suddenly hit Moki that they must have come from Kapiti Island. The survivors were rapturously greeted and hongi were exchanged. All were tearful.

Moki looked hopefully across the bay but the reflection on the sea made it difficult to see who else was coming off the boat. He prayed it might be Moana and Hone. As a woman clambered down into the cutter which had returned for another load Moki saw from the glint of the long auburn hair that it could only be Moana, and the man with her, surely not his son. Moki ran along the wharf and down the steps to await the cutter. As Moana stepped off the cutter, both nearly fell between boat and wharf as they clung to each other. Moki swung her on to the wharf and ten long years of separation vanished like the sea mist before the rising sun. Moki could not believe that the man taller and broader than himself was his son. But the ten-year-old boy who had defied Te Rauparaha himself, and lived, was now nearly twenty.

The thirty or so other released slaves had been brutally treated and it showed in the way they shuffled, bent from the waist, as if walking on all fours, back to the village. Looking at them, Moki was grateful for the special treatment his wife and son had received as a result of Waitohi's intervention.

Chapter 2
Land-based Whaling

It was Moki who, in the absence of the chief, had to meet the whalers. There were about forty of them led by a Scotsman, Robert Fyffe, who had previously had experience of whaling further north in Marlborough. The favoured deep-sea sperm whale was already declining in numbers but the right whale still moved along the New Zealand east coast, mainly between May and October, and could be caught from shore-based stations.

For the whalers, shore whaling offered several advantages: they were not at sea for months on end, the whales came to them, and there were home comforts of fresh food and water, and women. It was certainly a lot safer boiling out the oil in try-pots on land rather than at sea risking fire, which every wooden-ship mariner dreaded.

Robert Fyffe needed Moki's permission to set up a whaling fishery on the point of the Kaikoura peninsula, an ideal location to intercept the whales as they moved along the coast. He also needed the protection of Moki's Kati Kuri people, even though their numbers had been decimated by Te Rauparaha's raids. Moki was fearful of further raids by Te Rauparaha and thought that the presence of forty pakeha with muskets at Kaikoura might cause him to think twice before again invading the south.

Through Moana, who had picked up some basic English from traders and whalers whilst a prisoner of Te Rauparaha, Robert Fyffe reached an agreement with Moki. 'If you allow us to fish for whales' (Moana used the Maori word 'Tohora' meaning the right whale), 'then we can supply your people with trade goods, muskets, blankets, axes, rum and tobacco. We will buy food from you, such as wild pig and potatoes.'

As both parties would seem to benefit from the arrangement a deal was soon struck, and sealed with gifts of ship's biscuits, rum, tobacco, and a musket for Moki, the first he had owned. It was agreed that some of the Maori men would help in the building of whares for the whalers.

The question of women was raised reluctantly by Fyffe after his chief headsman gave him a nudge in the ribs and a toothless grin (the result of a whale's tail smashing his boat) and asked, 'Wha' abart some young fillies to look after the warries and cook the spuds and grunters?' Moana had encountered some of these terms in talking to other whalers so even when Robert Fyffe repeated the request in his broad Perthshire accent she was able to make a satisfactory translation. Again it suited Moki and the elders to have these pakeha grafted into the tribe and they agreed that some young women would be available, but only if they were willing to become 'wives'. In turn Moana, on Moki's behalf, assured Robert Fyffe that if they did not work hard at their house-keeping and cooking duties they would be replaced by others more inclined to apply themselves.

The whalers treated their 'wives' well, except when they were drunk. Since this happened both when they were bored through having no whales to capture and when celebrating a capture, it was a regular occurence. However their credit usually ran out first and Davey Jacobs, who acted as clerk for the fishery would not allow them any more rum on 'tick' until their share of the next catch was due to them. Sometimes supplies failed to arrive from Wellington by schooner and they would have to go without. When Davey Jacobs assured them, 'There'll be ten 20-gallon barrels of grog on the next ship,' it was small consolation after a day of rowing a whaleboat.

Naked breasts did not worry the Maori 'wives', but their whaling 'husbands' saw no reason for them to share their charms with the other whalers. Gowns and blankets became standard uniform. In the whalers' argot the wives were 'titters', from the sound of their laughter, which often echoed off the limestone cliffs behind the small settlement and out into the bay. To the returning whalers it was a welcome sound as they rowed across the bay.

Pickled pork and potatoes did not take much skill to cook. The Maori wives soon had vegetable gardens planted which added some variety to the meals. Kowhai, a young niece of Moki, had agreed to be the 'wife' of Ginger George, a headsman who had served on both British and American whale ships. He always kept himself shipshape, his red beard neatly trimmed in naval fashion. He had a temper which went with his fiery beard but he never vented his anger on Kowhai, saving it for his boat crew if they failed to lay him alongside the whale they were chasing. He admired Kowhai for her great beauty. Her rich auburn hair, which she wore long, she had inherited from her mother, Moana's sister. She was ever cheerful and if one of the 'Mourie wives' started to sing, the refrain would spread like a bush fire through the little huddle of whares. Kowhai had been brought up to respect warriors and these men who bravely faced the biggest animals on earth from a small boat armed only with a spear were as courageous as any chief.

Their whare, which they had built themselves, with some help from her village, was part Maori, part pakeha, in design. The wattle and daub sides and the reed-thatched roof, were almost purely Maori. The door was a little higher than the Maori style and had been made out of pit-sawn planks by Jack, the cooper, and the stone fire place was English, Scottish or Irish. A whaler who sat beside it with a tot of rum and a pipe of 'weed' felt at home. The floor was pounded clay and the window, at first, was without glass. One of Kowhai's tasks was to holystone the plank table in the centre of the room so that it looked like the deck 'of one of Her Majesty's ships of the line'. One jar on the mantelpiece labelled 'sand' and another labelled 'soap' provided the necessary ingredients. Ginger George told her, 'All you want 'sides', pointing to the sand and soap, 'is some elbow grease to keep the place shipshape.' She had no idea what this meant, except 'clean'.

It was a small but happy home. A dresser imported from Sydney held a few treasures. The bunks were at least an improvement on the hammocks in a whaling ship. Tools and clothes hung from the walls or from the roof. Oil lamps, ropes, harpoons and spiked boots for standing on the whales when cutting the blubber all spoke of the owner's trade. The musket was used for hunting pigs. Hams and flitches of bacon hung as trophies beside the fireplace.

George was accepted as one of the tribe and Kowhai's people brought them fat wood pigeon and wild pork. The wives were faithful and caring to their pakeha husbands. The Kaikoura whaling station received a report from their fellow whalers to the south at Banks Peninsula that at the time of the Wairau affray they had been saved from slaughter by local Maori when the plan to kill them had been revealed by their Maori wives.

A Sydney brig had brought news to the fishery of the capture earlier in the year by Taranaki Maori of a pakeha woman and her two children. They were the nineteen-year-old wife and offspring of a whaler, John Guard, who had been one of the earliest whalers on the Kaikoura coast. Both Ginger George and Robert Fyffe had sailed with him.

Neither had liked him. 'An ex-convict and a most disreputable rascal,' George confided to Kowhai. 'The captain of the brig told me Guard had got them to bring the navy in, HMS *Alligator* from Sydney, and they used cannon to blow their pa to splinters. The two children and Betty Guard were rescued. She seemed to have enjoyed her captivity.' George laughed, 'This is the best part. The captain tells me he heard from scuttlebutt going round the Sydney wharves just before he shipped out, she had given birth to twins and both are rather dark. Serve him right. Guard's on his way back but we don't want the likes of him here.' He patted Kowhai's hand, 'We've got a sweet berth here.'

Robert Fyffe, as owner of the fishery, was more than pleased with the contribution the Maori women made and Moki and his tribe, with the presence of the whalers, felt a little safer from another bloody sortie by Te Rauparaha.

The site of the fishery was a place of great natural beauty. The Wai o Puka stream from the peninsula ran into the sea here across a small sandy beach. It was on the north side of the peninsula, close to where Te Rauparaha's war party had landed, and provided calm water, sheltered from southerly storms, into which the dead whales could be towed. From the bay the carcasses could be winched up the gentle slope on to the flat, wave-cut rock platforms where the blubber could be cut off. Across the Kaikoura bay as a backdrop were the snow-capped, purple-blue mountains.

It had been an idyllic scene before the arrival of the whalers but was now transformed. Oily black smoke from the rendered scraps which fed the fires under the try-pots was blown inland by the sea breeze and obscured the view of peninsula and mountains. The stench of the rotting whale carcasses was intolerable. Heaps of whale bones, some already bleached white, others, more recently captured, with putrid flesh still adhering, littered the beach. The once-golden sand was soaked with a foul mixture of whale blood and oil. In the murky waters of the bay, masses of slimy blind eels fed on the blood and offal. The whale flesh, after removal of the blubber, was just a nuisance. When fresh it was considered a delicacy by the Maori but for most of the whalers the dark, almost black flesh was too strong, although to Peter Anderson it tasted much like the black puddings he had eaten in Scotland.

Pulled up on the beach in readiness to be pushed out as soon as a whale was sighted were the four whaleboats of the fishery. All were painted the same blue, since it was thought this made them harder for a surfaced whale to see. Clinker-built of half-inch planks, with both bow and stern pointed, they were immensely strong. Two were of the older type used by the whaling ships, pulled by five rowers, and two, built by Jack, the cooper, expressly for bay whaling, were larger, with space for seven oarsmen. Ginger George still favoured his 'five' as it was 'handier', as he put it, for approaching and getting out of the way after harpooning or lancing. His score of 'strikes' seemed to prove his point. The boat steerer guided the boat as close as possible to the whale then used the harpoon to 'make fast'. When the whale tired, they came up to it again and he changed places with George who, as headsman, came forward and killed the whale with the lance.

The oval-pointed, razor-sharp lances were stored under the thwarts. The barbed harpoon of soft iron was rested in a crutch in the bow as they approached a whale. Both bow and stern of the boats were planked over. In the stern a logger head in the planking was used to pass the whale rope round. In the bow the rope went through a small, lead-lined notch with an iron bar clipped over it to prevent it snaking out and tangling.

In the early days of the fishery the four boats would often be launched at first light and sit off the point until the signalman on the top of the peninsula signalled a sighting.

Ginger George's crew kept warm with some gentle rowing. The snow was well down on the Kaikoura mountains and a glistening white rime crusted the boat and the oars above the sea line. It was bitterly cold but George thought it a little early to allow a nip of rum. Long Bill stretched his legs. He was from New Bedford, and at six feet three inches, needed the extra space provided by his position as aft-oarsman or stroke. In front of him were Jonah and Blue Nose who were the tub men. Alongside them were the two tubs each with over 100 fathoms of coiled whale rope. Ahead of them were the two bow-oarsmen and at the bow was Hone who was bow-oarsman until the action started and then he became boat steerer as they pursued the whale. As they came close he would stand, brace his leg in the notch in the bow top planking and be ready to make fast his harpoon in the whale's side.

'Ar bart a drop of grog to keep art the cold?' suggested Jonah, so called because he drank like a fish.

'If we fasten into a fish you'll get one on the way in and we'll broach a cask tonight,' replied Ginger George. As headsman he demanded the same sort of discipline as a bosun in the Royal Navy.

'We're away,' shouted Long Bill who had been keeping one eye on the signalman. 'He's waving one flag for a right coming up from the south.'

All four boats were off, oarsmen pulling hard. George's boat held their initial lead but as Holy Joe was fond of saying, 'Who is first shall be last'. If the whale dived under them, the leading boats might pass over the whale, which would come up closer to the last boat in the line.

'Thar she blows, she be a right.'

'George is off again.'

'Follow them, he's picked her next rise.'

'There she breaches.'

'Give way in the lull – make her spin through it – there she spouts again – there go the flukes – clearly a right – I'll wager she makes eight tun – stand up, Hone,' shouted the headsman in the stern. Hone engaged his left leg in the notch and balanced the harpoon in his right hand.

The whale dived and the oarsmen on one side pulled back, the boat turned about, they rested on their oars and waited for the whale to reappear. It came up almost alongside the third boat. The harpooner threw and missed. The headsman threw a rope end in his face. The whale blew and sounded again.

Ginger George quickly estimated where it would reappear.

'Pull two, back three.'

The whale rose, water cascading off its back, a few metres from their boat.

'Look out. All clear.'

Hone put all his strength into the throw and the harpoon sank high up into the black mass of the whale's side.

'Peak oars.' The blades were lifted and the grip end was slipped under a notch in the opposite side of the boat as the crew braced themselves for a rough ride. A turn of the whale line was taken round the logger head in the stern and Long Bill poured sea water on it as it started to smoke as the line whistled out. Hone, still standing, now had an axe in his hand ready to strike the line if it tangled. The boat was racing away with veils of spray pluming up from the bow.

'Ten,' shouted Jonah, the tubman, as the marker indicating ten fathoms of line remaining flicked out of the tub. Hone braced himself to slice the rope if the whale sounded, they didn't want to be pulled under. A tub-man on one of the other boats had in the previous season been 'looped' by the rope and been taken down some 20 fathoms before the whale came up. He had coughed blood as they hauled him back on board but seemed otherwise unhurt.

As the line became slack, all hands heaved in and Jonah carefully laid the line back into the tubs.

'Veering away!' Out whipped the line again. As it tightened round the loggerhead the boat gathered speed again, but not as much. The whale was tiring.

The whale broached and spouted. In answer to a 'whiff' (flag signal), one of the seven-oared boats pulled across and its harpooner made fast with another harpoon. The whale lay wallowing in the gentle swell.

George moved his boat, *Swiftsure*, closer in for the kill.

'Come aft,' he cried and Hone moved back as George took his place in the bow.

He balanced the sharp, bright, oval-pointed lance awaiting his opportunity.

'Steady! Stea—dy. Pull! Row dry, boys.'

The whale slowly rolled one fin out of the water.

'Pull back three.' They were right alongside.

With all his strength, George plunged the lance through blubber and flesh into the spot where the life was said to be.

'Stern all lay off.' The tail swang round and landed with a smack where *Swiftsure* had been moments before. Boats were sometimes smashed. Hone had once been steersman on a boat headed by Robert Fyffe himself. They had made fast and, in the dying flurry of the whale, their boat had been lifted out of the water on the whale's flukes. All the crew, fortunately, were tipped out before the tail came down and turned the boat into matchwood. They had been a considerable distance from the other boats but all had been hauled in except Hone. The current carried him some way north. The other boats returned without him but Moana persuaded the crew of the *Kersage* to take her back out.

She directed them along the line of the current and after several hours they caught up to Hone, still clinging to a large piece of the bow.

The *Swiftsure* was never badly damaged and when whaling came to an end she had two hundred and sixty notches for the whales caught from her, two hundred humpbacks and sixty right whales.

'Thar she blows red!' The mortally wounded whale blew blood from her pierced lungs in a fine spray. George prepared a second lance and brought the boat in close again and sank it into the dying animal. Thick blood poured from the whale's blow hole and the sea turned red. Holy Joe, who some called a 'remittance man', as he received regular payments from England, and was also reputed to have gone to university, was usually heard to quote at this point, 'rather the multitudinous seas incarnardine, making the green one red,' which the whalers took to be another of his obscure Biblical quotations, not being well up with Shakespeare.

However they were skilled at versifying and putting their words to popular tunes of the time. On the long row towing the whale back to the fishery they sang verse after verse without, unless the tow was unusually long because of a tide change, repeating a line. As they headed back towards Wai o Puka and Kaikoura the voices from the four towing boats rang out in unison across the bay:

> Wounded and sore yet strength undiminished,
> He lashes the sea in his ire.
> A lance in the life and the strength is finished
> As he sinks down with his chimney on fire.

The next day the whale would be hauled up by windlass, affording an opportunity for more shanties and whalers' songs. The blubber was cut off with very sharp 'spades' in long strips and then cut into blocks for feeding into the try-pots. Most of the cutters were Maori, supervised by a 'tonguer', twice aptly named as he could often speak Maori and also received as additional payment the oil from the very large tongue. In 1838 this was worth forty pounds to him:

> I am paid in soap and sugar and rum,
> For cutting in whale and boiling down tongue
> The Agent's fee makes my blood so to boil,
> I'll push him in a hot pot of oil.

During the 1840s the Kaikoura fishery prospered. As a result, the Maori people gained materially but changes in their lifestyle were not always for the best. Many, at first averse to the rum of the whalers, later fell victim to it. The 'wives' of the whalers knew at first hand its bad effects and would not touch it but most enjoyed smoking a pipe of 'weed'. The arrival of children made living conditions in the whares even more cramped. The children were generally healthy, certainly more so than those of the 'native' village where an outbreak of measles was fatal for many young children, who had no resistance to European diseases. Moki believed that he was witnessing the end of his people as a race and this made him very bitter. Moana still held hope for her people and especially for her daughter Huia whose birth celebrated her own release from slavery on Kapiti Island. She allowed Huia to spend a good deal of time with her cousin Kowhai at the whaling settlement because although Moana taught her daughter the Maori language and lore she realised that to have a future her daughter would need to know the pakeha language and their ways. Though Moana had become a Christian she found that the Christian runholders who were starting to come into the area and even the occasional visiting clergyman were not very approachable. The visiting clergy preached equality but in her estimation did not seem to practise it whereas the whalers treated her with respect and as an equal. They referred to Moki as a 'nob', which she took to mean in English, 'chief'. Moki had no time for Christian gospel, particularly any suggestion that all men were equal, a sentiment he could see was so obviously untrue and completely out of keeping with Maori ideas on position and rank. He admired the strength and bravery of the whalers, identified with them, and failed to understand the arrogance of some clergy when they criticised the lifestyle of the whalers who were so obviously better men than they. Moki continued to be a stalwart ally of the whalers.

Nevertheless it must be admitted they had led hard, even harsh, lives. Young Dick, an oar-puller, only just turned twenty, had learned about boats running errands on the Sydney waterfront, and at sixteen had run away to sea on a Yankee whaler. His father had been sentenced at the Surrey Quarter Sessions in January 1800 to transportation to Hobart for seven years for 'feloniously stealing one cask and one firkin (8 gallon measure) of butter'. Dick had visited his father in Hobart before shipping first to Wellington and then the Kaikoura fishery and found he had been made Chief Constable for Van Diemen's Land. The truth, but not believed by his fellow whalers.

More Maori found employment at the fisheries. Hone, now in his early twenties, strong, well-built and a first-class seaman, had risen from ordinary oar-puller to steersman and harpooner. Most of the other Maori men worked on shore.

When whales had to be 'cut in and tried out' there was more than enough work for all hands, from dawn to dark. The wives rose an hour before dawn to prepare breakfast, usually bacon and potatoes or, for some porridge. The try-pots had to be stoked with scrap skin and blubber and, between catches, cleaned and repaired. The shears and scaffolding for lifting the blubber off the whale had to be set up. The spades for cutting into the blubber had to be constantly sharpened. If whales had not been caught there was still plenty of hard work for the shore crew. The whaling boats required constant checking and main-tenance, as any defect, such as a tangled whale line in the tubs, could have fatal results. The cooper and his assistants never finished the task of repairing or making barrels. The importance of the cooper's job was recognised by his receiving a set wage rather than a share, or 'lay', from the whales caught. His wage was many times that of an oar-puller, who earned a seventieth share. Hone, as harpooner, earned a fortieth and the headsman one-sixteenth.

Black oil was fetching up to twenty-four pounds a tun, a 250 gallon barrel, in Wellington and whalebone over a hundred pounds a ton. Whalebone was the springy plates of baleen cut from the jaws of the right and humpback whales. In his eight-ton schooner, *Fidele*, Robert Fyffe made regular trips to Wellington with oil and bone, returning with supplies. Most supplies for the whaling station and Maori village came in by sea. The pastoralists, who were starting to come in as squatters, landed many of their sheep and cattle from the sea. It was dangerous work swimming in cattle from a ship anchored off the beach but if the strength of the sea was respected no one was harmed. Bales of wool were ferried out in whaleboats to ships lying off shore.

Robert Fyffe's *Fidele* was overloaded with casks of oil as he set out from Kaikoura for Wellington with a southerly storm brewing. Battered by tumultuous seas off Cape Campbell, he ran before the wind and tried to beach his boat. The waves picked it up and rolled it up the beach. Some days later, a shepherd driving sheep down the beach discovered Robert Fyffe dead under his boat and his Maori crewman thrown high up the beach. They had been careless of, and disrespecful to the sea. Tangaroa had claimed their lives.

Disrespect had been shown to the sea in other ways. The whalers had hunted the whales almost to extinction. No sperm whales were now sighted and the right and humpback whale catch was declining each year. No effort was made to conserve the whale by sparing calves. In fact the right whale mother was so attached to her calf that to secure the calf was to secure the cow. According to whaling custom, a boat making fast to a calf had the right to the mother. It was easier to harpoon and tow the calf towards shore and allow the mother to follow, and then harpoon her when close to shore.

The whalers had brought about their own demise. By the mid-1860s whaling had ceased at the Wai o Puka fishery. Before he drowned, Robert Fyffe had already turned to sheep farming to supplement his declining income from whaling. He had also brought in, on the *Fidele*, goats which provided the fishery with fresh milk. The whaling men had to turn their backs on the sea. Except for a few who took up groper and crayfish fishing, they now became shepherds and shearers. George Fyffe, a cousin of Robert, had bought out the fishery but his main interest was in his sheep run. He had many of the Maori shore hands at the fishery taught how to shear sheep and employed them on his run. Before Catherine arrived as his wife from Scotland he built a two-storey addition on to the original cooper's house.

Fyffe's house marked the end of one chapter in the human habitation of the Kaikoura coast and the beginning of another. Trees that had grown for hundreds of years in the valley where Moki had seen a war canoe brought into being, were pit-sawn for its construction. Whale vertebrae were used as piles but there were insufficient to complete the piling since the whales had already gone.

George Fyffe and his bride lived in the house within a stone's throw of where the whales had been dragged ashore and cut up but for his livelihood he looked away from the sea to his inland run and the rearing of sheep. Moki and Moana stayed in the village but Hone and Huia would once again need to change their lifestyles to fit into the changing circumstances of the pakeha world. The pakeha, and particularly the pastoralists, saw nature along the Kaikoura coast as wild and pagan, something to be tamed and made into a civilised English countryside. Their aim was to accumulate monetary wealth: the more land they controlled, the more wealth they had. The spiritual values that the Ngai Tahu had placed on the land meant almost nothing to them. In fact most of the pakeha feared the dark green bush and swamp and felt threatened by it. It therefore had to be destroyed.

As the whales appeared more infrequently, Hone's well-paid job of harpooner was no more. He had learned fishing skills from his father and hapuku were still to be caught in the deep chasm a mile or two out. He could provide fish for his own family and sell a few to the smallholder farmers who were coming into the district, but not enough to make a living. Wellington and Christchurch were too far away by sea for wet fish to be sent there. His life would have to change direction and his mother encouraged him to accept this and take advantage of new opportunities.

'You know we always used flax for our clothes but now we think a blanket is warmer. So the pakeha can think of nothing but growing sheep for wool. He doesn't value the swamp land where we found flax, all he wants to do is to turn the land into grass to feed sheep. Sheep and wool are now valuable things and you should accept George Fyffe's offer to teach you how to take this wool off the sheep's back. You learned the ways of the whale and you must now follow the path of the sheep.'

Hone looked unconvinced. Moana continued. 'We worked hard to collect bracken fern root. Do you remember how we worked as slaves on Kapiti? Do you remember before then when at Kaikoura we put all that effort into growing some precious kumara in warm sheltered spots? Where are the fern root and kumara now? Gone, because it was easier for us to grow the pakeha potato and sell it to them. This is how Te Rauparaha earned muskets.'

Moana was right but she did not realise that the failure of a potato harvest in another pakeha land would bring to the Kaikoura coast a different people with different ideas of what was valuable in the land and what was not.

Chapter 3
The Land is Ploughed

The seagulls were a sure sign of a shoal of herring. James Adair and Davey O'Neill checked their net, pushed the skiff out and quickly rowed out to the shoal. Having had years of practice, they soon encircled the herring shoal with the net. The purse string was drawn in and the bottom of the net secured.

'Tis a good catch, James, a good meal we'll be having.'

'Aye, it will make a change from kipper and taties.'

The sky was grey, the sea leaden, and green hills rolled gently inland but although the coast was rocky, this was not the Kaikoura coast. It was on the opposite side of the world – Donegal Bay on the north-west coast of Ireland. Only a few years had passed since the Great Potato Famine of 1845-47.

The young men in the fishing skiff out in Donegal Bay were only ten years old at the time of the famine. They and their families owed their survival largely to the herring they were now catching and the three cows the two families shared. The Adairs and O'Neills were also more fortunate than the Irish peasantry in that they rented their own few acres of sandy soil and peat bog. Most of what they grew in the way of oats and potatoes went in kind to pay rents to the English landlord, but sufficient was left over to keep the family alive during the famine. However, even after the famine, life was still a constant round of hard work and grinding poverty for the survivors. In contrast, many who had left Ireland during the famine had struck it rich in the gold strikes in California and more recently in South Australia.

With nothing to hold them in Donegal except their families and one or two colleens who had invested some of their charms in the hope of becoming mistress of a farm, even if rented, Davey and James found it an easy decision to seek their fortunes overseas in the gold-fields. It was certainly easy to understand how they eventually came to arrive at the other end of the earth, in a far-off island, which the people of that land had called Te Wai Pounamu but which the diggers on the Australian gold-fields in the 1860s knew as 'the land of gold'. The big strikes were practically over by the time James and Davey reached Bendigo and Ballarat and they followed the rush to the far south of the South Island of New Zealand. From there they followed the rushes north and then west to the West Coast. Although they had become rich beyond the understanding of their families back in Donegal, both wanted to put down their roots in the land. In their hearts they were farmers, not gold-miners.

When they saw on a noticeboard at the diggings that land was for sale in the Kaikoura area on 'this Twenty seventh day of September in the year of our Lord, one thousand, eight hundred and sixty five', they decided to journey there and, if the land was suitable, buy some sections.

Another act in the drama of the Kaikoura coast was about to be written. The set was the same but the actors were new.

James Adair, Davey O'Neill and others of their family and neighbours who followed them, to this new land brought a different culture with them as well as new ways of using the land and the sea. In time the coast also changed them. The magical relationship of sea and land continued.

The land they bought at Kaikoura had been created by the sea: from the mountains overlooking the peninsula great rivers had brought down grey sand and shingle which was swept by sea currents along the coast to pile against the limestone reefs of the peninsula, once an island, but now joined to the plain. On this peninsula had stood the pa of Moki's people. Its palisades had long since fallen down but the trenched earthworks could still be seen. From this vantage point, whalers had hunted migrating whales.

The high shingle banks of the beach blocked the entry of streams to the sea and created a swamp between the coast and the seaward mountains. This was the land, so like the peat bogs of their homeland, yet created here by the sea, and so much more fertile, that James Adair and Davey O'Neill were to purchase at Kaikoura. The swamp had been a rich resource of the Maori, first people of the land, but now it was going to be used in a different way.

It was not the first time that the Adairs and O'Neills had left their homeland to begin new lives across the sea. Both families had originally come from Scotland. Their great-grandfathers going back some six generations had been rewarded with land in Ireland for fighting for the Protestant King William III against the Catholic James II and particularly for their participation in the victory of the Battle of the Boyne on 12 July 1693. Their transfer to Ireland had also enabled them to act as Protestant watchdogs of the Catholic Irish.

On a soft, spring Monday morning they left the lime-washed, stone-walled, thatched-roof huts in which they had been reared. Their parents had insisted that before they set out they be present for church on the Sunday. Then they walked two days over the moors of Donegal and took a ship from Londonderry for the gold-fields of Australia.

After arriving in Victoria, they walked the hundred miles to the gold strikes of Bendigo and Ballarat. In their moleskin trousers with their gold pan and carpet-bag, except for their handwoven Donegal tweed jackets, they looked much the same as the thousands of other 'diggers' who followed the gold trails to the latest strike.

They and some other Irish miners they met up with had some success but the easiest gold had already been won. They joined the new 'rush' to New Zealand and sailed on the *Phoebe Dunbar* from Melbourne, bound for Port Chalmers in the south of the South Island of New Zealand.

They faced another almost hundred mile walk to the new gold strike at Gabriel's Gully. On the west coast of Ireland the weather had been pleasantly mild with occasional winter storms but on the Central Otago gold-fields in the winter the Antarctic moved north. Snow was common and in their calico tents, clothes and boots froze as stiff as boards. There was no friendly peat fire to thaw out by, although some miners had found a brown coal which was a smoky and smelly substitute. The summer was also extreme and the mud of the gold-fields turned to choking dust. Rain seldom fell in summer and water was scarce. James and Davey pined for the green grass and soft rainy days of Donegal.

But when they followed the new strikes to the West Coast there was more rain than they had ever seen before. They were continually wet as they worked their claims and several of their friends were drowned in the swiftly flowing streams. The Arahura River had a particularly bad reputation. From the bed of this river the Maori had obtained their precious greenstone. Now from this and other rivers, terraces and even from the sand of the beaches, James Adair and Davey O'Neill panned for gold.

With 50,000 diggers on the Coast, Greymouth was a thriving shanty town with over a hundred hotels. James and Davey came into town regularly, as James quaintly put it, 'to dry out'. They would hand over their chamois bags of gold-dust at the bank to be weighed, bank most of the money, and with the balance repair to the Golden Bull to 'dry out'. Their favourite tipple was Irish whiskey, but as their ancestry was Scottish-Irish they were prepared to stretch a point and accept scotch. Unlike many of their Irish compatriots, perhaps because of their more puritanical Church of Ireland upbringing, they never overindulged. This was probably also why they kept out of the regular bar brawls that their Irish friends seemed to enjoy so much. It also meant, again unlike their fellow diggers, that their bank balances continued to grow so that they now each had more than two hundred pounds, by Donegal standards a fortune of unimaginable magnitude.

It was on one of these expeditions to Greymouth that they saw the Commissioner of Crown Land's notice that land was being offered for sale in Kaikoura. Their families had not owned land since they had left Scotland in the 1690s and they were both determined to own land that they could farm and pass on to their children. They had bitter memories of their childhood during the famine, of the bailiff threatening their parents with eviction when they could not pay their rents. The last of their oats and their pigs had been sold to pay the landlord. They had money now and would never again be beholden to any man, in particular, an Englishman.

'We'll have our own land, Davey. Cows, pigs and a flock or two of geese, just as we had in Donegal, but we'll not be having to doff our hat to any bloody bailiff or landlord.' Davey was just as excited. 'It's on the east coast and there should be some fish in the sheltered waters there. They told me when we were at Gabriel's Gully that the Maori natives on the east coast grow taties. This Kaikoorie place is further north, it should grow taties no trouble at all — not at all.'

James had set out almost immediately to walk north to Nelson, following the swiftly flowing Buller River, and thence to Kaikoura to inspect the rural sections available in the swamp and to bring back a report to Davey who was working out a rich gold vein on the diggings. On his return he told Davey enthusiastically:

'Tis the most beautiful flat land, easily ploughed, and some sections on the higher part of the plain are quite dry. The swamp is much richer than the bogs at home, the rushes and flax are taller than a man. Drained, the bog would grow anything. We could grow giant taties there. Do you remember the "Elephants" dad used to grow in Donegal? There are snowcapped mountains rising steeply behind the swampland and you would never believe the colour of the sea. The peninsula, where there is a whale fishery – we can get supplies there – is pure white limestone which we could use to sweeten the soil if it is sour.'

Davey was equally enthusiastic. 'What about fresh water?'

'No problem,' replied James. 'There are springs rising up everywhere. In fact you need to be careful in the swamp because in parts the water is quite deep. We can buy some sections on the drier land and then later we can perhaps tackle the swamp.'

'How much will it be costing us?' enqired Davey.

'Well, it's hard to say as the fifty-acre sections will be sold by a sort of auction. The lowest price has been set at two pounds an acre to stop the sheeprun owners buying up cheap land, but we, between us, have over four hundred pounds and money talks. Unless, like us, they're from the gold-fields, no one will have the cash to push the price much above the two pounds. With potatoes now fetching two pound ten shillings a ton, in a year or two we could get our money back. What we must do though is buy ourselves a good strong horse. You wouldn't believe how thick the flax, rushes and cutty grass are on the blocks I thought we could buy. We couldn't plant a single tatie until we got it cleared. There's a sort of rush they call 'niggerhead' that keeps building up a stump, and these are 15 feet high in the swamp. If later we're going to drain the swamp we'll certainly need a horse.'

In Nelson they bought a chestnut mare with some Clydesdale blood, a sturdy animal which they could use to transport their worldly goods to Kaikoura and when they arrived there she would make clearing the land so much easier. James named her Ellen. As he said, 'A hard worker, with red hair and a short temper, she could be me mother herself.'

'You be sure you are getting on that horse right way round?' asked Davey, after James had landed on the ground for the third time. Ellen was unused to being ridden and each time James dug in his heels to urge her forward she pig-jumped and tipped him off. But her flighty nature was later to save his life.

'You are quite as stubborn as me darling mother and perhaps if I coax you with some sweet words and not dig you in the ribs you will oblige me by moving forward.' So it proved, with a shake of the rein and a few 'giddups' and a 'come on, me gentle Ellen', off she set with the easy, rolling buttock action of the Clydesdale.

Davey and James had persuaded two other Irish miners, John and Pat McAndrew to apply for land at Kaikoura and all four set out with James on Ellen ambling along in front. The saddle and saddle-bags had cost them a small fortune but with them Ellen was able to carry most of the party's meagre belongings. At the bottom of one saddle-bag was their savings of almost five years' gold-mining, nearly five hundred pounds. As the three behind plodded along James was still thinking about farming on the new land in Kaikoura. It was rich land and they would own it. They would never again experience famine as they had known it in Donegal as boys. He remembered the day his father had come into their stone cottage, his sleeves rolled up and his arms stinking of the putrefaction that was all that was left of the potatoes in the storage pits. They thought they had escaped the blight and had harvested sound potatoes. That was the beginning of almost three long years of near starvation. He remembered going out with snow on the ground to the granite outcrops above the valley, taking cabbages to feed the wild rabbits that, once the pigs and geese were sold, were their only source of meat. He also remembered the almost daily processions he used to watch as a boy, and the carryings-on of the Catholic priest as the famine dead were taken for burial. However, unlike many in the valley, they had been able to stay on their farm and did not have to go 'out on the road'. He thought, we must buy some seed potatoes in Blenheim. The Suttons and Dakotas – oh! the taste of those lovely red potatoes we used to grow in Donegal. They'd do well here. We must buy some tools too.

These thoughts were interspersed with snatches of Irish songs: 'I met her in the garden where the praties grow' and then in more serious vein, 'The Mountains of Mourne' or the sentimental 'Donegal Bay'. The three trudging behind suspected that James had a bottle stowed in a saddle-bag because as the day wore on his recital was extended to include items such as 'There was an old lady from Kilkenny, who would not spend a penny' and similar ditties that had been popular on the gold-fields.

As they left Nelson and the coast track behind they headed into the steep hills that separated Nelson from their destination, the Crown Land Office at Blenheim where they would purchase their Kaikoura sections. They followed an old Maori trail, the Maungatapu Track, through dense rain forest and up and down across steep ridge and valley.

James had used this track a few months earlier when he had made the journey to Kaikoura to inspect the land prior to purchase but that time he had walked all the way. The Pelorus River had been carrying its usual heavy volume of water, and James had been up to his chest as he lunged from giant boulder to boulder as he made his way across.

James remembered he had been none too happy as he approached the Wairau valley on his solo walk. Near the mouth of the river was the pa that Te Rauparaha had sacked some thirty years previously. James knew nothing of this but had heard on the gold-fields of the Wairau 'Massacre'. As he made his way through the manuka scrub of the Tuamarina river flats he remembered the lurid stories of the killing by Te Rauparaha and Rangihaeata of twenty members of a surveying party because they had in some way offended the 'Maoryies' as James called them. However the only 'Maoryies' James saw were further down the coast just before he came to Kaikoura. A small group, mainly women and children, were gathering some sort of food from amongst the rocks.

There had been a bridle track from Blenheim to Kaikoura which made the long walk for James a little easier but the many swiftly flowing streams and great shingle-bed rivers, though not as frightening as those he had crossed while seeking gold on the West Coast, were hazards not to be taken lightly by a lone traveller.

When he had come to cross the wide and turbulent Clarence River he was relieved to find a primitive ferry boat operated. The boat was attached to a steel rope anchored on each side and could be pulled across by the ferryman. He was a Maori of ample build and it occurred to James that had he been of average size more passengers could have been carried.

'Want to go across?' James considered this rather a stupid question as he stood on the bank and looked across the river swollen with melting snow water.

'Cost you half a crown.' Although James had amassed what in Donegal would have been regarded as a fortune, he, because of his upbringing during the famine, and his canny Scottish ancestry did not take kindly to paying two good shillings and sixpence to cross a stream when he had crossed hundreds on the West Coast. He regarded the rolling, milky torrent before him, assessed its depth as being about three times his height, remembered that he had never learned how to swim and stepped gingerly into the ferryboat and was pulled across.

James was more fortunate when he came out on to the coast as the tide was low and he was able to move round the rocky headlands but on several occasions he slipped on the seaweed. The salt water did nothing to improve the sorry state of his boots. At one very high and steep bluff the sea was too deep but he was able to scramble through a cave over heaps of rotting seaweed, from an earlier storm, to get through to the other side.

This would surely make the praties grow. As he was slipping and sliding over the seaweed he remembered the donkeys and carts they had used in Donegal to bring home the seaweed to put on the potato patches.

It was with considerable relief after a four-day journey that he scrambled around the last major headland and saw the flat outline of the Kaikoura peninsula projecting from the coast. He quickened his pace as night was coming on and the inland hills and mountains were already throwing long shadows across the sea. The white caps racing in to the beach suddenly entered the hill shadow and their light was extinguished. Like snuffing out a candle, thought James. He hurried along the beach, being slowed by having to cross yet another of the great shingle-banked rivers. On his arrival at the whaling station he was given a meal of a marvellous fish, the best he had ever tasted. One of the whalers told him that it was known by the Maori name of 'hapuku' and that was also the name of the last great river he had forded earlier that evening.

The owner of the whaling station at the end of the peninsula lived in what to James's eye appeared to be a mansion. He was not invited inside but could see that the house had an imposing gable with at least one room upstairs and a chimney at each end of the house. The owner, he learned later, was a Mr George Fyffe, who though a Scot, was not particularly hospitable, although he offered James a meal and a bunk in one of the whalers' huts.

Early the next morning James set out, after another memorable meal of pan-fried potatoes and the same fish, to inspect the site of their proposed land purchase. He would never forget the beauty of that morning: the sun blazing across an almost flat sea, sea birds wheeling, a banner cloud half way up snowcapped mountains which must, he reckoned, have towered six thousand feet, and below them, with just the slightest mist above it, was the plain and swamp, part of which he hoped to own, to farm and to make his home.

As he told Davey on his return to the gold diggings, he had been very impressed with the possibilities of the land available at Kaikoura. For both of them, obtaining land there would fulfill a dream and forever erase the nightmare of the famine years.

Now, as he swayed easily in the saddle as Ellen plodded sedately along, James had great expectations for the land sale in Blenheim in two days' time.

Well, the Adairs have waited three hundred years to own their own land again and no one is going to stop me now. James's life almost ended at the very moment of this thought.

Ellen undoubtedly saved his life as she bolted in fright. The bush-rangers who leapt out of the dense bush on to the track had between them already killed and robbed some thirty diggers for their gold or money. They had stabbed to death one digger only the previous day for the three pounds in his swag. They confronted James and Ellen with one 'balding and black-bearded fellow of villainous appearance', as James later described him, 'presenting a pistol at me.'

'Not a muscle did I move. My thoughts immediately went to our money in the saddle-bag. I also thought that the Adairs might never become landowners.' This he related later to the three walkers of the party. 'However, that may well have been, but Ellen, bless her sweet nature, saved me. I must have tightened me heels for she took off like a rocket on Guy Fawkes Night. She sent those rascals reeling and I galloped away like Tam O'Shanter with Cutty Sark after him. Not a shot was fired as the villains were tumbled by Ellen's stampede into the fern. She kept going for miles and it was only by God's grace that I wasn't knocked to the ground by overhanging branches. I got her head round and we came back here, praying that you others would somehow safely pass those villains.'

Davey, John and Pat had not been far behind when the Kelly-Burgess gang ambushed James but far enough to gather their thoughts and work out a life-saving strategy. John was carrying a small quantity of gold-dust in the usual chamois bag and this he promptly hid under a stone. All their money was in the saddle bag on Ellen so their best defence seemed to be to plead that they were poor Irish miners who had met with no success on the diggings.

There was no point in trying to leave the track. The surrounding bush was just too dense to force a way through to put any distance between them and the bushrangers. They had no choice but to keep moving forward. They had no doubt when they met the bushrangers what the four were after. They had picked themselves up by then and one again presented the gun, another held a large bowie knife.

Pat did not hesitate 'You should have shot that cheeky bugger on the horse. Nearly ran us down too. With a fine horse like that, your honour,' Pat admitted afterwards that he might have overplayed the simple Irish peasant, ' 'e be one of those what made themselves a fortun on the diggins. If you'd of shot him then it's us all you'd have done a favour.'

The balding bushranger with the black beard who had presented the pistol at James was obviously the ringleader of the gang and spoke to Pat, who recalled later his eyes like flint and as 'black as the divil's waistcoat'.

'Are you carrying gold?' was all he asked.

'If we had won any gold we would still be back at Nine Mile Beach. We got some colours but only enough for a glass or two of ale. We hear there might be gold through this way near Renwick town. All we have is the clothes on our back. And you be welcome to them.'

Their 'best' clothes, including the jackets James and Davey had brought from Donegal, were in the saddle-bags on Ellen and all three of the walkers were wearing the ragged clothes they had worn at the beach diggings as they worked the black sand. Burgess (they learned his name later, when all four were captured, tried and hanged at Nelson) accepted their story and, without even searching them, sent them on their way with a wave of his pistol. After they had met up with a very relieved James they set up camp under a large overhanging rock well back off the track in case the bushranger gang came back that way. After dark and after being called 'a two-times damn fool' by James, John went back up the hill, through the fern and bush, found the right stone, and retrieved his gold poke.

Two days later they were in Blenheim where they pitched their tents close to the Crown Lands Office. The auction was a mere formality. There were few other bidders and for one shilling over the set price of two pounds an acre, each of the Irishmen was successful in purchasing a fifty-acre block.

They were not early to rise the following morning. Even after the sun was well up all four showed a marked reluctance to be on the track south to take up their land. This reluctance no doubt owed much to their celebrations of the previous night, a double celebration in fact: first for their becoming landowners and second for their miraculous escape from the Kelly-Burgess gang. They learnt how miraculous when they heard from other diggers sharing their celebration that a number of miners over recent weeks had just disappeared.

They finally succeeded, albeit with some difficulty, as each of them seemed to want to clutch one hand to his head, in striking their tents and saddling up Ellen. Ellen stepped out bravely for the new land to the south but there was little spring in the step of the three miners following behind.

James, having previously walked it, knew the track well. For him it was easier this time. At the ferry at the Clarence River the saddle-bags went with them and Ellen swam across in great style. In the cave that James had used to get round the bluff at full water Ellen's performance was less impressive.

James unsaddled her and led her in with not much difficulty, although she still had to lower her head and she shied at the heaps of seaweed. In the dark she was quite placid but became terrified by the sudden appearance of light from the outlet, reared, hit her head on the rock above, and then backed all the way out.

'You God-forsaken creature,' shouted James, 'you were nearer the end than the beginning!'

Pat did nothing for James's temper when he added, 'She be coming out faster than she went in.' However this gave James an idea which in the end proved successful in getting Ellen through. He blindfolded her with his spotted bandanna. Then with gentle coaxing he backed her into the cave and successfully out on to the beach on the other side.

Before nightfall on the second day they had crossed the Hapuku River, followed the sweep of the bay towards Kaikoura Peninsula, turned inland towards the steep face of the Kaikoura Range and before it was too dark located the survey pegs 181, 182, 183 and 184 that marked their land. Their land! Their land! It was hard to believe but there it was. Covered in scrub, flax, and other plants they could not name. Red-legged, peacock-blue swamp hens were feeding everywhere. Some with a flick of their white tails dashed into the thicker vegetation of the central swamp. There in the failing light they could see hundreds of ducks wheeling in. This

land was theirs. No bailiff, no absentee English landlord, no government and no famine could take it away from them. While Pat and Davey pitched their tents for the last time James and John went to the whaling station at Fyffe Cove to purchase flour, salt, rising, tea and sugar. They were promised some of the delicious hapuku for the next day but this would depend on the sea.

Everything here depended on the sea. The coast had been created by the sea. From across the sea a different people with different customs had arrived and would become part of this coast. James, Davey, John, Pat and the many who followed them from Ireland took possession of new land but the land also took possession of them. They would live and die here, be buried here, never to return to live in the green valleys of Donegal.

The next morning they agreed to put up a whare on James's land. Timber for roof rafters and corner poles was obtained from the bush at the foot of the mountain; the axes they had purchased in Blenheim were put to good use. The walls and roof were thatched and flat beach stones plastered with mud formed the floor.

'If we had a cow and had a bit of her dung mixed in with that lot we'd have a bonzer floor,' suggested James.

Until they were able to clear the land and plant crops they would need to live off the land and what food they could buy at the whaling station.

'Look you, the food is all at hand,' said Davey who, soon after their arrival, had dashed after some overly curious weka, flightless birds like the kiwi. He had caught two by hand with no difficulty, wrung their necks, gutted them and in no time they were boiling in the billy over the open fire.

The weka had been less than a success as they were tough and much too oily, but James made a mental note that their oil might prove useful for waterproofing or softening leather. The handsome dark blue pukeko could not be caught by hand. When pressed too hard they would fly a few metres, but were easy game with a light charge of bird shot in the shotgun. They made excellent soup.

Pigs had been introduced very early on, some said as early as Captain Cook's first voyage when he had anchored off the Kaikoura coast and given the name 'Onlookers' to the backing mountains, because Maori in canoes had pulled out from the shore but had done nothing but 'look on' the strange sight that Cook's ship presented to them. Introduced by the early sealers and whalers if not by Cook himself, the 'Captain Cookers', as the pigs were called, were kept, escaped and bred in increasing numbers. There were hundreds of wild pigs in the swamp providing James and the other smallholders with an abundant supply of fresh meat and bacon for the winter. The smell of the curing bacon hanging from the rafters of their whare always reminded James and Davey of Ireland. There, except during the famine, they had always kept pigs, feeding them on potato scraps. When the potatoes rotted during the famine then that too was the end of the pigs, and when both were gone then it was starvation for the people.

The wild pigs in the Kaikoura swamp were easily hunted. Early morning was the best time when they came out to root in the more open ground; then they could be easily shot.

It was pig-hunting that brought James and Davey into contact with Moki and his family and later with the family of Captain John Browne.

Captain Browne was one of the sheepmen who were starting to move their flocks on to vast leasehold stations in the hills and interior mountains of the coast. The expectations of these pakeha invaders were totally different from those of Moki's people. To the sheepmen bush and swamp were something to be burned and cleared to make way for grass so that merino sheep could graze and fortunes could be made from sheep. The whalers had different ideas. Except for the food grown for them by the Maori, they had turned their back on the land altogether and hunted the whale for its oil. They each left their mark on the land in different ways. But the land was not passive in receiving their imprint: it in turn changed their lives.

As for James and Davey, they were intending to farm their land the way it was done in Donegal. They intended to grow both potatoes and oats as their forebears had done in Ireland and in Scotland before that. But before they could even start, the land had to be cleared. This was land and vegetation almost untouched by humans – a near-impenetrable tangle of fern, flax and scrub.

They followed the lead of George Fyffe, whaler turned pastoralist, who had partially cleared similar land to provide grass for sheep by firing it. 'Slash and burn' was the catch-cry. The dense cover of huge toetoe, flax, bulrushes, fern, manuka scrub and occasional large trees did not always burn well but James and Davey kept attacking the green wall and with repeated firing and constant onslaught with slasher, axe and grubber, a small area was cleared. Ellen proved her worth by pulling out some of the larger stumps using an iron hook made for James by a whaler with blacksmithing skills. Drains had to be dug by hand and the hollow trunks of the giant niggerheads were laid in the trenches to act as drainage pipes. Both James and Davey earned additional land by gaining draining contracts for the central part of the swamp. Draining the swamp areas was hard, wet work. Both would return to the whare covered in mud and plunge into the small stream behind the whare, strip off their clothes, and put them to dry in front of the open fire ready for the next day. They would then have to cook a meal, always with damper bread cooked in the hot coals of the wood fire. Manuka wood gave the bread a tangy, smoky flavour and if 'rising' was available from the whaling station James and Davey reckoned it better than yeast bread. However they had to admit to the whalers when invited to Fyffe's Cove for a meal that their bread cooked by deep frying in the whale oil pots and accompanied by groper steaks was, as James put it, 'best food in the world. It would stand alongside the home-cured bacon and taties with farm butter me dear mother used to cook us in Donegal.' On the way home Davey agreed but complained, 'twould have been a damn-sight better if it were not for the stench of the whale oil and rotting whale flesh.' The need to cook their own food and memories of home, naturally enough, turned the thoughts of both men to marriage. Davey immediately saw a picture, as he came home wet and cold from the swamp, of a dark-haired colleen tending a stove with roaring fire and a steaming soup pot on the hob. Other no-less-warming pictures came to mind. As for James, he had plans to build a 'proper' house and then seek a bride from one of the Irish families now moving into Kaikoura, some, like themselves, from the gold-fields as the gold petered out.

After the ground was cleared, the main crops of potatoes and oats were planted. Ellen again proved her worth by dragging a primitive plough to open up the virgin soil. Blue Derwent potatoes were planted and when they were harvested James estimated they yielded more than 30 tons to the acre. Oats also yielded heavily and wheat, when they planted it the following year. The ever-patient Ellen was again employed to turn a millstone to grind the wheat for flour.

The first crops of oats were harvested just as they had been in Ireland. James would take a handful of stalks and use a toothed sickle to cut off the bunch. In this way no grain was lost and any weeds, such as the poisonous tutu could be left.

The oats were also threshed as they had been in Donegal. A tarpaulin, borrowed from the whaling station, was placed on the ground then the oats beaten on it with a wooden flail, consisting of two sticks hinged with leather.

'These', said James proudly, 'are the finest oats you ever be seeing. Ellen will be right pleased to munch on some of these. We've come a long way since we last harvested oats in Donegal. Do you remember during the hard times the donkey carts piled high with bags of oats being taken out of the country to England while our people were starving? And the police carrying rifles to prevent any attacks by the people? Well, Davey, these oats are ours and this land is ours. There's not much point in fencing it yet because we have no stock but we can split some timber and make a shelter for Ellen, and I would dearly love some geese like we had in Donegal.'

Once the crops were in and most of the land cleared and ploughed there was really insufficient work on their combined hundred acres to keep both James and Davey fully employed, though they both earned five pounds a chain constructing a road through the swamp. Moki's people had used the swamp for hundreds of years taking only what they needed, and the swamp could sustain, in the way of flax, and birds and eels for food. Within a year or so of arrival the pakeha was changing the face of the landscape. The Maori tracks skirted the deepest pools in the swamp and threaded their way carefully through the tangled vegetation. The pakeha roads had been drawn in when the subdivision was made by the Commissioner of Lands in Blenheim. Unlike the coast road, when it was eventually constructed, which was forced to conform to every bluff, rocky outcrop and indented bay along the coast, the swamp roads were uncompromisingly straight. They were driven straight through trees and secret places that had been tapu to Moki's people.

The first step in road-making was the digging of six-foot deep ditches on either side of the surveyed road. The excavated earth was mounded up between the ditches. Manuka scrub bundles were thrown on top and then another layer of earth added. As the swamp dried out and the level dropped the roads needed constant building up. At five pounds a chain Davey was resolved to seek some other form of work but his opportunities were limited.

It was the wild pigs that provided him with another job and the opportunity to meet the dark-haired colleen of his dreams. James had become quite expert at hunting the wild pigs. Rather than using a gun he would stick them with a long knife, but catching them was difficult.

'What we need is a dog to find them in this cursed flax and to hold the pig while I use me priest. James referred to both his knife and the club he used to kill eels by this term as they both 'administered the last rites'.

By asking about at Fyffe's Cove they discovered that a bitch from the village had visited the whalers' settlement some time ago and in particular a remarkably ugly bull terrier in which one of the whalers must have seen some virtue. When James had seen one of the whalers whirling the dog about him as it gripped a length of whale blubber he had exclaimed, 'That's the sort of dog we'd be wanting. He would certainly hold a pig.'

The offspring of this union had been given away except for one, which was even uglier and stronger than its sire, that had been kept by a Maori owner of the bitch. James then enquired further around the pathetic cluster of whares which was all that remained now of the Kaikoura pa and in this way met Moki and Moana. A price was soon agreed, with Moana translating. James had his pig dog.

Moki, through Moana, assured James the dog hated pigs and would be excellent for his purpose but failed to point out, for obvious reasons, that the terrier also hated pakeha. However it seemed to make an exception of James. Because of either his soft Irish brogue or his knowledge of handling animals, it submitted to the rope halter that James slipped nervously over the massive head.

As he was about to leave, James asked, 'And what would you be calling him?'

'Raha,' replied Moana without hesitation but with the hint of a smile.

'Why Raha?' asked James, whose knowledge of the Maori language was almost non-existent. Moana replied, 'Because he is ugly, stupid and a dog, and "Raha" is short for "Te Rauparaha".' As an afterthought she added, 'But the dog is not a runt like that one,' and spat to emphasise her point.

Raha proved a splendid pig dog, with but two minor limitations. First, he had difficulty locating the pigs in the dense scrub cover and second he was quite uncontrollable, and would chase after anything in the swamp that moved. Weka were sent desperately running and pukeko and ducks flew in all directions. None of these, nor any pigs, fell to his enormous jaws.

In discussing their problem with some of the whalers who, with fewer whales being sighted, were turning more to land-based interests, it was suggested that what they needed for their pig-hunting was another dog to use as a 'finder'. This time their search for such a dog took James and Davey inland to the sheep station, Winchester, where Tom Gill, one of the whalers, thought that a shepherd's bitch some time ago had come to town and also succumbed to the considerable charms of their brutish bull terrier.

So it proved, for when they had reported to the back door of Winchester, 'as befits our station in life,' remarked James with a wink at Davey and been directed by the cook to the shepherds' quarters, they found that one of the shepherds, Jake Anderson, had saved a pup from the litter, because of its fine black and white markings.

'Yes, she'll do just that. Her mother is a Scottish Border eye dog and she'll find pig for ye, and round them up, and 'twouldn't surprise me if she drove them back to ye. She don't bark none though, gets that from her dam.'

James asked if he would be prepared to sell, as he was obviously fond of the dog.

'Aye, she's a grand dog and does as she's told. Sit, Kate.' And she did. 'I wouldn't be selling 'er but the boss, Captain Browne, has seen her once or twice grab the ear of a sheep and he don't like that, although he 'ardly knows one end of a sheep from t'other. 'E's told me to get rid of her and threatened to shoot her hisself.'

And so James acquired the second dog of what was to prove a very successful team. As they headed out the drive from Winchester with Ellen pulling the dray and just about to break into a sedate trot, Captain John Browne, gloved and booted, came cantering in on his hunter.

James and Davey had to stop but they had no intention of doing any cap-doffing. They civilly passed the time of day and James was about to shake the reins for Ellen to move off when the Captain noticed the dog tied behind the dray.

'Jake's at last getting rid of that pesky dog, I see. Not before time, much too rough on the sheep. You've not got any stock down in the swamp, have you?' he asked, almost as an accusation.

James explained that they were going to use Kate to hunt pigs. James wasn't quite sure what magic word he had used to change the country squire attitude of Captain Browne to one of farmer neighbourliness but he immediately insisted they return to the homestead 'for a drink, or cup of tea or whatever you would like.'

James wheeled Ellen about and soon they were climbing down and being invited inside. 'Through the front door,' whispered Davey under his breath.

The magic word that had so quickly thawed out the frostiness of Captain Browne proved to be 'pigs'.

'I have coming up to 10,000 sheep on Winchester but I am sure by the damage they do we must have about the same number of wild pig. They come out of the scrub and root up good grazing tussock land. Can't canter over it, damn dangerous for horses. I would be willing to pay for each snout or tail you bagged.'

Davey said he would be interested in the job at a shilling a tail. James afterwards suggested that as they were his dogs Davey intended using for the hunting then perhaps he could pay James sixpence a tail.

'But to be serious, Davey, you'd be better employed here than in the swamp digging drains and making roads and there's not enough work for two on our farms yet. But the time will come. Meanwhile you could make a few bob out of this pig-hunting.'

The next week Davey moved into a bunk in the shearers' quarters and took over a couple of empty kennels for the two dogs. He kept Raha on a heavy chain as he felt, given the opportunity, he would have made short work of Captain John's baconers.

Chapter 4
Sheep on the Land

It was hardly a road, just a rutted track, but the two-in-hand bowled along in fine style, a cloud of dust swirling behind. The cobs were a matched pair, gleaming black and high-stepping. The gig had left the few straggling cottages and whares along the beach of Kaikoura town, had climbed over the peninsula, descended to South Bay and was now following the Kowhai River inland. The river flats under their cover of dun-coloured tussock looked like a billowing golden sea broken by grey islands of Wild Irishman scrub. Here run-holders were taking up vast areas of land, some of it mountainous, on which to graze merino sheep.

Captain John Browne had ordered Davey O'Neill to take the carriage and pair into Kaikoura town, more a collection of huts, to pick up the new servant girl. His wife, Elizabeth, had stressed the need to act promptly if they were to secure the girl's services before another runholder offered more than the thirty pounds a year she would cost them.

'A disgraceful amount, and her keep,' complained Elizabeth, 'but we just have to have a house maid. Cook says she will pack her bags if she doesn't get help. These people in the colonies are beyond belief.'

Captain John's thoughts were centred on the horses. 'Give them a bit of exercise. Been eating their heads off. Too much condition on 'em. Get going, man.'

Davey was tempted to give his forelock a pull but just smiled. Captain John Browne, Browne with an *e*, had served with the 27th Foot in India, and managed his sheep run and homestead with the same military style and inefficiency that he had displayed in the disastrous retreat of his company from the Punjab. Fortunately his regiment had not taken part in the Crimean campaign or the disaster there would possibly have been worse. He knew practically nothing about farming, except about horses, because riding them and looking after them were expected of the landed gentry. His family owned a number of estates in Dorset but as he was the youngest of a large family it was strongly suggested to him that he should seek a career in the army. When his colonel suggested, even more strongly, that he had little chance of being promoted past captain, he decided to seek his fortunes in the colonies and sailed with his wife Elizabeth and family of two sons and a daughter from Southhampton for New Zealand. They had arrived at the port of Lyttelton.

'Know the fellow well (referring to Lord Lyttelton), at school together, you know,' said Captain John Browne to his wife as they and their luggage were being rowed ashore.

'Yes, dear,' in public she always addressed him as 'Captain John', 'but have you arranged for our conveyance to Christchurch? You realise the town is on the other side of those hills in front of us. There, you can see where they have begun the tunnel through the hill.'

Such details seldom bothered Captain Browne. It was fortunate that the financial transactions for the purchase of land at Kaikoura for their homestead and for the lease of nearly 15,000 acres stretching inland from the Seaward Kaikoura Range, together with 10,000 merino sheep already on the run, were arranged by Elizabeth. Her father had been the member of parliament for Nottingham, and his rather liberal ideas included a good education for his daughter. It was a pity that after training as a teacher the family also insisted on a 'good' marriage. That the marriage worked in their younger days was probably because Ensign, then Lieutenant, then Captain John spent most of his time with his regiment. However, when he was posted to India she and Mary, the baby, accompanied him. The boys, Charles and George, were both born in India.

They cleared customs, where Captain John expressed the view that the customs officers seemed rather slack. Elizabeth hurried him on to securing a wagonette to take them up the winding Bridle Path across the Port Hills to Christchurch. Captain John did not demur when the men were asked to get out and walk at the steepest part, in fact to assist the two straining horses, he at one stage was seen to push. He was not to know that it was over this very track that the Ngai Tahu who had been farewelling chief Taiaroa had returned to defend their pa at

Kaiapoi against Te Rauparaha. There was, as yet, no armed Maori opposition in the South Island to the pakeha invader from overseas.

Wet and cold from a 'southerly buster' Captain John, Elizabeth and their three children enjoyed that night the warmth, supper and real beds that, as Elizabeth said, were not undulating, provided by a Christchurch boarding house.

Captain John was quite excited in chatting with some of the locals to learn of the possibilities of hunting in the province. There were pigs to be had in great numbers inland and one sportsman had shot, a few years back certainly, native quail in the marshy areas of the town itself.

As for Elizabeth, when she explored the town the next morning, she was quite surprised that Christchurch was so much developed. It boasted well laid out, if muddy, streets, gas lighting and red pillar boxes. She and her family were solidly Church of England and she intended to rename their sheep station Winchester after the cathedral and town she loved so much. She was therefore disappointed to find that although a foundation stone had been laid for a Christchurch cathedral in the town square, work had stopped. It was even rumoured that the foundation stone had been lost. People told her that it was hard to get workers in the colony but easier here because, as she explained to Captain Browne, 'the Canterbury Association who planned the colony charged a sufficient price for the land and the working classes, thank goodness, cannot acquire it easily. However, I've noticed the people in the streets are quite well fed and clothed and I've seen no paupers. We might have trouble, though, obtaining servants for our residence at Kaikorie.'

She had arranged for the homestead to be cut out in Christchurch. The builder had told her, 'Framing and weatherboards will be kauri, madam, a fine straight timber shipped down from the north.' He also told her before she could bring him back to considering whether a bay window could be included in the dining room, 'Most of both fleets of ships at the battle of Trafalgar had masts of the same straight timber.' He assured her that once 'cut out' and the joinery made, their homestead would be taken by horses and drays to 'Kaikorie' and there he would personally undertake its fitting up and finishing to her complete satisfaction.

She outlined to the builder some additional features to the plan. 'Could you put a window in the smoking room adjacent to the billiards room on the second floor so that the gentlemen could look down on the sitting room when we use it for balls? The walls of the smoking room, you remember, will be decorated with some of the Captain's trophies from India.'

Her father had made a settlement on her which would finance, as Elizabeth put it, 'a residence suitable for an English gentleman and a courageous officer of one of Her Majesty's most distinguished foot regiments.' Elizabeth had tried to interest Captain John in the planning of the house but his participation stopped short at the stables, of which Davey later was heard to remark, 'They be finer than the cottage me parents had in Donegal. They had no fancy bricks on their floor.'

Elizabeth insisted, when she had finally managed to get him to talk about the house, 'It must have at least a small music room, John, and a large formal sitting room that we can clear the furniture from to use as a ballroom. In our position we will be expected to entertain.'

Captain John was not convinced. 'You realise our nearest neighbours will be miles away, Elizabeth, that is, anyone worth inviting. At Kaikoorie', Captain John never bothered to pronounce Maori names correctly, 'there are a few farmers, mainly uncouth Irish, out on the plain, and whalers, the very roughest characters, in Kaikoorie town. You certainly would not be wanting to invite the likes of them to a ball or musical evening!'

Captain John had driven his two-in-hand the hundred miles north to Kaikoura and selected a suitable site for their homestead on a higher part of the coastal plain. From there, if time allowed between the social events Elizabeth was planning, he hoped to supervise the running of sheep on the hill and mountain country inland. He and Elizabeth had discovered whilst visiting several runholders during their time in Christchurch that the idea was to buy small 'spots' of favoured land from which large tracts of Crown leasehold land could be controlled. 'Gridironing' had the same effect by surrounding leasehold property with narrow strips of purchased land, thus locking out any other graziers. Even Captain John was able to appreciate this strategy.

'Just basic tactics,' affirmed Captain John. 'Capture the high ground then you control everything in range of your guns. In Afghanistan we did it all the time.' He had put the strategy into practice at Kaikoura by arranging to purchase a number of small 'spots', including a well-favoured site for their homestead, which effectively made a large area of Crown lease land unavailable to other graziers.

In discussing the purchase of the land with Elizabeth, Captain John had expressed his admiration of James MacKay, the Native Secretary, who had purchased the land from the Ngai Tahu.

'Did a splendid job. Bought the whole coast, over a hundred miles you know. George Fyffe, who was whaling at Kaikoorie, and later took up a sheep run, was telling me that MacKay, another Scot of course, with a keen eye for a bargain bought from the natives about two and a half million acres for three hundred pound. The richest part is that the natives were allowed to keep about 5,000 acres: sounds a lot but most of it was quite useless, for sheep anyway. Mind you, from what I can gather, they never used the land properly – we can make better use of it. I don't know what the natives are like as workers. You know they never had any livestock so probably they're not much good with sheep and I certainly wouldn't trust them with any of my horses. I hear from George Fyffe they are very clever though at whaling and fishing. If you are going to take any of them on as servants, Elizabeth, you will need to jolly them along if you are going to get any work out of them. They're all the same, these coloureds, you've got to keep chivvying them.'

'They're not quite as bad as you paint them, George. Look at that Moorie girl the Langleys had. You remember Mrs Langley's last baby was taken ill, she'd already lost two others, and the Moorie's husband, he was a Scot, tried to cross the Cowtra in flood to go for medicine at Kaikoorie. He nearly drowned. Then the Moorie girl pulled him out and tried to get across herself, a strong swimmer she was said to be. She drowned and they found her body on the boulders when the river went down. They lost the baby too.'

'Well, why don't you take a look at the Moorie girl George Fyffe was telling me about. She's been broken in to housekeeping as she's done some work for the whalers. Her parents live in the Moorie village at Kaikoorie and her brother is a harpooner on one of the whale boats.

Elizabeth followed her husband's advice and a day or so later reported back.

'Davey drove me into Kaikoorie and I spoke to her and her parents. The mother was hopeless, wouldn't look at me, kept her eyes down all the time. Her father was of a better type but he could not speak English but George Fyffe had brought with him a half-caste native who spoke the Moorie language and English, of a sort. He was able to explain that we wanted their daughter as a servant, her name is Hooheha, by the way, it's the name of a bird they said. The father became quite angry but after the half-caste explained in Moorie that we would be paying and keeping her, the mother was able to pacify him and they agreed Hooheha could come to us this week.'

Huia had acquired some English, not at home where her mother and father spoke only in Maori, but she sometimes helped out by cooking at the whaling station in Fyffe Bay, where her brother Hone worked as a harpooner. There she picked up the rudiments of English, including some words which when freely used in her new position caused Mrs Elizabeth Browne several attacks of the vapours.

Huia was a beautiful young woman who had inherited her mother's fine features: large, brown eyes which Moki said when she was a baby were as knowing as a dolphin's, high cheek-bones and a strong jaw line. Her crowning glory she also owed to her mother: rich, dark auburn hair cascaded almost to her waist.

'You will need to put that hair up,' sniffed Mrs Elizabeth Browne.

And so she did when Mrs O'Flaherty, the cook, had finally managed to get her into her uniform. This consisted of a plain black frock Cook had made from some cotton lengths that had come up on one of the drays from Christchurch, a white apron so stiffly starched it would stand without support, topped by a lace-fringed white cap that only just managed to confine the auburn hair. Her 'nether garments', as Cook referred to them, must have been non-existent or in a sorry state because Cook had given her some of her own.

Huia and Davey had driven in silence from Kaikoura back to Winchester. Davey was much impressed by Huia when she had first come timidly out of the whare. As servants they had of course not been introduced. As Davey expressed it later when visiting James back on their farm, 'I've not seen the like since we left Ireland. I would have spoken to her but you see she was in back and I was driving in front with the Captain. Every time I turned prepared to pass the time of day with her the Captain told me to watch the road. I felt like telling him not to be daft as there wasn't no road to watch though them big bloody tussocks can tip a cart in a twitch of a tail.

'When we pulled up outside the main doors, the Captain tells me to take the girl round the back to Cook. You should have seen her after Cook had done her up. I went to the stables to unhitch and feed the horses, they eat better oats than we had during the hard times, and then

I went round the back to the kitchen to get a cuppa tea. And there she was. You have never seen such a picture. She was all brown and white. A smile as white as sea spray, brown eyes, white apron and a white cap from which every time she laughed, which was most of the time, gold-brown hair tumbled down like a waterfall.'

'You daft fellow, you're sweet on her. You realise she's Moki's daughter. He's a tough one, that. Was a chief and quite a fighter in his day. The drink seems to have got him these days but if you're thinking of courting this girl you'd best watch out for her brother, too, by all accounts a hard man. Not pleasant to have a whale harpoon through your middle.'

'Oh, it's nothing like that at all. I just think...' Davey stammered and even through his weatherbeaten face the heightened colour showed.

'You've not been and taken advantage of the poor girl, have you, Davey?' James teased with a broad grin. 'If her family finds out they might have you for supper.'

Davey, in spite of these warnings, made a point of visiting the kitchen at 'smoko' mid-morning and afternoon. As he told James, 'I've never tasted the like of Ma O'Flaherty's scones straight out of the wood range with freshly made butter.' He failed to tell James that Huia also joined them for tea. While carrying out his duties, Davey saw a good deal of her. One of his jobs as station handyman was to milk the three Jersey cows that had been brought into Kaikoura and unloaded with a great deal of bellowing at the wharf. They had employed the loading crane used to swing out the bales of wool to hoist the protesting beasts ashore. Davey delivered the milk to Huia whose job it was to skim it and churn the cream into butter. He and Cook had instructed Huia how to operate the churn. She seemed to have some difficulty turning the handle, or so Davey said, and he had to hold it too, with his arm around her waist, for some time before she got the knack. He put it down to her lack of experience of mechanical things and continued to give her regular refresher courses in its operation.

He also delivered to her the manuka wood he had sawn and chopped for the wood-burning stove. It was designed to burn coal but although some coal was starting to come in through the port of Kaikoura it was far too expensive compared to the readily available wood. It was one of Huia's duties each week to blacken the stove with a paste that Mrs O'Flaherty made up herself from lamp black and whale oil she had

Davey pick up from the whaling station.

'It smells worse than the whaling station,' complained Davey who didn't think Huia should have to do such a dirty job. He had to admit, though, she looked most impish, without her apron and cap, brown hair cascading to the floor as she knelt before the stove. As she wiped the hair out of her eyes the blacking was transferred in streaks across her face. Davey could have kissed her and resolved to do so at the first opportunity.

When Huia rose from her position of worship at the altar of the now-gleaming black stove, Mrs O'Flaherty clapped her hands and came as near to smiling as she had ever come since the famine riots when she had seen her young husband sentenced to deportation to Australia. She had told Davey that she had obtained an assisted passage to New Zealand, tradespeople, including cooks, being in short supply in the colony. What she had not realised was that she would still be a thousand miles from her husband. Neither could afford the fare to reach the other.

'Oh, that be joost woondiful. You've got the idea now, lass. Now get yourself cleaned up and in your pinafore so that you can serve tea to mistress and Captain John. And now that you have had your tea, Davey O'Neill, you can fetch in some of that mutton you butchered t'other day. A nice leg for roasting would be fine. Sweet Jasus, would you be listening to me, Davey, and you, girl, be on your way. Make sure your face is clean. You can use some of that lye soap we made yesterday.'

Mrs Browne did not approve of Davey coming into the kitchen. One of the features she had insisted on having in the new homestead was a window in the kitchen for the receipt of food deliveries. Steps were provided on the outside so that the delivery boy or tradesman could deliver supplies there to the kitchen. No delivery boys called at Winchester but Davey made good use of the delivery slide. He told Huia that kitchen maids usually kissed the delivery boy through such windows. Huia thought this a strange custom but went along with it as part of learning the job. One day Davey handed through six chickens, for one of Mrs Browne's dinner parties, and received six carefully given kisses.

Davey, except for orders to tend the horses from Captain Browne, was left to organise his own day. Although he enjoyed a good deal of freedom, he nevertheless looked forward to when he would be able to join James on their farm. Huia, on the other hand, worked all hours.

She started at six each morning in the shed that had been built as a dairy on the cool side of the stables, skimming yesterday's milk for cream and setting out in pans the morning milk that Davey brought her. She could never understand why he brought her the milk after he had milked each cow: she thought it would be quicker if he brought it all at once, but perhaps, she thought, that was the way it was done. Kissing Davey anyway was no hardship. She had so much to learn.

She was at the beck and call of the entire household. Cook directed her in the kitchen and taught her some of the elements of cooking. In the house Mrs Elizabeth Browne expected her to be housemaid and to wait at table. The children were also very demanding. Elizabeth's daughter, 'Lady' Mary, as Cook called her, was twenty, and although something of a tomboy and a good horsewoman, was very clothes-conscious and kept Huia busy ironing and mending. Huia hated the ironing as she got so hot heating the big cast-iron 'smoothers' on the stove, particularly in the summer months when the nor'westers blew. The two boys, Charles and George, couldn't have cared less about clothes but as a consequence theirs always needed mending and so added to Huia's work load. The whalers, fortunately, had taught her the art of mending.

The family dressed for a formal eight o'clock dinner each evening. Huia had at first been quite overwhelmed. The dining room, with the bay window that Mistress Elizabeth had wanted, was an elegant room: timber-panelled, high-ceilinged, with some of the Captain's Indian trophies on the wall and red and white damask curtains across the bay window. The heavily embossed dark red wall covering looked like leather. It was another world to Huia. To her the most startling object in the room was the tiger skin, with its head of ferocious teeth, spread before the great stone fireplace, which was decorated with crossed lances.

When she had first been shown into the room by Elizabeth and Captain John she had stared at the snarling head so fixedly that Captain John had said, 'It won't bite you, girl, not now anyway, but that's what it had in mind before I shot it. A close-run thing at the time.' Huia had not dared to ask what sort of animal it was although it resembled the pet cats the whalers had to hunt rats and mice. It was Davey who told her about some of the things in the room, including the weapons on the wall, and Huia added the word 'tiger' to her growing vocabulary of English.

An Irish woman from the Kaikoura swamp came in two or three times a week as governess to the boys. She had been educated in a church school and left Ireland at the same time as James and Davey but although she came from the same country as them she seemed to have no time for them and Davey referred to her as a 'mick'. Huia's vocabulary was limited in regard to colloquial terms, and Davey had to explain that even though most Irish were Christians (Huia had received some Christian instruction) there were important and irreconcilable differences between some factions. Davey's actual words had been 'us and them don't agree and we don't hold with their papist nonsense', from which Huia gathered that it must be like their tribes: they might all be Maori but that didn't stop one tribe hating and killing another. When Mistress Elizabeth learned that Huia could not read or write, this information having been leaked to her by Cook, who had given Huia a recipe for scones, and been rewarded by her bursting into tears, she arranged for Annie, the governess, to give Huia some lessons with the boys.

Huia was most grateful for the instruction she received in English and after several lessons showed her gratitude by sharing with the boys some of the English she had picked up from the whalers. When the boys at dinner asked if a 'whore-house' was another type of Maori whare, Mary laughed, Captain Browne choked on his port and Elizabeth, not knowing what to do, pretended to faint. Huia's English lessons with the Browne boys did not continue.

Huia was proud that she and her parents were Christians although only nominally in her father's case. Davey was not very impressed that she had been received into the Church of England, but as he said, 'Tis better, but not much, than the Church of Rome. We will be having to put you right on some matters, lass.' Huia wondered whether she would ever understand the pakeha world.

Huia's introduction to Christianity had come about in a strange way, and even more strangely for her mother, Moana. Te Rauparaha had cast a giant shadow over her life but it was his son Tamihana, by his senior wife Te Akau, who had converted her to Christianity. Tamihana had become a convert of Church of England missionaries and had taken his life in his hands to visit the South Island to convert the Ngai Tahu enemies of his father. As a very young boy he had been with his father when his war party had attacked and captured the pa at Kaikoura. Tamihana had come ashore again at Kaikoura during his missionary journey to the south. Huia was only three years old but she remembered this imposing figure addressing the forty or fifty survivors of the sacking of their pa. Only some years later did her mother tell her of the subject of his sermon which was on Christian love and forgiveness. She also told Huia that she had convinced the tribal elders to allow Tamihana to land safely at Kaikoura and speak to them. 'I hated Te Rauparaha,' she had declared to Huia, 'but his sister, Waitohi, shielded us from the worst trials of slavery and helped us gain our freedom. As a boy Tamihana was a friend of your brother. If the sorry remnants of our tribe are to have any future we must abandon tribal rivalries and learn pakeha ways, and this includes their beliefs in the teaching of Jesus Christ.' At eight years of age Huia, with her mother, attended the first European church service at Kaikoura, held at Fyffe's whaling station.

For her father the old ways were sufficient. The old gods answered his needs. Whether it was the 60-pound hapuku or the rock lobster or the flashing, leaping kahawai, the sea off the Kaikoura coast provided all he wanted and he said a prayer to Tangaroa in thanks.

Whakatau, paramount chief of the remaining Kaikoura Maori, had also been converted to Christianity and attempted to influence Moki to change his ways but without success. Whakatau was a wily character and saw it was in his interests to keep in with the pakeha. He did not intend, however, to change his own lifestyle too greatly and often used biblical text to justify some of his more questionable activities.

Captain Browne had made available one of the larger whares at Winchester to which Anglicans, both Maori and pakeha, were invited. When other neighbours of the 'squattocracy' visited and 'natives' were not present, a service was held in Elizabeth's dining room. Occasionally the clergyman based at Cheviot, sixty miles away, would bravely make the journey on horseback to take the service but generally Captain Browne officiated. Whakatau was a regular attender but he and Captain Browne did not see eye to eye. Both Captain John and Elizabeth spoke to the bearded old warrior after the service but had no intention of inviting him into the house and had upbraided him on several occasions for having two 'wives'.

'Not done, sir. Not a thing a Christian gentleman does,' were Captain John's final words, as Whakatau hoisted himself into the dray that had brought the Maori group from Kaikoura. Whakatau had taken some offence at these remarks and at the church service the following week, at which he had been asked to read the lesson, he substituted one of his own selection:

'I read to you this morning from the first book of the Holy Bible: "And Sarah, Abraham's wife, took Hagar her maid and gave her to her husband Abraham to be his wife".'

Whakatau then proceeded with a sermon of his own, pointing out that Hagar's son Ishmael ' "shall twelve princes beget, and God will make him a great nation." The pakeha', he pointed out, looking directly at Captain John, whose colour was now turning from red to white as his anger mounted, 'has brought muskets and disease into Aotearoa resulting in the deaths of my people. If we Maori are not going to die out altogether I, Whakatau chief of Kaikoura, need to do something about it. My final words are: It is part of God's plan, as it was for Abraham, for me to have two wives, that I may multiply my seed as the stars of heaven and as the sand which is on the sea shore!' Captain John had suffered many defeats in his military career and did not raise the matter of wives with Whakatau again.

Moki, after Whakatau, was the senior chief of their hapu and they were good friends. They had both gone south to Kaiapoi, the journey bringing back many bitter memories to Moki, to put forward a claim before the commissioner of the Native Land Purchase Department for a share of the money being paid to their Kaiapoi cousins for the purchase of their land. The northern part thereof the Kaiapoi Maori acknowledged was Kaikoura land and consequently Whakatau's people were entitled to a share of the payment being made by the Crown.

Two or three hundred Maori assembled near the old Kaiapoi pa site. Moki looked towards where the palisades had been and remembered the three months during which they had withstood Te Rauparaha's siege. He did not venture on to the pa site. The bloodshed was too fresh and the whole area was tapu.

Moki turned his back on the ruins of the once great pa at Kaiapoi and joined the several hundred local Maori and his own Kaikoura people where they were gathered for the negotiations with the Crown Commissioner. His people, even to Moki's eye, were an ill-assorted lot. Most were old women, tribal elders, in an assortment of black cotton and blue silk pakeha dresses, some affecting velvet and lace. Many were smoking a pipe or had a cutty pipe thrust into their flowered bonnets. Most were wrapped in coarse grey blankets. There were fewer old

 warriors as not many had survived Te Rauparaha's muskets and ovens. The more bent of them were returned slaves from Kapiti. Some were in their finest cloaks, some dogskin, some feathered. Children, with nothing on at all, ran about wildly. There was great excitement as the gathering discussed their expectations. Moki joined a group of Kaikoura people who were listening to Whakatau holding forth. He again felt the occasion appropriate for a biblical quotation. From memory he first gave it as he had read it in English:

'Timothy said, "And having food and raiment let us therewith be content", and then repeated it in Maori adding, 'We cannot take anything out of this world, let us take the money now and enjoy it.' He sat down with some satisfaction but was dumbstruck when one of the younger women rose to speak. This was not a normal marae meeting but it was unheard of for a woman to address such a gathering. Whakatau was about to rise and order her to sit down when she, in almost faultless English, also quoted from the Bible. This so dumbfounded Whakatau that he remained motionless and speechless.

' "While the earth remaineth, seedtime and harvest, cold and heat, and summer and winter, and day and night shall not cease".' She gave a free translation into Maori then asked them, 'What will you have left if you sell your land to the pakeha? You will have gold now, but what of your children?'

Whakatau, on making enquiries after the meeting discovered she was an orphan of the Kaiapoi sacking and had been looked after by a Maori 'aunty' who worked for a pakeha clergyman in Christchurch. It was he who had taught her both English and a knowledge of the Bible. Moki's English was not good enough to follow her in that language but he agreed with what she said in Maori. He said so to Whakatau who had been considerably shaken by the experience of being out-quoted, particularly by a young woman. Moki felt ever after that Whakatau had lost something of his mana and was not the strong figure he had been. It is certainly a different world when a young Maori woman dares speak to her elders in this way, thought Moki.

However, the older women and warriors sided with Whakatau and pointed out that they would keep as Maori reserves the land, including the coast and sea, from which they obtained their food and would sell the rest which was not of much use to them. The sum they eventually hit upon as reasonable for this land was two thousand pounds.

The commissioner stepped forward and addressed the meeting, with an interpreter translating into Maori. 'The government has enjoyed the use of this land', (over a million acres stretching beyond Kaikoura to the Wairau River in the far north from the mountains to the sea) 'and has authorised me to pay a good price in an honourable and fair way. The government will pay you now in money one hundred and fifty pounds.' There was an immediate silence as his listeners sucked in their breaths. This was broken by angry shouts and a buzz of conversation. It was obvious to the commissioner and his government group that his offer was going to be rejected. He went to the front of the assembly again, held up his arms and as discussion stopped declared, 'I cannot offer you more than two hundred pounds, I am not authorised to pay you more.'

Most of the Maori group were now on their feet and at a signal from one of the older warriors turned their backs and slowly headed back to the village. Talk went on there for most of the night.

Whakatau led about one hundred Ngai Tahu out to the meeting the following morning. Without further quibble the Crown's offer of two hundred pounds was accepted. An immediate payout was made of ten pounds (in bags of half crowns) to twenty of the senior warriors. They in turn divided it among the populace.

Whakatau had got his way. He persuaded Moki to accompany him and some others to Christchurch where they could make immediate use of their newly won fortune. They celebrated by obtaining lodgings at the White Swan close to Cathedral Square and there Moki was introduced by the more experienced Whakatau to the pleasures of pakeha drink. Moki had already been introduced to rum, 'grog', to which the whalers at Kaikoura were most partial. Hone had brought a bottle home and Moki, the next day, had sworn then never to touch pakeha liquor again. But on this occasion, in the public bar of the White Swan he was no match for Whakatau's powers of persuasion.

'In the fifth book of the Bible it says, "Thou shall bestow that money for whatsoever thy soul lusteth, for strong drink, or for whatsoever thy soul desireth; and thou shalt rejoice."' In Maori the message lost none of its impact on Moki.

By the second day of their stay he and several of his companions had become wildly drunk, had been taken in charge by the constabulary and the next morning appeared before a magistrate. Most of the half crowns they had received for their land found their way into the Resident Magistrate's Court, and so back to the Crown.

On his return to Kaikoura Moki sought comfort from the sea. He rowed far out from land in his dinghy and from there looked back at the land of his people: the white cliffs of the peninsula, a smoke haze over the plain, the mountains soaring up. Those white cliffs are nothing less than the canoe thwart on which Maui had braced himself to fish up the North Island. How can my people have lost it all? We suffered defeat and humiliation from Te Rauparaha but now, far worse, we have lost our land! What is left? Almost in answer to his question the sea suddenly parted a few canoe lengths away and the black bulk of a sperm whale exhaled. Great breaths were taken for some minutes then the mighty back curved, the tail rose high above him and the whale slid down to the depths.

There are some good things left in this world but for me there are only the scraps of the old world. But I still have three things remaining, thought Moki, my pride, the freedom of the sea, and my whanau. These I will protect with my life. He stood facing forward and skulled the dinghy in so that he could continue to drink in the beauty of the coast, fearing that as it was no longer his it might disappear.

 Davey O'Neill, was also thinking of the land. His own land. He wished he could be doing more to develop his 50 acres in the swamp. 'I am a land-owner now, perhaps not one of the gentry, but at least a freeholder, not a tenant. But the time will come when I will be my own boss and not be at the beck and call of the Browne household. He grinned, I don't mind giving Huia a bit of a hand but I'm dammed if I'll run and fetch for that jumped-up Captain Browne and his wife Elizabeth. We left the likes of them back in Ireland. Lady Mary is a different kettle of fish, she's got some spirit and she's a grand horsewoman, wonderful hands, but I'm not here to be her stable boy. When I've made a bit more out of me pig tails it'll be back to me own farm and thumb me nose at all of them.

Davey had settled in well at Winchester and his tally of pig tails was mounting daily. Some wild pig had been seen rooting in the tussock close to a thicket of 'Wild Irishman', a woody, prickly plant, and manuka scrub, only a mile or two from the homestead. Davey set out at dawn with Raha on his chain and Kate at heel. He carried a double-barrelled 12-gauge shotgun purely for emergency use as he hoped to stick most of the pigs with James's knife. This had a hilt on it so that if a bone was struck the hand did not slip forward across the blade. In one barrel of the shotgun he had a cartridge into which he had poured mutton fat to solidify the shot, making it a single bullet of enormous stopping power.

On reaching the thicket, he could see no pigs but plenty of evidence of their rooting. With a whistle he cast out Kate as if she were heading sheep. She disappeared into one side of the thicket and all was silence. Suddenly a great deal of squealing and snorting broke out and Davey slipped Raha off the chain. He had only to make for the commotion in the thicket. Davey followed hard after him but more slowly as he forced his way through the scrub. He could see nothing in front of him and after a couple of barks from Raha, the squealing became louder. The pair had baled up an enormous sow. Kate was holding one ear, but only just, as she was flung this way and that, and on the other, Raha clung grimly with no intention of letting go. Davey called off Kate from her side of the sow, which she left immediately. Raha, with feet braced, was pulling the sow's head over. Davey dived in at the open side and stuck the pig under the rib cage. She went down with a great oof! of expelled air and was dead. She still appeared alive as Raha continued to worry the head so that it shook about. Davey had to get a stout manuka branch and beat Raha off the body before he relinquished his grip and could be rechained. Kate was meanwhile whining to be off after the rest of the herd. Davey sliced off the tail and whistled her on and within minutes she had another baled up.

He returned to the homestead for a morning cup of tea with Cook after tying up the dogs and feeding them some choice cuts of pork. He had become a handyman on the station and was well regarded by Cook though she was sorry that though Irish he was not Catholic, for which she hoped 'Sweet Jasus' would forgive him. For his morning's work he had almost twenty tails which, at a shilling a time, meant he had earnt a pound.

As Cook fussed over the scratches Davey had got in the scrub and a long but not deep gash from a boar's tusk on his arm, he said, 'Tis a lot easier work than digging drains in the swamp. It would take me two weeks' work to earn that much.'

After only three months, Davey and his dogs had killed over 1,500 pigs. Captain Browne was pleased enough to be rid of the pigs but the shilling a tail was another matter, although in the end Davey was paid. Like most of the tradesmen, he had to wait for his money until payment came in for the station's wool clip.

The only serious injury Davey, or his dogs, suffered was in an incident which in no way did they bring on themselves.

Lady Mary, Captain James's daughter, was the cause of the incident; a role in which she was often cast as a result of her headstrong nature and her having been utterly spoiled by both doting parents.

In the house she was insufferably rude to both Cook and Huia and hardly raised a finger to do anything for herself.

'Make sure my crinoline is well starched and put out my pink velvet dress for dinner. Come to my room at seven to do my hair and help me dress. After dinner put the warming pan in my bed.' A string of such orders kept Huia almost constantly on the run. But Lady Mary was a different person when she was going riding. She would rise early and often get out her short riding skirt, hunting jacket and boots. She was a skilled horsewoman, Captain John having lifted her on to her own pony before she was five years old.

Lady Mary had seen Davey about the property and knew he was hunting pigs. Davey had cleared most of the pigs from close to the homestead and was now riding out on one of the station hacks into the higher hill country. Lady Mary saw no reason why she should not accompany him. Her mother remonstrated, 'A lady does not ride out with a station hand,' to which Lady Mary replied, 'Bosh.'

Huia had witnessed the scene as it unfolded during dinner.

'Father,' appealed Elizabeth, 'tell her what her duty is as a member of this family.'

Captain Browne would sooner have faced the tribesmen on the Indian north-west frontier than oppose his wilful daughter. He was also secretly pleased that she showed, as he put it, 'some real grit'.

'Watch your manners to your mother, girl. I don't think pig-hunting, particularly the barbaric way this fellow does it, is the sort of sport a young girl should be taking an interest in. On the north-west frontier we used to use a lance and stick 'em on horseback, good sport, but this fella is only out for the money. The rabbits we got from Keene's are establishing themselves well on the back flat and we should be able to get some rough shooting over there shortly. You can use my 410 gauge, which is an excellent lady's gun.'

Captain Browne had never had much faith in diversionary tactics and against his wilful daughter they usually failed.

'Papa, I shall be going just for the ride out there. Bess needs a good workout. I shall take a picnic lunch that I can have while your pig-hunter goes about his business. I have no interest in pig killing, it sounds simply disgusting.'

Captain Browne looked intently at the crossed lances above the fireplace, got no inspiration there and switched his gaze to the floor and the tiger's head, but even this evidence of his one-time courage did little for him now.

Huia stood ready to serve the next course and followed the conversation, of which she had understood the main drift, with some interest. She had a strange feeling that had something to do, she thought, with Davey being involved, which she had not felt before, and she awaited the outcome of the family altercation. There was little doubt in her mind who would prevail.

'Your man Danny or whatever his name is, is riding out to the back range, my horse needs exercising, you would not be happy if I were to go alone, so I can ride with him and ride back. We will be home by afternoon and I shall not be taking part in any pig-hunting.'

Captain Browne pulled back his shoulders, as if he had made the decision himself, and declared with some authority, 'Well, put like that I see no reason why she can't go, Mother, but you stay put with your picnic lunch and leave Davey to get on with his pig-hunting.'

Huia saw Lady Mary and Davey ride out the next morning and again experienced the unidentifiable feeling of the previous evening. As far as Huia could determine, it seemed to be made up of a considerable aversion towards Lady Mary and a corresponding regard for Davey. Huia had no further time for such musings and returned to her duties.

'You don't have much to say for yourself, do you?' said Mary as they cantered across the river flat towards the tussock hills. 'I thought you Irish had the gift for talking. Is it because I am a woman or English that you have lost your tongue?' Her horse stumbled as they crossed the dry, stony bed of the Kowhai River and she dug it sharply in the ribs with her spurs. 'Watch your step, Bess!' Mary did not ride side-saddle as was the custom with ladies and affected the spurs her father wore.

Davey's eyes hardened but he set his jaw and still did not speak.

'Father tells me you Irish breed some very good hunters but that not much else of worth comes out of Ireland.' She was deliberately trying to provoke Davey, whose early silence was simply because he was unused to speaking to women, particularly a spoiled daughter of the English landed gentry. This time she succeeded in drawing a response.

'Madam, you are entitled to your own opinion of Ireland. As for England, it must be the paradise of women, but the hell of horses,' looking pointedly at her spurs, 'and the purgatory of servants.' They rode on in silence up the river valley.

At the head of the valley was a pool in the shade of black beech and here they tethered the horses. Mary took from the saddle-bags the lunch, mutton sandwiches with mint sauce, that Cook had put up for her. She offered a sandwich to Davey, which was refused, kicked off her boots, and sat with her feet dangling in the stream. Davey, with Kate at heel, and Raha on the chain, set off up the hill.

Kate soon located pigs, which had been sleeping in the bracken fern. The whole herd broke down-hill towards the stream. Kate held a young one which was easily stuck. Down on the bed of the stream the squealing indicated that she had quickly located another. Davey crashed through the undergrowth downhill, accompanied by Raha. It would have been more accurate to say that Davey slipped and stumbled downhill dragged by Raha. As they arrived, the pig, a grey boar of monstrous size, shook Kate off and scrabbled up the bank on to the tussock river flat. Kate hotly pursued it and again secured an ear hold and hung on awaiting the arrival of Raha. Mary, who had heard the commotion upstream, had struggled into her boots, leapt on Bess, and galloped towards the angry squeals. She arrived just as Kate was again losing her grip on what was now a very tattered ear. The boar was terribly enraged and opening and closing his jaws, which displayed razor-sharp curved tusks.

Davey burst from the brush along the stream bank some hundred yards down stream. Girl and horse were frozen as Kate finally lost her grip and was sliced from shoulder to ribs as the boar swung its head. Kate lay winded and almost motionless, fortunately, as the boar now turned its attention to the horse which stood only feet away, trembling.

'Go,' screamed Davey, mainly to horse and rider but also to Raha whom he had released at the same time. Mary pulled the horse round, it pivoted, she dug in her spurs and was off, the boar close behind. Raha gave out a fearsome bark as he realised this was a pig actually coming towards him. They met with an impact which Davey heard clearly. Raha was a large dog but not a quarter the weight of the boar and he was bowled over in a confusion of threshing legs. The boar was hardly checked and was close on the heels of the horse. Davey marvelled afterwards how Lady Mary had managed to stay on the horse. The ground had been rooted over by the pigs but Mary's hunter just flew over the ground with Lady Mary crouched low over her neck. As horse and rider, with the boar snorting behind, crossed in front of him, Davey fired his right barrel. He had aimed at the body but the solid charge must have hit the rear leg, as the boar slowed and then Raha, now also roused to great anger, threw himself at the boar's head and held tight. The beast was almost sitting, probably favouring its broken leg, and propped on its front legs with its head held high. So high, in fact, that Raha's back legs, as he clung to the head, were off the ground and he was being swung wildly round by the boar. Davey dashed in but the beast was so large he failed to kill it with his first blow. He dropped on to the ground to avoid Raha as the boar tried to throw him off. The boar was squealing horribly, its head blood-covered, and its great tusks scything back and forth. Davey stepped in but mistimed his thrust and a tusk opened his arm to the bone. He changed hands and with an awkward left-handed stroke finished the struggle. There was so much blood he could not tell whether Raha was also injured but as he continued to vent his anger on the boar's head, Davey assumed he had escaped serious damage.

He still had little to say to Lady Mary except when she asked, 'Are you all right, Danny?' to reply 'Davey'. But he acknowledged, when relating the story to James later, that, 'She didna' stand on any ceremony, ripped up her chemise and bound up both me and poor Kate. She be covered in blood but didna turn a hair, rode her horse the whole way home without reins holding Kate in her arms, a remarkable woman.'

Exactly the same account, when related to Huia, drew a very cool response. Davey was puzzled.

Their arrival back at the homestead caused an uproar. Cook had rushed out into the stable to provide first aid and entreaties to 'Sweet Jasus'. Captain John flew into a towering rage. A shearer, with great experience of patching up sheep cut by a slip of the shears, coolly sewed up both Davey's and Kate's wounds and finished his handiwork with a dab of hot tar. Neither Davey nor Kate showed any appreciation of his ministrations at the time but both were grateful later. Cook added, 'And thanks be to gentle Mary.' Huia held Davey's other hand as he was sewn up, tucked him up in a shearer's bunk and did the same for Kate with two warm, thick sheepskins. Her two brothers quizzed Mary on the boar, 'Did its head really come up to your stirrups?' Mrs Elizabeth Browne contributed to the confusion by also joining the group in the stable yard and, at the sight of so much blood, fainting. This time the swoon was genuine.

The next day station life settled back to the normal round of tasks. Huia had more than her share of these. One, at least once a week, was doing the washing, a bloody one after the pig encounter. It was back-breaking work. She was helped by Cook but it was still a major task. After Davey arrived she no longer had to fetch and chop her own wood to heat the copper boiler mounted in the shed alongside the stable that served as a wash house. After the 'whites' were boiled with some of Cook's homemade soap they were fished out with a 'copper stick' into wooden tubs for rinsing. All the water had to be fetched by pail from the brick-lined well beside the stables. Particularly in the hot summer months, Huia, as she struggled with the wash, and the sweat ran down her face, and her hair became bedraggled in the steam from the copper, wondered why people wanted to change their clothes so often. Especially Lady Mary, who was always asking Huia to carry in hot water from the copper, to fill the bath in the wash room and yet still changed her underlinen every time she bathed. She knew from the time she had spent with her aunt Kowhai at the whale station that it was necessary to wash her face every day and that 'duds', as the whale men called their clothes were washed each week or so, but Lady Mary's demands were just too much.

After washing the clothes, and Mistress Elizabeth insisted that the 'whites', especially the table cloths and napkins, be 'blued' in the final rinse, Huia had then to hang them out. When she first arrived she had had so much to learn. Some of the strange customs of the pakeha she still did not understand. What did it matter how she pegged the clothes on the clothesline? But to Cook and Mistress Elizabeth all had to be pegged in the right order and right way round. Even before they were carried out to the clothes line all the washing was folded, each in its own way. The clothesline stretched from the stable roof to a bluegum tree in the cow paddock. Huia had now mastered the several wooden props so that she could hang out the washing without sheets and such like dragging in the dirt. A magpie, a large black and white bird recently introduced, so Huia heard, from Australia, used to make a habit of sidling up the clothes prop, on to the line and then would move along sideways pulling out the pegs. The linen had to be pegged away from the 'smalls' and Captain James's long johns on no account, according to Cook should be hung next to Mistress Elizabeth's pantalets. Huia was greatly taken by the mangle and when first shown how to use it by Cook put her apron through it several times to obtain a variety of pleats.

Starching and ironing completed the washing for the week. Lady Mary had no notion of the work involved and changed clothes without giving it a thought. Huia started her wash day often by six in the morning. Davey, with one good arm, brought her fire wood. Lady Mary often did not rise until noon.

Whilst staying with her cousin Kowhai at the whale fishery, Huia had picked up some of the rudiments of pakeha cooking and laundering. When Cook had introduced her to the mysteries of ironing it was a culture shock of some magnitude.

'Now these be flat i-rons on the stove here and be 'eating,' explained Cook. As Huia still looked mystified she explained further, 'we be gettin' 'em 'ot.' Mrs O'Flaherty's Irish brogue and her tendency to leave off key consonants did nothing to improve Huia's understanding of this new pakeha ritual.

'Cap'n John's most p'ticlar of 'ow we do 'is shirts. These you've starched joost abart right, not too stiff but will come up grand with an i-ron. Collars is another story. They've gotta be stiff and shiny.'

Cook encased her hand in a sugar bag cloth mitt and clipped the detachable handle on to the furthest away of the three irons on the hot stove.

'Na not too 'ot,' as she spat on her fingers and quickly dabbed them on the sole of the iron. Huia stepped back in alarm. 'A bit 'ot, give it a wave and a blow and try again.' The ritual of the spittle fingers was repeated but Huia gathered that as Cook used her favourite saying of 'Sweet Jasus', the iron was still too hot for the work in hand.

'Check it on the i-roning blanket, and then away we go,' and, to Huia's astonishment, Mrs O'Flaherty broke into song:

'Dashing away with a smoothing i-ron she stole my heart away.' Huia had not much idea what the words meant and she winced at Cook's far from melodious voice. Huia sang like a bellbird but the nearest she had heard to Cook's voice were the frogs of the swamp.

'Na that's the way you do all the starched whites, table cloths, napkins and such like. When the i-ron cools you grab another off the stove and put this one back. Keep shifting them to the centre of the stove.'

This was all too much for Huia who was close to tears.

Cook continued, 'Na for the collars use this smoothing i-ron,' and picked up an iron with a boat-shaped sole and an upward curve each end. She went through the same spitting performance but Huia was ready for the hiss of the spittle this time and did not start. She was still not sure why this was done as the irons, having sat for some time on the stove, were clearly hot. Why burn one's fingers to discover this?

To Huia's consternation Mrs O'Flaherty then declared, 'Now we'll go on to something a bit more difficult,' and pulled a red-hot poker out of the fire box of the stove and brandished it round her head. Some of the pakeha, thought Huia, might think the haka frightening but most Maori would have fled at the sight of Mrs O'Flaherty as she whirled the hot poker round her head a number of times. Huia thought the first time that this might be to appease the laundry god, but learned later that it was a variation of the spitting-on-fingers ritual and was intended to cool the iron. Cook, like an expert swordsman, then thrust the poker into a finger-like metal sheath on an iron stand. To avoid this deadly lunge, Huia used the side-step she had seen her younger brother use when their father was demonstrating the way in the old times he had used a spear. She was beginning to think that this 'i-roning' was somewhat more dangerous than war-like games.

'This here now is called a "goffering iron," and this is the way it works. Y'see with one of the big irons you wouldn't be able to get into all the nooks and crannies,' (Huia had no idea what they were anyway) 'of this ruffle of Lady Mary's. But we can use this hot finger here, by Jasus', she had obviously come too close to it, 'this way we can i-ron it but still keep it all wavy and lacy-like. If we used a smoothing iron we would flatten it.'

The lesson over, and with a 'Na get on w'it', she left Huia to practise with a flat iron on the smalls, as on these the odd iron burn might go unnoticed.

Ironing was not as bad as Huia had feared. As she grew in confidence she was able to think of other things as she worked. Looking with dismay on the veritable mountain of laundry piled before her, she wondered, why did Lady Mary have to change so often? Why did the family have to change into formal wear for dinner every night? How did the boys get so dirty? Why did Mistress Elizabeth wear so much lace on the top and bottom of everything? I'll have to finish all these before I can get out to see Hone.

Huia tossed her hair and seized another iron, 'i-ron' she said to herself, off the hot stove and 'dashed away with the smoothing iron', but the song she sang was a Maori canoe song which had a rhythm, she thought, more appropriate to her actions. These stopped instantly as Davey came into the kitchen with another load of wood for the stove. The action was resumed at great speed as she smelt the burning coming from the shirt beneath the iron. But it was too late and the front of Captain John's dress shirt would never be the same again. Huia gave a wail that almost precipitated Cook, who had been listening with approval as Huia sang, into the pot she was stirring.

Even 'Sweet Jasus' deserted Mrs O'Flaherty in her search for words. She seized and held up the shirt to determine the damage done and looked clear through it to the tearful Huia. Her Irish sense of humour won the day, her eyes twinkled and the crow's feet puckered. 'Well, girl, God said he did not want burnt offerings but the only sacrifice he desires is a contrite heart. You will need to make your p'ace with Mistress Elizabeth.'

Lady Mary had come into the kitchen in time to witness the tragedy. Perhaps she had been attracted by Huia's cry but she had been coming into the kitchen quite regularly ever since Davey had been doing the same. To report the scene exactly it would have to be said that Lady Mary had noted that Davey was in the kitchen long before she was aware of a burnt shirt and Huia's sobbing figure collapsed in a chair.

Once she had noted the shirt, she also could hardly stop smiling. She did not take after her father and was a woman of action and of courage.

'Give me the shirt,' she said and stuffed it with the poker into the open fire box. 'Father has drawers, of these he won't miss this one. Now, girl, pull yourself together, I am sure it was an accident. Mrs O'Flaherty, what about making us all a cup of tea?'

And that was the end of the matter, for which Huia was most grateful, but she did not like the way Davey looked at Lady Mary, nor how she looked at Davey.

Huia's fears were not without cause as Lady Mary, after the encounter with the boar, was given to seeking out Davey to attend to her on the slimmest pretexts.

'My girth seems rather loose and I can't tighten it,' or, 'Matilda seems to have something bothering her in her left fetlock. Could you do something, Davey?'

On this occasion the request for assistance concerned sheep rather than horses. It was the first big muster for shearing on Winchester and she had asked her father if she could visit the shearing sheds when the shearing gang arrived and watch them at work. Her mother had replied, as she often did, for her husband. 'A shearing shed with the sort of men they have in their shearing gangs is no place for a lady. They're all sorts of riff-raff: one-time whalers, Maori, even ex-convicts from Australia. And their terrible women, mainly Maori, work in the shed too, picking up the wool. You just keep right away from them, my girl, and keep away from the shearers' quarters too.' Drawing a deep breath she continued, 'And they overindulge in liquor after they have finished work for the day.' Mrs Elizabeth Browne sniffed in disapproval.

Lady Mary appealed to her father. 'I should know how the sheep are shorn. I've ridden for the last three days with the muster. My backside is so sore I can't even sit down to pee.' Her mother was rendered speechless by her daughter admitting the need for such bodily functions and she breathed in, outraged, almost bursting out of her corset.

Lady Mary, unperturbed, resumed her frontal assault on her father. 'One of the shepherds could take me over to the shearing shed in the morning.' As he had done on a number of military occasions, Captain Browne did not capitulate but negotiated a compromise. This involved Davey being asked to escort Lady Mary the following morning on a tour of the shearing shed. Davey had been Lady Mary's suggestion and when it was accepted by her parents she had promptly marched out to the kitchen, where Davey had been sitting in front of the coal range with Huia and Cook, and led an embarrassed Davey back into the dining room where final arrangements were made for the next morning.

It was Davey who suggested they could start the day by breakfasting with the shearers and then move over to the shed with them at six o'clock. Mrs Elizabeth Browne thought it unlikely the shearers would be 'taking drink' at such an early hour and agreed to the arrangement. Lady Mary could hardly back out of the visit but did not relish the thought of being out of bed and dressed before five o'clock. Fortunately it was midsummer and the morning would be warm.

Huia, for very good reasons, was not happy at all for Davey to be escorting Lady Mary in the morning and resolved to stage a counter-attack of her own.

She was not barred from visiting the shearers and she slipped out of the back door with a kerosene lantern and went past the shearing shed round the back to their quarters. Here she found Hone playing cards with three of the other unmarried shearers. An upturned box served as a table and they were sitting on the edge of the lower bunks.

His job with the pakeha as a harpooner at the whaling station had gone with the demise of the whales. As shearing shed rouseabout on George Fyffe's station he had learned shearing and was now a 'top-gun' shearer with a local itinerant shearing gang that had arrived at Winchester by horse and dray early that morning and was settling into the shearers' quarters.

Hone was now twenty-six, and whaling and shearing had con-tributed to his fine physique. His features were more those of his father, Moki, with high cheek-bones and hawk-like nose. His hair, black with auburn glints was undoubtedly from his mother. He wore it slightly longer than the fashion for workmen and tied it back with a red bandanna when he was shearing. He had the same ready and gleaming white smile as Huia.

He greeted her warmly in Maori. 'Tuahine, good to see you. Huia.' He had picked up more than a smattering of English from the whalers then the shearers, particularly a fine repertoire of curses for difficult sheep, but he felt more at home speaking Maori. After almost ten years of captivity on Kapiti Island he spoke Maori more like their old enemies of the north, with an accent his Maori friends found strange. For example, in speaking of his own tribe he sometimes used the softer northern 'Ngai' pronunciation rather than the 'Kai' they used. He had received no formal education. This in one way was not a disadvantage as his Kaikoura friends attending the local mission school, while he had been a captive, had been forbidden to speak Maori at school and now spoke it poorly, if at all. They either mispronounced local Maori place names or used the English equivalent. Hone used the Maori names which meant much more to him. The shearers referred to the highest mountain in New Zealand (to Hone, Aotearoa) as Mt Cook but to Hone it would always be 'the cloud piercer', Aoraki. Hone was a natural athlete and handled the shearing shears as ably as he had wielded the harpoon against the whales, and his ancestors before him, taiaha and mere against their enemies. In a fourteen-hour day he could shear 120 merino sheep, the average for his gang being about 80. He was supremely fit as this rate would have to be maintained for almost three weeks to remove the wool from the 50,000 sheep run on Winchester.

Huia had wanted to see her big brother but thought that she could also ask him to keep an eye on Lady Mary, or, more importantly, on Davey, during their planned visit the following morning. She was sure Davey had special feelings for her but she mistrusted Lady Mary and particularly the effect her blonde hair and china blue eyes had on the station hands. As it turned out Huia had no need to worry on this score as at the first sight the next morning of Hone, Lady Mary had eyes for no other. Whether she saw him as 'the noble savage', black singleted, rippling biceps, hair taken back, shining eyes and a ready smile, or as one of the Greek gods she and the other young ladies had tittered over in art classes at school she was completely smitten, and Davey ceased to exist.

Lady Mary had at first been overwhelmed by the strange sounds and sights of the shearing shed. She thought that she might very well lose the substantial breakfast of mutton broth and mutton chops she and Davey had shared with the shearers for breakfast. She held hand to mouth as one of the shearers, wielding the razor-sharp blades, nicked a sheep and blood spurted. The blood seemed unnaturally red against the pink-white shorn flank of the sheep. One of the Maori women shed-hands was quickly on hand with a tar pot to dab the wound and the sheep, none the worse, was pushed, scampering and skidding over the greasy floor, through the trapdoor.

Davey explained to her that each man's shorn sheep went through the trapdoor to a small outside pen where the station manager could check on excessive cutting and count each shearer's tally for the day. He explained that they were paid a shilling a hundred sheep shorn. Lady Mary had done a quick calculation based on the 50,000 sheep on the station and declared, 'They seem to be over-paid, don't they?' Davey refrained from commenting as he knew from the shilling a tail he was paid for killing wild pigs what he would sooner be doing.

After gazing with undisguised awe at the sight of Hone in full flight on the boards: the sweeping blows of the shears as they peeled off the grey fleece, the easy rhythm as with the other hand and legs he turned the sheep this way and that as the fleece seemed almost like magic to fall on to the boards, she seemed little aware of Davey's commentary.

Lady Mary was still gazing in undisguised admiration as Hone, with a deft sideways kick, sent the now snow-white sheep skittering through the trapdoor. He smiled at her, the warmest, most beautiful smile Mary had ever experienced. She continued staring at this magnificent creature with mouth open, forgetting all she had been taught of etiquette.

Hone immediately understood why Huia was anxious about the effect of this golden goddess on Davey, in whom his little sister obviously had some interest. Hone had no doubts of the effect of this apparition on the station men, particularly Davey.

His mother had given him English lessons out of fashion catalogues but he had never imagined that those women in the magnificent wasp-waisted dresses existed in reality. But here one had materialised in front of him like a wairua. And she was in colour, not like the black and white illustrations in the fashion catalogues. She had takakau hair and kahurangi eyes.

He picked up the sharpening stone and with easy strokes swept it across the blades. He continued to smile at Mary and she was transfixed, mesmerised by the sensual interplay of brown arm and wrist and the whisper of stone against steel.

A 'scuse Missee' by a large Maori woman in a black, shapeless, long singlet-like dress swooping on the pile of fleece at Hone's feet, for the moment, broke the spell.

Mary followed after Davey as if in a trance as they continued their tour of the woolshed.

'The rouseabouts pick up the wool and throw it on to those shelves according to its quality and where it comes off the sheep. Then when the bins fill they put all of the same sort into these presses and then screw this down so the wool is forced down into the bale. When it's full, you see that woman there, she's sewing down the top, then she pulls out those four iron pins and the sides fall away. Bang! There you have a bale of wool. Like to stencil the Winchester brand on it?'

Mary had barely been following Davey's account and had been somewhat startled when the wooden sides had fallen off to reveal the bale. She declined the offer to brand the bale, not quite sure what was expected of her. She felt less self-assured than in all her life. She thought that the enormous breakfast and the shearing shed smells may have made her queasy but she was more light-headed in an excited sort of way and any feelings of unease seemed to come more from a tightness in her breasts and loins rather than her stomach. She looked back along the shearing floor and could see the bent form of Hone, the bright fleece falling about his feet.

As they came outside to the dip her stomach did do a turn. Whereas in the shearing shed there had been a silence except for the steady click of the shears and the wool-sorter's decisions as he flung the fleece behind him, outside, all was dust, noise and confusion. Having taken part in the muster she was prepared for this and spoke to some of the shepherds she knew by name as they filled the 'skillions' from which the shearers caught and dragged out the 'woollies'.

White, clean and somewhat bewildered-looking, they emerged to face the dip.

Mary knew that the sheep had to be dipped and on Winchester the flock had already been dipped three times that season, but this was the first time she had seen what was done and she was horrified at what she thought was the cruelty of the operation.

Davey assured her that it was necessary. 'In Kaikoura we have the worst scab problem in the whole of New Zealand. Your father thinks the wild pigs are a menace but they're nothing compared to scabby sheep. Laws have been passed making it an offence to have scabby sheep.'

Mary took her hand away from her mouth to ask old Peter Anderson, the shepherd who seemed to be supervising this scene from hell what he was putting in the water which had such a foul smell.

'Well, we be trying a recipe of me own. We was using lime and sulphur, that ponged even more ye ken. But this be 10 pound of baccy and a pannikin of arsenic to every 100 gallons, or thereabouts of water. Does the trick but they've got to be held under,' as another bleating sheep was tossed down the planking leading into the large hole that contained the evil-smelling liquid, and he pushed it under with the long pronged pole he had for the purpose. 'Got to give 'em a bit of arse over tip while they're under, like this,' and he demonstrated. Davey hoped that Mary would not be reporting to her mother the actual words of these conversations.

'But arsenic is poisonous! Don't some of the sheep die, if they swallow it? And what about the men? Isn't it dangerous?'

'Well, some of the sheep get a bit crook but a spell of coughing seems to see them right. And as for the men, I've told them for Christ sake, sorry Miss, if ya fall in keep your blo… blessed mouth shut.' Davey was grateful the old shepherd had not used with Mary the actual version in which he detailed the other orifices they should also endeavour to close.

One after another, the sheep condemned as scabby by the large 'S' branded on them continued to be thrown into the dip. Mary could hardly make herself heard over the bleating of those being seized and tumbled in and those coughing, retching, draining and shaking themselves on the slope leading out of the dip.

'How do they get it?'

Old Peter handed his prod over to another of the torturers, took out his pocket knife, cut off a slice from a plug of tobacco and kneaded it in his palm.

'Well, it's caused by a tick that burrows under the skin. Drives 'em mad. The flesh festers and then gets covered with a green scab. The sheep spread it by rubbing themselves on trees and posts. Ruins the wool and even for tucker they're not much good.' He filled an ancient pipe, struck a wax vesta on his moleskins, and lit up with a series of short puffs. Mary was glad that she had temporarily lost her sense of smell. She was amazed that he was so little affected by the stench: she could barely breathe.

'If they're too far gone, like them ones,' and he pointed with his pipe to a mob separately fenced, looking even more dejected than the rest of the dip victims, 'they'll be going to the boiling-down works and end up as talla.' When she had visited the port at Kaikoura Mary had noticed the barrels of tallow awaiting shipment to Wellington.

'Trouble is, not all of the owners will fence and their scabby sheep can infect others. But the 'spector can fine 'em now. Bert Cullen 'cross the Kowtra cleaned up his whole flock of 35,000, clean as a whistle they were and this mangy 'spector found one sheep in a small mob with the scab. Up went old Bert before the magistrate. But he only had to pay a fine on the number in the small mob. Just as well as it would have cost 'im something between threepence and a bob for every sheep he owned.'

'If we're ever to be free of the scab, Miss,' Davey came into the discussion, 'we have to be hard. It may seem cruel but it is the only way. Your father has told me when I'm hunting for pigs to shoot any stray woollies as they could be infected with scab'. Lady Mary seemed to be away with her own thoughts again and Davey explained further, 'A "woolley" is a sheep that was missed in the last muster and wasn't shorn.' Mary seemed as distant as ever.

The cook at this point came out from the shearing quarters kitchen with some freshly baked bread, which Mary thought looked delicious, and some cold tea.

'Rattle your dags, you jokers, and get stuck into this lot while the bread's hot an' the tea's cold.'

'Christ,' exclaimed old Peter, 'I'm as dry as a wooden god. Nothing like tea.' The dipping stopped, but the bleating continued and Mary returned to the homestead. She refused tea and went to her room. Later she wondered if Davey had escorted her back, but couldn't remember and little cared. But she could recall Hone in vivid detail.

When Huia visited her brother again that evening she was disgusted to find that he was as besotted with Lady Mary as the rest of the entire male work force of Winchester. She would have been even more enraged if she had heard old Peter Anderson, who was well into his 70s, declare, 'Her father wouldn't know a two-tooth ewe from a randy ram but that one's a bonnie lassie!'

This as Huia perceived seemed also the opinion of her brother, Hone. He was badly smitten. 'How can I see her again?'

Huia gave him a pitying look. 'You can't. She's the daughter of the owner. You're a shearer. Not your class. She wouldn't give you a second look.'

Hone remembered the look he had exchanged with Mary and didn't agree.

'Isn't there some way you could arrange that I could meet her? She was just like those pictures in Mum's fashion catalogues, do you remember them?'

Huia had learned some of her English from the same well-thumbed catalogues as Hone. 'You might just as well hope to meet the girls in those fashion pictures as have any chance of meeting Lady Mary.' She then used a coarse phrase in Maori meaning that Hone should pour cold water on a certain part of him to cool his ardour.

'Just forget her. I can't help you I'm only a maid and the only time I see her is when I'm serving at table.' This last phrase was in English as there just didn't seem to be a Maori equivalent. 'What do I say to her? "More devilled kidneys, Miss? And by the way that shearer you saw is my brother and he wants to meet you." '

'Right, I give in. But she did notice me, I know.'

At this stage one of the three other shearers in the bunk room called him back to the cribbage they were playing.

Huia returned to the homestead and was surprised to learn that Lady Mary had been asking for her. Huia ran through in her mind what omissions or indiscretions she may have committed. She may have skimped a little on the ironing of Lady Mary's crinolines, but they wouldn't show under her dress anyway.

From the kitchen Huia made her way up the back stairs to her tiny but, to her, sumptuous bedroom in the attic and tidied herself before presenting herself to Lady Mary in the drawing room.

She bobbed the curtsey that Cook had taught her and waited for Lady Mary to look up from the book she was reading.

In fact Mary was only feigning to read and was working out how she would ask this Maori girl about her brother. When she had commented, 'That one looks a strong worker,' Davey had told her he had been a whaler and was Huia's older brother. She could not tell this girl that it was not only the strength of her brother that she had admired. It was all so silly. She had seen him only once. He might be perfectly horrible. After all they were savages but a generation ago. But

142

no one with eyes like that and such a smile… Mary looked up and found herself looking at the same eyes and, as she continued to stare, at the same smile, although this one was not one of supreme confidence but rather one expressing some doubt and concern. Huia was sure now it was the rushed ironing of the crinolines – she had been hurrying to finish so that she could meet Davey – that had led to this meeting. As Cook put it, 'You'll be on the mat.' Huia wasn't quite sure what this meant, except trouble. The thought went through her mind that this would not be a good time to say to Lady Mary, 'My brother is smitten with you. Would you care to meet him?' Huia smiled and it was such a wonderful smile Mary laughed.

'You have a brother who is shearing here, I believe?' Mary was always direct but the effect of this question on Huia was shattering. As she related to Hone later, 'I stood there speechless, opening and closing my mouth like those big blue cod we used to catch.'

'Yes, Miss, Hone is my big brother.'

'I have been considering, Huia (she deliberately mispronounced her name), that I have no knowledge at all of the Maori (she carefully botched this word too) tongue and believe as part of my education I should learn some. I have heard you speak it at times and it sounds most melodious.'

Huia was again thrown into confusion as she tried to recall some of the occasions she had used Maori. Once, she recalled vividly had been when Davey's great brute of a pig dog had followed him into the kitchen and had seized a cured ham and bolted out the door. Another occasion, when Lady Mary had been present, was when she had held the iron too long on the starched front of one of Captain Browne's dress shirts. It had been Davey's fault both times. But the Maori she had used on both occasions would not have borne translation for Lady Mary's ears. The Maori alone would have shocked her but she remembered having embellished it with some Maori versions of terms she had picked up from the Kaikoura whalers when cooking for them.

'I don't speak Maori too good, Miss. We weren't allowed to speak Maori at the mission school and I've just picked it up at home. Some of the words I use – it wouldn't be right for you to use them, Miss.'

Mary had known Maori was not taught in schools and that Maori children who spoke it there were often punished if they forgot themselves and did so, as she had recently offended her father by having an 'unladylike' discussion, he said 'argument', with the Reverend Patrick O'Shea when he had been a dinner guest. He had declared that 'no good will come of allowing the natives to speak their own barbarous tongue whilst at school as they will never bother to learn English and they are a dying race anyway. There is no future for the Maori language.' Coming from a well-to-do family, Mary could afford to be liberal in her views and had opposed the reverend gentleman's opinions. He had been even more shocked when Mary declared that she, herself, intended to learn Maori.

Mary had little intention of learning Maori seriously but thought the stratagem might enable her to see Hone again, and to confirm one way or the other if he was as remarkable a young man as she had first thought. The deception of learning Maori might also not raise too much suspicion with her parents. Though, Mary reflected, her father had never thought it worthwhile to learn any of the Indian languages or dialects, except a minimum of basic commands for both army and home use, when they lived there.

'Is there perhaps someone else in your family who has a better command of Maori who could provide me with instruction?' Mary was ashamed her question was so obvious in its intent but Huia was a simple-minded girl and would accept the request at its face value.

Quite the contrary, though Huia's English was halting, her mind was as sharp as a barracouta's teeth. Her mind raced: Maori and pakeha thoughts scrambled in a mishmash with a phrase she had picked up from the whalers, 'as randy as a bitch on heat'. Not him! Not Hone! Oh no! They're both mad. It's just not possible. Dear God, let them each find someone else.

'My father is very old now, Miss, and he does not speak English. My mother might be able to instruct you, she speaks beautiful Maori and also speaks good English.' Huia awaited the effect of this suggestion on Lady Mary. If she acted stupid enough she might save her brother from this folly.

Mary was reluctant to take the next step as even this chit of a Maori girl would guess at her motive if she came straight out with a request for tuition from Hone.

'Perhaps you could arrange for me to meet someone suitable from your people in Kaikoura who might be prepared to come out here to give me some instruction.' Mary knew of Huia's friendship with Davey and saw a way of using him as a lever. 'We could ask Davey to take us in the carriage and pair for a picnic and you could ask this person to accompany us. Have you been on a picnic before?'

'I don't think so, Miss. I don't know what a 'pic-nic' is.'

'Well, we'll get Cook to pack us a special lunch in a hamper, and then we'll go somewhere in the countryside and picnic. We spread out rugs, put up parasols, sit on the ground, and in the secluded place we have chosen, perhaps in the shade near a stream, we eat our lunch from the hamper.'

Huia was not at all impressed by the idea of a 'pic-nic' but the thought of being driven out to a secluded spot in the country by Davey had considerable appeal. As to a suitable tutor for Lady Mary, she knew just the person: a cousin who spoke Maori quite tolerably. Fat, ugly and bad-tempered, she was just the sort of teacher Lady Mary deserved. Initially Huia had no intention of allowing Hone and Lady Mary to come anywhere near each other.

However, as her mind continued to race and she began to explore the possibilities of a picnic, and in particular the opportunity to be with Davey in what Lady Mary had described as a 'secluded place' she saw some advantage in the fourth party of the picnic being someone who could hold Lady Mary's total attention. She did not think her fat cousin, though of threatening manner, had the required qualities. Cook had used the expression 'two's company, three's a crowd' on one occasion when she had left her and Davey together in the kitchen and had later explained its meaning to Huia. But if Hone were to come, she mused, then she and Davey would become wairua and become invisible.

'Come on, girl, has the cat got your tongue?' Huia was a little puzzled by this expression too. However it was obviously a question and Lady Mary was expecting her to say something.

'A pic-nic would be bonzer,' (a term she had picked up from the whalers), 'Miss, I think I could get someone who could teach you Maori good. He was captured and lived as a boy with a North Island tribe, although he is Ngai Tahu, and so could teach you the way we speak and the way they speak'.

'I don't think an old man would be appropriate, Huia. I have seen some of those bent old men who were slaves and am sorry for them but couldn't bear them near me.'

'Oh, no, Miss, I thought my brother could teach you. He is quite young and not bent at all.' Huia was as much a woman as Lady Mary and was quite prepared to play her games. Hone was old enough to fend for himself and he was a necessary sacrifice to the Goddess of Love if there was the chance of an outing to a 'secluded place' with Davey.

The following evening, when she had completed washing up a mountainous pile of dishes after one of the Browne dinner parties and the silver had all been checked and locked away, Huia intended again paying her brother a visit. Mr Grimes, a whaler who had served some time in his career at sea as a steward and had been taken on by the Brownes as butler to improve the image of Winchester in the eyes of the local squattocracy, was charged with checking the silver and the crystal glasses back into his pantry. On this occasion he took an age and Huia was becoming frustrated as he slowly counted in the cutlery.

'We seem to be one pearl-handled fish knife short.'

'Check the copper sink, Huia,' suggested Cook as Huia stood there looking flustered.

Huia ran her fingers through the wash water and the knife surfaced catching the light from the kerosene lanterns. 'Here it is, Mister Grimes, just like a freshly caught kahawai.'

'Them knives are expensive. I'll be obliged, girl, if you'd take some care.' Mr Grimes, though Australian, and his father of convict origin, endeavoured to act the part, as he saw it, of butler.

When she finally made it out to the shearers' quarters, Hone was delighted at his sister's news although he had doubts as to his ability to act as tutor to Lady Mary.

He grinned at Huia, 'There may be some things I can teach her. Eh? They say even the kea can be taught new tricks.' Hone warmed to the topic. 'It's hard to explain some things. I may have to show her.'

'You may be older than me brother but just remember who pays you fellows,' and she looked past him to where the card players were again waiting impatiently to resume their game. 'Her father's the owner here and he can throw us all out.'

The carriage with its two-in-hand bowled along the roughly formed clay road in fine style. The two blacks stepped out eagerly and the dust cloud billowed behind. Davey kept the carriage in the ruts and avoided tussocks and rabbit holes. He recalled an almost identical day when he had picked up Huia from Kaikoura. Beside Davey, who was driving, sat Huia, clasping a straw hat, borrowed from Cook ('don't want you

getting sunstroke, girl' – a girl who had never worn a hat in her life). In the back seat were Hone and Mary.

The day had started disastrously. Mary had decided that the following Sunday would be a suitable day for the picnic and had requested Davey to have the carriage and horses ready for an early start. This did not suit Cook, who had some time off on a Sunday morning as the family usually had cold cuts on a Sunday. Lady Mary had ordered an elaborate hamper to be prepared with cooked chicken, mutton pies and freshly baked bread rolls.

'I don't hold with this gallivanting around. Particular as I've to get out of me bed hours before usual.' Huia had also come down early and had at least got the fire in the range lit before Cook had come in grumbling.

Captain Browne was not pleased about the expedition either. At breakfast he came down, and remarked to Huia, there being no one else about to complain to, 'It's not good enough. Mary knows we have a regular church parade scheduled for 10 o'clock on a Sunday. Relying on her to read the lesson. If he's made it down from Blenheim, the Reverend McAra should be coming out from Kaikoura. Jolly poor show,' as he helped himself to more bacon from the side board. 'Taking you,' he glared at Huia, 'and Davey. Although it's Sunday, there's still work to be done, my girl. And what's this about one of the shearers, and this cock-and-bull story of Mary learning Maori?'

Huia retreated to the comparative safety of the kitchen just as Lady Mary must have entered the dining room. Both Huia and Cook stood transfixed, not eavesdropping, but unable to prevent hearing the ruction in the next room. As Cook exclaimed, 'What a Donnybrook!'

'It is only a picnic, Father. It will provide me with an opportunity to see if this Maori person is suitable to teach me some Maori. I could not go unaccompanied and so Huia is going as my maid. Davey is needed to drive us.'

'You should not be associating with this type of person. Your mother is most concerned. After all, two of them are natives and the other fellow, admittedly a good horseman, is a pig-hunter and the station handyman.'

'As they are on the station, Father, I would think we associate with them already. We are not in India or England now and must change our attitudes to these colonials.'

'But it is ridiculous, unthinkable, that a Maori shearing hand should be employed to teach you Maori. You have been educated as a lady.'

'But I should be learning new things, useful to me here. Anyway, a picnic will be fun. I have hardly been off the station since we arrived. I've already told Davey to harness up the horses and we're going.'

The next disaster in the expedition's departure occurred after Davey had picked up Lady Mary and Huia at the front of the homestead. As Huia climbed up beside him, Davey whispered, 'You wouldn't be daring to come out the front door would you, now?' Huia collapsed against him in a fit of giggles. They then drove round to the shearing quarters and picked up Hone. He was waiting and vaulted up alongside Lady Mary who, as Davey later confided to Huia, 'shied away like an unbroken filly.' Huia twisted round from the front seat and made formal introductions as she had been coached by Cook. 'Miss, this is my brother Hone, Hone, I would like you to meet Miss Mary Browne.' Huia was pleased with her effort. Lady Mary smiled although obviously finding Hone rather close. He responded with a boyish grin and, in his most correct English, 'Pleased to meet you, Lady Mary.' She, though pale in complexion, turned paler and then rosy patches appeared on her cheeks and she burst out, 'I am not a Lady, you will call me plain "Mary".' Huia's jaw fell open, Davey doubled up and nearly dropped the reins and Hone was completely bewildered. He then added insult to injury by asking with complete innocence, 'Please, but why is your name "Plain Mary"?' Davey shook the reins over-vigorously and they all held on as the carriage lurched away.

Davey followed the rutted track heading for the Puhipuhi valley a few miles north of Kaikoura township and the 'secluded spot' Mary had in mind. Mary was still nursing her wrath. Huia and Davey were in the highest of spirits.

They followed a track made by the dragging out of trees for the local timber mill. Davey remembered when they had built their first cabin and they had pit-sawn timber. He and James had taken turns, one on top of the log, thrusting the great cross-cut saw, while the other looked up from the pit into the falling sawdust. The native bush in the valley, except for the larger timber trees, had been spared the burning-off by the sheepmen. Punga ferns reaching twenty feet high overhung the track. They moved further into the green, cool bush.

'There's a stream with a small waterfall and a pool just ahead, Davey.' Mary (after the outing both Davey and Huia dropped the Lady) gave the directions.

Davey helped Huia down from the box seat and, not to be outdone, Hone clasped Mary by her wasp-waist and effortlessly swung her to the ground. Huia braced herself for another outburst from Mary, but she had only laughed and seemed to have enjoyed the experience.

'I know this place,' exclaimed Hone as he turned round. 'Our father as a boy saw them bring out from here a great totara to be made into a waka.' Suddenly remembering his new role as tutor, he went on, 'Waka Mary, is our Maori word for canoe. It was a great war canoe. I'm sure the stump is not far from here; we could find it.'

Huia had heard the story many times before and anyway preferred to have Davey to herself. 'You take Miss Mary to see the stump, Hone.' She faced Mary. 'It's a tapu place for Maori women but you will be all right if you go with Hone.' Huia thought she had managed that quite well as Mary and Hone plunged into the tangled bush. She heard Hone's receding voice explaining that 'tapu' meant 'sacred' or 'forbidden'. Huia was surprised at Hone's command of English and thought that both might learn something by being together. Meanwhile she had Davey to herself.

They sat on the bank above the pool. Huia hated shoes and had kicked hers off and was trailing her feet in the water. Davey lay back and looked up at the canopy of creepers and bush above them. 'You know this is altogether different to Donegal. It's still a wild and untamed land. But there are opportunities here that we would never have had back home. You know I own a block of land in the swamp. It only needs draining and some fences and we'd have a farm. I need a bit more capital, which I'm getting from my pig-hunting and then I'll go back to it. We'd need a house, of course.'

Huia had not interrupted these recollections but noted that he'd said 'we'd' do this and 'we'd' do that and wondered if he had been talking about his partner, James, or whether she was included in his long-term plans. She decided that it would be in their best interests if she gave Davey a little assistance in making a firmer commitment that included her. She knew she loved him and nothing would suit her better than to be able to help on a farm. A house with the chooks, ducks and geese he was so keen on running round outside seemed 'bonzer' to her. She calculated the time she would have before the return of Mary and Hone.

She threw her dress, which was all she was wearing, over her head, and dived like a seal into the limpid water. When she surfaced Davey was standing on the bank seemingly ready to come to her assistance but also not quite knowing where to look. Huia laughed and swept her long auburn-black hair back from her face. 'Come on in. It's a bit colder than the sea but it will make you feel great'. There was nothing wrong with the way Davey felt and although he might shave with water or have it in whiskey there was no way he was going to swim in it. Huia laughed again, pushed off from the bank and swam on her back to the far side. This was not done by chance and she was pleased to see that the effect on Davey was most promising.

'If you don't want to come in you could make yourself useful instead of just gawping and fetch the towel. It's under the back seat by the hamper.'

When he returned Huia had hauled herself out and was sitting on the bank. 'You are quite a useful fellow, you know. You can dry my back now.' As Huia recalled later as she snuggled into Davey on the drive back to Kaikoura, all had gone very much to plan and she was sure she would be included in Davey's future plans. She did not find it strange that a Maori woman and a man from a country on the other side of the world should come together in this way. It was the mana, the standing, the magic of this Kaikoura coast that had made it possible.

As for Mary and Hone, they also enjoyed each other's company. Hone had succeeded in finding the stump of the waka tree, much overgrown with fern. His excitement communicated itself to Mary and she found much to admire in Hone. He showed her the plants that were good to eat, and told Mary their Maori names: the tiny red berries of the giant totara, the lettuce-tasting green ferns, the mamaku or black tree fern, the trunk of which was split to extract the thick, slimy pith. To Mary this was a new and strange world. Hone's knowledge seemed inexhaustible. He pointed out the poisonous plants: the kernels of the karaka tree that could cause paralysis and plants good for medicine such as the koromiko and the rata vine, the sap from which could be used for flesh wounds.

A large wood pigeon, Hone told her it was the kereru in Maori, with its green head and white breast flapped heavily by. Hone told Mary how the old time Maori snared them by putting out wooden drinking troughs in the forest to attract the thirsty birds after they had been feeding upon the berries of trees such as miro and kahikatea and he pointed these out to her.

As had Huia and Davey, Mary and Hone certainly came together but more as a meeting of minds. Mary, as she also nestled into Hone as the carriage rattled homeward, gave a chuckle. She might have succumbed totally to this fine, strong fellow but today she had fallen in love with the New Zealand bush and had also gained a new respect for this remarkable young man. She laughed aloud and Hone smiled down at her. She thought, I may have that the wrong way round, perhaps today I have gained a new respect for the bush and have fallen in love with this fine fellow.

As they followed the coast she wondered at the series of events that had brought her family to this country and what her so-very-English family would think if she announced she intended to marry what her father would call a 'native'? She foresaw a considerable battle on that score. Mary smiled again. As far as she knew her father had not won a battle in his life but getting round her mother might be another matter.

It was easier than Mary had expected. Her mother was undoubtedly a snob but she was not racist and her prejudices were firmly rooted in the English class system. In India she had been only too happy to entertain any nabob, no matter how spurious his title, irrespective of his colour. However, she scorned the 'lower classes' who were where they were in the social scale 'as a result of their own wilfulness'.

Mary demolished her father's attack on her proposed marriage by a frontal counter-attack in which she announced that she intended to live with Hone no matter what. She had earlier ambushed her mother along another path.

'Mother, you remember Hone, who is helping me in my studies of Maori. I have just learned from Huia, who is a member of the same tribe, the Kai Tahu (she, for obvious reasons did not mention to her mother that his sister was their own kitchen maid), that he is the son of a chief, in fact the paramount chief of all this part of the coast.' A slight exaggeration but for a good cause.

Hone had been invited to dinner: a most uncomfortable experience for him. Elizabeth was astonished that he could recite his whakapapa back a thousand years to Rangi, the Sky God. That was certainly better than her genealogy back to the Wars of the Roses when her ancestors had acquired land. Captain Browne still regarded Hone as a 'native' but viewed him in a kinder light when he heard some of his whaling experiences as a harpooner and also some of the stories of Maori battles.

'I'll be blowed, had no idea you chaps were so clever in warfare. Could have taught us a thing or two in tactics, eh?'

He was only a little put out when Hone replied, 'Yes, actually we did in the North Island when we were fighting to get our lands back in the wars of the sixties.'

The energy and the magic of the Kaikoura coast, as evident in its teeming marine life culminating in the mighty whales, is derived from the conflict of disparate elements. The mixing of cold and warm ocean currents produces the plankton on which the food chain of the ocean is based; the conflict between land and sea creates spectacular coastal scenery. The conflict between polar and semitropical air masses spawns great storms.

Storms are as much a part of the Kaikoura coast as the daily breathing of the tides, although less predictable. Nothing can impede the wild southerlies that blow up from the Antarctic seas and savage the warm air that blows indolently from the north.

Many ships have been wrecked and many people drowned along the coast. Other than the peninsula of Kaikoura there was no shelter, no safe haven, for two hundred miles. The navigators Maui, Kupe and Cook, and the whalers and sealers, had all recognised the value of the Kaikoura peninsula as a safe anchorage. It was one of the few features along this part of the coast that stood between the opposing winds. When the wind blew from the north, South Bay offered shelter, and when the wind turned southerly, the northern bay, along which the town straggled, gave welcome refuge.

The sea god Tangaroa had apparently not taken kindly to the idea that Fyffe Cove, near the whaling station, should become an officially recognised port of entry. When the *Sea Bird*, carrying marine surveyors from the capital, Wellington, arrived off the Kaikoura peninsula,

Tangaroa summoned up such mountainous seas they were forced to run south to Amuri Bluff and there when the southerly struck they were forced to abandon ship, take to the boats and flee shoreward. The tide, or Tangaroa, spared them and the seas swept them over the reefs below the cliffs and they landed more dead than alive.

This same storm, gaining strength and sweeping inland, was to have dire consequences for those such as James and Davey who were attempting to break in and tame the alluvial plains of the interior. The plain that they had started to cultivate for the first time had been laid down over thousands of years by the great rivers with proud Maori names: Kahutara, Kowhai, Hapuku, which rose in the Kaikoura mountains. More rain was going to fall in this area than had ever fallen before in the memory of man. No stories in Maori oral history spoke of such a terrible storm and resulting flood as this one.

The wind had veered from south-west to south-east and blew steadily against the coastal hills and mountains. In four days over thirty inches of rain fell. The Maori would have explained the storm as Rangi crying, and this was near the truth as it was the moist warm air above belaboured from below by the cold that over several days released the torrential rain. The major rivers came down in tumultuous flood. Nothing could stand against the spate of water. Boulders as large as houses were rolled down the river beds. The force of the water carried all before it. Trees, as if drowning, thrust arms above the boiling muddy-yellow flow and were tossed end over end. Rivers lost their form and became continuous sheets of rolling water that spread out over the shingle fans they had in ancient times created. Millions of tons of sand and shingle were brought down from the high country and spread over the flood plains. Islands in the centre of braided rivers were swept away. Good topsoil on the lower plains was carried away and deposited in the sea.

The Kowhai River which had flowed to the south of the Kaikoura peninsula built up a new, higher bed of shingle and then the main flow of water shifted to the north side of the peninsula. This had been a natural sequence of events in geological time past and had resulted in the island of that time becoming a peninsula tied to the mainland. But now, in February 1868, human habitations had been erected in the ancient path of the storm waters.

James looked out from the doorway of his whare and saw that muddy water was already racing over the potato fields. The potatoes were a month or two from harvest. James shook his head and wondered if he would get a harvest. A few hours later as under leaden skies the rain continued to fall without pause and the last of the potato tops disappeared under the rising waters James realised that not only might he lose his precious potatoes but the very soil in which they were growing. The whare was on a slight rise, which gave it some protection, but James believed it could at any moment be swept away. It was too late for him to move out and seek refuge in the Kaikoura village or the whaling station. They in any case were almost at sea level and although protected by the peninsula from much of the direct force of the overflowing rivers would nevertheless be flooded.

The Maori village on top of the peninsula was above the flood waters, although their fishing canoes on the beach were swept out to sea. Good use was made of the four whaling boats at the fishery to evacuate some of the settlers from the town, which had grown up along the beach, to the higher ground of the peninsula. The Adelphi 'Hotel', consisting of two mud-hut whares with gin case extensions, was evacuated before it sank in to the waters of the flood. A rival establishment, the Caledonian Hotel, bore the full brunt of the assault by the Kowhai River and one side slowly toppled into the flood waters. The shepherds and shearers staying there were ferried out to higher ground by the whale boats. The rising waters soon became too swift for even these hardy boats to operate and they were hauled up on to the top of the peninsula. The town was abandoned to the flood waters.

The Clarence River, which James had crossed by ferry on his first journey to Kaikoura, was thirty feet higher than had ever been known. Many houses were washed away.

James had waited too long to possesss his own land to give it up without a struggle but it seemed as if it was going to be taken from him. There was little he could do during the long night except listen to the rain steadily driving against the thatched walls and roof. As the flood waters came up to the lower bunk he climbed into the top one and remained dry there but during the night he had put out a hand and touched water. James could do nothing, except pray. Although the scene next morning was one of utter devastation, he did have something to be thankful for: the flood, which was now obviously subsiding as the rain eased, had brought down from up-river and deposited great heaps of sand and shingle, one of the largest of which was piled on the inland side of James's whare. It was ten feet high and almost higher than the roof of the whare and it had provided protection for the whare. The main spate of flood water had been turned aside and both the whare and James had been spared. James later found the large stone used for a doorstep wedged against a flax bush on the edge of the swamp.

Much of the topsoil, together with the potatoes and oats, had been swept away and would now be at the bottom of Kaikoura bay. James joked when he later saw Davey, who was still working at Winchester station, 'If we can get out and catch some fish in the bay the taties should already be inside them.' But there was little chance of catching fish. The sea, for miles out, was discoloured with mud and the beaches were littered with driftwood. Dead sheep were entangled in the confused mass of branches and barbed wire.

James was disappointed at the loss of their crops but there was much on the plus side. Ellen had stood against the whare throughout the storm with her back to the driving wind and a high water mark high on her chest indicated how great a flood they had survived. James was optimistic, ' 'Twill give me a foine foundation, those stones, for me new house.'

Davey, inland at Winchester, although they had suffered some flooding, had not realised the damage that had resulted down country and to his own fifty-acre block. Shingle had buried much of his 'farm' and his potatoes and oats had also been washed away. The fresh water spring they had used was buried. The remaining soil was buried under a layer of boulders and shingle. This could be removed with a great deal of effort and Ellen's assistance but there would be no crop this year and Davey would need to continue his employment as handyman and pig-hunter at Winchester. His relationship with Huia was such since the 'Great Snow' that he was only too pleased to be back there.

For the Browne family and Davey and Huia at Winchester, their time of trial had come the previous year, in August 1867.

Again the cause was a storm. Tangaroa could not have been held responsible as the sea and snow have nothing to do with each other and are antagonists. The sky god may have had a hand in it, as the sky from a brilliant blue had turned leaden and then it snowed as had never been known before, or since.

On the Wednesday the snow storm began, Mary looked out from the bay window of the dining room at Winchester, at the great flakes of swirling snow that settled softly on the home paddocks. Even as she watched, the paddock fences became progressively dwarfed. The five-barred gates lost one bar, then another, and another, until only the top bar remained. The garden gate disappeared and snow started to build a wall across the veranda. Soon the snow was up to the window-sills.

The next day fences and out-houses had completely disappeared under the snow and it continued to fall throughout the Thursday. No one stirred on the station. A deep blanket of snow filled the valleys and smoothed out cliffs and promontories. All animals had been completely buried. The dogs' kennels were under feet of snow and the house milking cows had disappeared.

When Huia, who had never before seen snow so close, looked out of her open attic window on to a landscape that was featureless, white and silent, it was a frightening experience.

On the Friday, Davey and John Anderson, the shepherd, dug their way out of the shearers' quarters and reached the stables. They were able to feed out some oats to the starving horses that had managed to keep a few yards of clear space around them by moving about. A snow wall surrounded them. They then dug across to where they thought the dog kennels might be and by calling encouraged them to dig their way out to the surface. Kate's dam, the old black and white Border bitch, did not appear and Davey presumed her dead. They dug down and found her body quite stiff.

With the aid of the dogs, although they had difficulty staying on the surface, the house milk cows were found, dug out and with much pushing, dragging and bellowing were brought to the enclosure made by the horses. The cows were also starving and Davey and John Anderson struck out in the general direction of the nearest haystack. Although only 200 yards away it took them four hours to dig a track through to it. They then tried to find the fowl house but had to give this up.

Having done all he could for the animals, Davey thought he had better check on the situation of those in the homestead. It was another long dig, to the back door of course, thought Davey, with a grin. By crawling on top in some places and digging a trench in others he came to where he thought the back door should be, found it and opened it inwards. As he tumbled in he was seized with joy by Huia and hugged and kissed. Davey said afterwards he had been too weak to defend himself and submitted without a struggle.

The family were in quite a bad way as the dray had been expected up from Kaikoura the previous week with supplies but storms had held up the boat from Wellington and the result was they had run out of practically all supplies. They were completely out of rice and flour and Huia had taken a tea chest apart to get the last few tea leaves from the corners to make the Browne family tea that morning. There was no meat in the house.

Mrs O'Flaherty had taken one look at the snow and had returned to her bed from which she had not stirred, declaring, 'Oi'll die in me bed warm, be Jasus. If there's nothing in the pantry to cook I'd be wasting me time to get myself out of bed.'

Huia eventually released Davey for which he in no way seemed grateful and suggested that he could perhaps return into the snow to forage for some food for the family.

Davey expressed some reluctance. 'It would freeze the... the...' Davey changed his line to one more suited to Huia's ears. 'No one could persuade me to go out into that again.' Huia persuaded him nevertheless, almost without uttering a word. A kiss and a promise that she would warm him when he returned was all it took.

'I've broken up the last of the boxes for firing, Davey. We need wood and we need meat. There was some bacon hanging beside the fire place in the wash house.'

Davey had located the garden fence as he had dug his way in and returned to it and knocked down all he could reach and returned with it for fuel. He failed to find any bacon in Huia's wash-house. However, he had more luck with the fowl house which he managed to find this time. He dug down, prised off the roofing and reached the hens. They were near to death and mere bundles of feathers. However, he gathered in as many as he could reach and returned to Huia. He was well rewarded by Huia for the scraggy hens, sorry as they might be. Davey found it difficult to get through the snow but there were certain advantages he found in making a number of separate trips. On each return he was warmly received. It was coming on night and the temperature had already dropped below freezing. Davey made one last journey to the shed where he butchered sheep for the house. He couldn't open the door as it opened outward so again he lifted off some of the rush thatching on the roof and got in that way to retrieve a leg and chops. This was a most fortunate find as Huia was quite carried away with the sight of this food and rewarded him extravagantly. She had already used the fence to good effect in the stove and had made some chicken broth. Davey stood in the kitchen before the fire to thaw out and took in great lungfuls of the steam from the broth.

Davey stayed the night. Candles and oil for the lamps had almost run out so when Huia took him up to her room he agreed with her that they would make do without lights. In spite of the snow still lying deeply ouside Davey had never spent a warmer night. They had chicken broth again for breakfast.

The wind shifted from south to north-west and outcrops of rocks began to appear on the hills as the snow was being blown off in clouds like spray. Davey continued his foraging activities. He discovered one of Captain Browne's baconers and promptly turned it into fresh pork. He also found some Indian meal intended for the fowls, but as these had all been turned into chicken broth, Huia made some very acceptable hot cakes out of the meal. Captain Browne declared Huia's pork curry, made to a recipe told to her by a whaler's 'wife', was 'top notch' and the fowl-feed girdle scones to be 'as good as any chapati he had tasted in India'. What these were Huia had no idea but Captain John obviously intended it as a compliment. Cook at first rejected them outright as 'heathen food and only fit for the divil.' However, the curry and the change in the weather raised her spirits sufficiently for her to contemplate getting out of bed.

By Tuesday the snow was melting rapidly and, around the homestead, turning into slush. Davey's clothes were soaking and as there was no fire wood to spare to dry them Huia had come up with a solution which meant his having to put on wet clothes each morning but spending the night warm and dry. Davey thought the morning agony of wet clothes a small price to pay for the warmth and comforts he enjoyed in Huia's bed.

On the Wednesday, after a severe frost, the day dawned bright and clear. All the men prepared to go out to rescue what stock might still be alive. Mary was also anxious to help and treated her own riding boots with weka oil and set out with the rescue party. They walked right across the five-barred gate, the top rail was just visible. On the hills streaks of the taller tussock were starting to show through. As they trudged through the snow and came over the brow of the first hill Mary could see dusty patches close to one of the deepest and widest creek beds. Another patch lower down would seem to be in the creek itself. Swamp hens hunting for food made splashes of peacock blue against the white snow. The grey patches indicated where sheep had 'mobbed' for protection against the snow.

 Some of the men had shovels and rakes. The dogs were greatly excited and started to burrow down. Mary used her hands. When they reached them the ewes were packed solid. Here, most of them were still alive and the men lifted them out and carried them over to a tramped down area of packed snow on the other bank. Mary could lift only the lambs but few of these had survived. She noticed two ewes leaning towards each other, a lamb under them alive, another one beside them dead. They rescued 1,400 ewes and a handful of lambs.

The dogs helped to find others in drifts but only a few of these were alive. The grey area in the centre of the creek was a graveyard. The sheep had mobbed in the creek itself and had either been suffocated or had drowned. There were no survivors here.

The rescue party returned to the homestead absolutely exhausted. Mary's hands were blue with cold and her feet ached as snow had fallen inside her boots. The men had tied their moleskin trousers above their boots and this kept out the snow but they were cold and wet. However, all soon rallied when Captain John insisted that all, even Cook, ('Thank you kindly, sir, a drop will help me a treat') shared his French brandy. However, the crisis was now almost over and Captain John dismissed his staff with a brisk, 'Thank you all for pulling together, things will still not be easy as we have lost a great many stock and almost all of this year's lambing, but you will all be staying on.' Cook and Huia returned to the kitchen, Davey and the shepherds back to the shearers' quarters and the Browne family prepared, after almost a week under seige, to dress for dinner. Dinner was again curried pork, but this time on a bed of Indian fowl meal, food which Captain James again pronounced as, 'Capital!' and launched into a discussion with himself as

159

to whether it had been Rawalpindi or Peshawar where he had tasted no better.

Most of the snow had thawed from around Winchester homestead but when Davey rode inland some weeks later he still found the main tracks impassable and snow a hundred feet deep in the gullies. Davey and the shepherds were kept busy skinning the dead sheep. All the fences around the homestead were festoned with sheep skins.

Although both these storms did great damage to the countryside and resulted in considerable loss of stock they could be credited with two positive outcomes.

First, a consequence of the snow storm, was that Davey, once of Donegal, Ireland and Huia of the Kaikoura hapu of the Ngai Tahu tribe were married by a visiting clergyman. Bride and groom arrived for the ceremony in the only spring cart in the Kaikoura township at that time. Captain Browne had made available his pair of blacks from his own carriage. The local spring cart also served for the delivery of meat and fish in the township and as a hearse for funerals.

The wedding was celebrated in a building in the Kaikoura township which served as a church but had previously been stables and retained features of startlingly unecclesiastical architecture. Captain Browne, who attended, thought the building 'first class'. He had made some contribution to drink and victuals for the occasion as he believed his horses may have suffered badly in the snow if Davey had not rescued them. More people gathered for the wedding than had ever assembled in one place in Kaikoura since the Ngai Tahu marae meetings before Te Rauparaha's attack. The Brownes were all there and some other neighbours from adjoining sheep stations, including George Fyffe. The entire Maori village, now numbering about sixty, attended. More smallholders had taken up land in the swamp and some of James's and Davey's relations, who with their financial assistance had emgirated from Donegal, were also present. As James declared, 'It was a foine occasion.'

It was an uncomfortable gathering in one way, however, as for the most part the 'tribal' groups that made up the growing Kaikoura populace kept to themselves. The landed 'squattocracy' did not mix with the 'swamp' Donegal Irish and neither group had much to do with the remnant Maori 'native' population. Shepherds and shearers were further sub-groups. Methodists, Presbyterians, Anglicans and Catholics were happier each in their own company.

Davey and Huia's marriage flew in the face of the religious, social and racial prejudices of that time but they brought together two proud blood lines, one Scottish-Irish, the other Ngai Tahu Maori.

Mary's marriage was also a 'mixed' one but only for the first few months a happy one. For Captain and Elizabeth Browne the prejudices of race and class they had known as children and that had been entrenched over a lifetime were too strong. Hone, to Captain Browne, still remained one of the 'natives'. As a chief he had some status in the eyes of Mrs Elizabeth Browne but when she discovered he was Huia's brother, 'His sister a pantry and chamber maid!' he was damned. When Hone's father died, Mary accompanied Hone and joined him to sit with the body and remained for the funeral. Captain Browne and his wife could not bring themselves to attend.

Mary never returned to Winchester. She and Hone were married at a small wedding attended by his people but none of hers. After the wedding Mary felt uncomfortable living in Kaikoura and they moved further north to one of the large high country stations, where Hone was employed as a shepherd. They had their own station cottage, not what Mary had been used to, but she enjoyed riding out to muster with Hone.

Mary reluctantly ceased her riding out into the hills she had come to love so much when she realised she was several months pregnant. When Mary's time came, Hone drove her in the station's gig the long, dusty miles to the imposing wooden building in Blenheim that had been the homestead of one of the earliest runholders of the district, and which now served as a maternity hospital. After the two-hour bone-jarring ride on iron-clad wheels Mary was white-lipped and in agony. Hone was not unduly worried as he accepted that some pain for women was just part of the natural process of a child entering this world. He had carried her into the hospital and had wanted to stay for the birth but was driven out by a number of what he referred to later as, 'old bags of great girth in stiff white starched uniforms that crackled as they waddled'. They bundled him out the ornate stained-glass bordered main door. The birth of a child had never been like this back at Kaikoura, thought the bemused and downcast Hone.

'Come back in an hour or two, young fellow, and it will be all over.'

Hone untethered the mare, one of Mary's favourites, stroked her muzzle and confided, 'Well, girl, we'll just have to wait.' At the first hotel in town he tethered her again and found refuge in the public bar to wait the long hours.

Mary died before Hone returned. The midwives had sent for the local doctor when it became obvious that the task was beyond Mary's failing strength though not, to the very end, her courage.

Whether the doctor made any conscious decision to save the baby at the cost of Mary's life or whether as a country GP he just did his best, Hone, still at the pub looking into an untouched schooner of beer, would never know.

The life had ebbed out of Mary with a massive, unstoppable haemorrhage. Her death was not an exceptional occurence at that time, as testified by the several orphanages even in a small town like Blenheim, but the doctor felt he needed to determine the exact cause of Mary's death and did not immediately sign a death certificate.

Hone knew something was wrong the moment he came through the massive front door of the maternity home. The nurses again appeared in force but seemed gentler and less stiffly starched.

'You have a beautiful son.' To Hone it was said as one would offer an apology. 'But we are so sorry…'

Hone had faced death before. With his whanau he had often provided support for those near death and had spent days and nights with the dead on the marae before a tangi. Now he was confused, plunged into the depths of anguish and guilt. Mary had been alone, with none of her family to help her as she set out on her final journey. Her soul would now have cleaved sea and seaweed through the rock hole, leading to the path of no return. Hone saw her spirit plunge into the surf along the Kaikoura coast. She may already have reached Cape Reinga and taken the final leap.

Mary had enjoyed no warmth of family, seen no familiar face, heard no karakia chanted to free her spirit. Hone hung his head and tried to shut out the image of the agony of her lonely death and the coldness of the hospital mortuary, alone, alone until he had come to weep for her. He had loved her free spirit and also her fair features which now in death were set as marble and as cold.

For Hone the final horror was when he was being prised from Mary by the same white-uniformed 'hags from hell' to hear the pakeha word 'post-mortem' of which he had first learned the meaning, in disbelief, when one of the whalers, whilst cutting blubber, had suddenly collapsed and died.

For the post-mortem, this obscenity, the funeral was delayed and Hone suffered dreadfully.

In the end he buried Mary in the Blenheim cemetary in the pakeha way. Hone himself saw that the grave was dug early and the casket closed before sunrise. The day before he had argued unsuccessfully with the hospital staff to allow him to take his baby son to join him in a last farewell. That he had asked for the afterbirth of his son so that he might respectfully return it to the earth had offended the hospital authorities so much they now regarded him as being little better than a savage.

Huia arrived from Kaikoura that day, having ridden the near hundred miles on horseback, and gave her brother some consolation. A southerly storm was lashing the coast and she and her horse had swum most of the fords.

Hone was glad it was still raining on the day of the funeral. The station manager and four of his fellow musterers, the only other mourners, stood about awkwardly, their sou'wester oil skins shedding rivulets of rain. Hone saw in the reflected puddles the shining tears that would have fallen on the rocks rimming the sea pool where Mary's spirit had started her journey of no return.

The pakeha clergyman struggled to provide some glimmer of hope but failed to reach Hone.

Huia's waiata tangi caused tears to mix with rain on even the craggy faces of the sheepmen.

As for Hone, he, in Maori, called after her spirit with an assurance of his enduring love but ended his lament in black despair with a cry of bitter anguish:

Ki te po uriuri, ki te po tangotango, ki te po oti atu.	To the dark night, to the intensely dark night, to the final night.

Huia stayed a week with Hone and then returned with his baby to Kaikoura. Hone never returned to Kaikoura. Davey welcomed Hone's son into their own growing family.

From the beginning along the Whale Coast there had been times of darkness, of black night, and despair; and times of bright day, and happiness.

For the family of Huia and Davey O'Neill happier times lay ahead.

Huia had no difficulty having babies and within ten years her brother's son had five brothers and three sisters. Davey each year extended their original cottage. With a large, happy family, and the flocks of ducks and geese in the yard outside, Davey often thought of Donegal but as he just as often said to James, 'They were good times but we're a sight better off here, and the land is ours.'

Just as it had been the shared trials of the great 1867 snow storm that had brought Davey and Huia closer together and led to their marriage, so for James Adair, in an odd way, it was the 1868 rain storm that benefited him. The shingle and sand deposited on James's swamp land, though first thought a disaster, provided him with the incentive of the near destruction of his original whare and some higher, well drained land on which to build himself a new house.

He and Davey built it with pit-sawn timber as a much grander version of their home in Donegal. It had a second storey with bedrooms upstairs and wooden floors throughout. It was no sooner finished than James proposed to Mary Buchanan, who had recently come from Tipperary with her family. She was only sixteen but in Ireland it was the custom for the husband to be older.

James and Mary's house became the social centre of the Donegal Irish and on Sundays most of the Irish families would gather there. There was always a great pot of taties over the fire and all were welcome. There was boiled meat on the stove. A large boiler always had thirty or forty hard-boiled eggs to share with visitors, another custom brought from Donegal.

Word would quickly go round that it was 'party night' and James and Mary would greet everyone at the door. Dancing and singing then started with the accompaniment of accordians, concertinas, violins, Jew's harps and mouth organs. The purchase of a German piano was a major event.

It arrived by the schooner *Ruby*. She had been a gunboat during the Land Wars in the Waikato and was one of the fastest coasters operating. Getting the piano to Kaikoura had been no trouble but James had his heart in his mouth as it had been swung first on to a whale boat then up on to the wharf at Fyffe's Cove with the crane used to load wool bales. The dray and Ellen completed the journey to Carnbouy, as he had named his new house. The piano was well worth the trouble.

Old and young all joined in the dancing. The older O'Neills, after a few home-brewed whiskeys, would move into the centre of the room and do an Irish jig, holding their glasses high and kicking their heels behind in a sort of skip.

Songs were sung between dances and there was no dearth of soloists. James's nephew prided himself on 'I met her in the garden where the praties grow'. Brother Charlie would sing 'I am a wee boy from Athlone and wish I had never left home'. About eleven o'clock Mary would start into 'The Mountains of Mourne' and all would join in. There was hardly a dry eye among those who remembered Donegal, but a cup of tea prepared the visitors for the walk home along the dark, narrow, drain-bounded swamp roads. Charlie, who lived furthest away, had a cart and horse. The horse knew the way home even if on some party-nights Charlie did not. On one occasion he was lucky as cart, horse and Charlie all slipped off the steep crown of the road into the ditch. The cold swamp water sobered Charlie immediately and he recovered horse and cart and walked the rest of the way home, cursing his horse for its stupidity with rich Irish oaths. The horse plodded sedately along behind, knowing it would be rubbed down and given oats when they arrived home.

Chapter 5
Land for Soldiers

To Moki and the survivors of his Ngai Tahu people, his son Hone, who had fished for whales, for the people from Donegal who farmed the swamp, the squatters inland who grazed sheep, the problems that they had faced seemed of local origin, to have arisen from the coast itself or at least in the land that the Maori had known as Aotearoa and the later settlers as New Zealand.

But often events that affected the Kaikoura coast were merely reflections or extensions of worldwide occurrences. Even the birth of the coast in ancient geological times was part of greater global earth movements: it just so happened that Kaikoura was at the interface between one great earth crustal block and another.

That Te Rauparaha had practically destroyed Moki's people was mainly the result of his being able to trade flax fibre for muskets from a people who had come from the other side of the world. The enmity between their tribes was but the spark to the gunpowder. Hone harpooned whales because their oil and bone had a value on the other side of the world and the same could be said for the sheepmen who made a profit out of wool. But when prices for these commodities fell the livelihood of people on the Kaikoura coast also suffered.

In the northern hemisphere three great disasters occurred in the years after 1900 which should not perhaps have affected the Kaikoura coast but it had become caught up in the economic and political affairs of the wider world and could not escape these disasters and it too suffered the consequences.

The first of these disasters is commemorated at Kaikoura, as it is throughout New Zealand, even in the smallest hamlet, by a list of names, usually on a bleak stone monument, sometimes on something more useful like a community hall. The commemorations all have similar wording: 'In Glorious Memory to those from this District who Gave Their Lives in World War I 1914-1918.' The names are different. In the Memorial Gardens at Kaikoura beside the path beneath the archways of ageing whale ribs a simple, natural stone monument bears both the names of those who served and survived the slaughter and those who died. At Kaikoura the names half way down read:

Pte Mu J.K. Killed
Sgt O'Neill D.A. M.M.
Pte O'Neill R.K. Killed
Spr Prince J.A.

The third name is that of the grandson of Davey O'Neill and his wife Huia. He was 20 years old when he died and had little idea why he was fighting against an enemy he did not know and did not hate, in a place called Gallipoli he had never heard of. The seventy-five-year-old Davey, on being told of his grandson's death, cursed the English politician who had conceived the idea of such a lunatic attack on the Dardanelles and the incompetent English general who had led, from the safety of a warship, the landing at the wrong beach. Young Roy with others of the Maori Battalion, fresh from Malta, had arrived at Sulva Bay to reinforce the Australian and New Zealand Division (ANZACs). They climbed the tortuous slopes and scaled the cliffs almost to the crest and then were pinned down by Turkish fire. Some New Zealand troops passed through them and captured the crest of Chunuk Bair. Old Davey, before he died a few short years later, never tired of telling the story of their bravery.

'There was the Dardanelles spread out before them, the whole object of this wretched expedition, and the English generals failed to give them support. Malone, the Irish colonel of the New Zealand Wellington battalion, did a grand job. The Turks showered them with grenades. Do you know,' he would declare, 'that only 70 of Malone's 800 came back from that hill, and my grandson Roy was one of them. Malone himself, a good man for sure, was killed. They should have sent some of those milksop English generals up there.'

Thirst, vermin and flies in the fierce summer heat were enemies as pitiless as Johnny Turk. Young Roy's death was neither romantic nor gallant. On coming down from Chunuk Bair he had contracted enteric fever and within a week was dead.

The name above his on the monument is 'Davey O'Neill', the youngest grandson of old Davey. After word had been received that his brother had died at Gallipoli 'on active service', he added a few years to his age, enlisted and fought in most of the victories and defeats on the Western Front. He undoubtedly did know what he was fighting for. In the manner of his grandmother Huia's family it was for utu for the death of his brother. At the battle of the Somme he had gone into action with the 2nd Canterbury Battalion on the first day behind two of the new tanks. The next night he led a bayonet charge with a display of bravery and ferocity which would have delighted his Maori warrior ancestors. In twenty-three days the New Zealand Division had suffered, in this 'famous victory', 7,000 casualties with over 1500 killed. Young Davey, against all the odds, was not one of them. For his gallantry on the Somme, he was awarded the Military Medal. Old Davey would have been very proud of him but before young Davey returned home, he died in the great influenza epidemic, one further outcome of the Great War from which Kaikoura was not spared.

It is only right that the stone monument in the Memorial Gardens on the beach front should record and honour all those who fought in this 'war to end all wars'. Those who survived were as brave as those who died. On the opposite side of the memorial tablet is another list of names of another generation from Kaikoura who perished in a second world war.

World War I had little visual effect on the Kaikoura landscape, certainly not in the way that Flanders fields had been turned into a lunar landscape of shell craters and mud but increased wartime demand for two products, butter and whale oil, had far-reaching effects on the people and the land.

Whale oil increased in price making it again worthwhile to hunt the returning humpback whales who were attacked with all the weapons of modern warfare. Fast motorised launches which could easily keep up with either humpback or right whales were armed with a powerful harpoon gun in the bow. These monstrous guns, looking much like enormous duelling pistols, hurled massive barbed harpoons.

Henare Tai was tempted to apply for the job of harpooner on one of the new chasers. Henare's father and his father before him, going back to Moki, had been fishermen. Henare was proud that his grandfather,

Hone, had been a harpooner on one of the early whale boats putting out from Wai a Puka on the northern side of the peninsula. The new, modern whaling was based in a bay on the southern side of the peninsula. But Henare did not apply for the harpooner's job, because he did not approve of the modern methods used.

The whales had no chance of outrunning the fast chaser boats as the harpoon gun had a range of up to twenty yards. There was no need to lay alongside as in the old days. Instead of the lance to kill the whale, bombs were carried which could be electrically detonated. Henare was most upset at this sort of 'fishing' which resulted in the killing between 1917 and 1920 of some thirty whales, mainly humpbacks. Henare was particularly enraged by the killing of a mighty sperm whale, none of which had been killed along the Kaikoura coast in the previous sixty years.

A modern factory was established at South Bay for processing the whales. A traction engine was used to haul the carcasses out of the water. The stench combined that of rotting flesh and fish, which had been a feature of the old whaling station, with that of the coal smoke from the traction engine as its great fly-wheel spun and the steel hawser drew another humpback up the slipway. After the blubber was removed with old-style cutting spades it was loaded into a large chopping machine and then into the one large tank for rendering down. The corrugated iron-clad factory, the litter of whale bones, the smoke and the stench did nothing to enhance the still beautiful limestone cliffs and reefs in their setting of blue sea and sky.

Except then for the World War I memorials and the litter of bones in South Bay, the war had left little mark on the Kaikoura coast. But there were sorrowful gaps in many families where there had been shining young men with golden futures. Their loss was a terrible price for a young country to have to pay to participate in world affairs. What also could not be seen was the new way the Kaikoura people were starting to think of themselves – as citizens of a country that was entitled to stand on its own two feet, to make its own decisions on the world scene and never again to be involved in a European war.

But the brave new world after World War I was not to be, or was at least postponed, because in 1929 another world disaster was, like the shock wave of a massive earthquake, to reach round the earth and affect the lives of the people of the Kaikoura coast. The economic Slump was the second world disaster the Kaikoura coast could not escape.

The Depression is usually attributed to the Wall Street crash of 1929 and that in turn was attributed to the failure of an obscure Austrian bank. This remote world event, just like the circumstance that enabled Te Rauparaha to buy muskets and go on the rampage, was just the incident that worsened the effect of a series of events that had already occurred in New Zealand and that had started the country on the slippery downward economic slope, the Slump of the late 20s and the early 30s.

There had been a change of government in 1928 and increased unemployment was already a problem. Wool and dairy prices were falling. By 1929 wool was down to fourpence a pound and butter prices had halved.

 Young Davey O'Neill, after his return from the war, had obtained a bank loan with his grandmother as guarantor and bought, for a dairy farm, two of the original fifty-acre swamp blocks that his grandfather had helped to drain and break in. His grandmother had told him how they had decided to try a few cows on their swamp block. She would prepare the morning porridge on the coal range and, before going out to hand-milk their twenty black and white Holsteins, would breastfeed Davey's father, and then it would be out to the milking shed, rain or shine. Davey remembered her showing him the heavy white china shallow bowl in which she settled the milk. The cream separated on top and the whey was poured out of the spout half way down the side of the bowl. Butter was then made in a wooden churn. Davey couldn't help thinking how much easier dairying had become with the invention by Swedish Alfa Laval of the cream separator and the introduction of the vacuum milking machine.

Young Davey milked over fifty Jersey cows, sleek brown-eyed beasts which were suited to the mild Kaikoura coastal climate and gave rich, creamy milk. When Davey first started dairying the whole milk had to be transported in milk cans by horse and dray to the co-operative factory of which Davey was a shareholder. The whole milk was made into an excellent cheddar cheese for export.

Dairying was certainly easier than in his grandmother's day. Electric power was produced as early as 1922 in Kaikoura township from a coal-fired generator but was not available to the outlying rural districts. The generator stopped at midnight and many a visitor to the town was caught as the lights went out. Davey had one of the earliest vacuum milking machines driven by a single cylinder petrol motor. Davey, although an old soldier, seldom swore, but his language on some cold frosty mornings when the engine failed to start was horrendous, and his 'flaming' this and 'flaming' that should have been suffcient to provide ignition even if the magneto once again would not.

For Davey and his wife, Maggie, the 1920s were desperate times. Davey received so little for his milk that after they had met the cost of the bare necessities of life there was nothing left of the cheque from the co-op to spend on farm improvements. The peaty, sour, once-swamp land cried out for the sweetening of lime and the phosphate it lacked. But even though the grass was running out and the milk yield per cow was dropping, Davey could not afford fertilisers. It was a vicious circle with the income from the impoverished land falling each year.

But like most New Zealanders Davey had a flair for mechanical invention. He assembled from an old water tank and a truck axle and wheels a primitive water cart for transporting liquid manure from the cow bails out to the paddocks. The same pump he used to fill the tank with effluent from the cow bails he also used to spray it on to the land. By dint of hard work Davey kept the farm going but by the third year of the Depression the evidence of penny-pinching was beginning to show. Fences were in a sorry state and calves often escaped down the road. One of Davey's pedigree Jersey cows escaped and in her need sought out the services of his neighbour's bull. A very fine bull, with a noble sweep of horns, but a Hereford. Davey's hopes of a prize-winning Jersey calf later in the year for the Kaikoura show were dashed. The bitter argument between the two farmers over the incident was a reflection of the hard times they and their families were going through. In better times they would have laughed at the episode.

Maggie had to scrape and save. These were certainly the 'sugar bag' years when everything was made of the ubiquitous jute sugar bagging: aprons, oven mitts and sun hats. All were decorated with the brand name, stencilled in red, 'Chelsea Sugar'. Maggie had not had to resort to using the bagging for blankets but many of the poor in the town were reduced to this.

Maggie's daughters, Sarah and Grace, born in the first two years after Davey returned from the War, were now eleven and twelve and before and after school helped on the farm. The whole family milked the herd of fifty cows by hand as this saved the cost of fuel for the milking machine.

The work was not easy: up in the early hours in pitch black, the cows appearing out of the gloom into the light of the kerosene lamp, their breath steaming, the smell of the frothing milk in the bucket. In wet weather the concrete floor of the four-stand milking shed was a morass of mud, urine and cow dung. The udders had to be washed down and on frosty mornings, hands ached. It was a relief to seize the warm teats and strip out the milk.

As a sideline which brought in some cash − the most precious commodity during the Slump − Maggie had organised Sarah and Grace to deliver milk to the town. The few pence a pint was cheap for townies. With porridge it made an economical, sustaining meal. Cost was everything during the Depression. The few pence they got for the milk was all profit to the O'Neills. Maggie had purchased two ancient step-through ladies' bicycles for the girls and they would set off after milking down the shingle road into town wobbling dangerously as they balanced the cans of warm milk on the rear carriers.

During the hard years of the Depression, selling door-to-door was a fact of life. One family in Kaikoura made soap from sheep's tallow, packed it in treacle tins, and hawked it not only in the town but throughout the entire county so almost every farm had tins of it on their wash-house shelves. Many bought the tins of soap, and perhaps even the O'Neill girls' milk, as a form of charity. However, the fierce competition for the little cash available was 'the school of hard knocks' attended by many who in the better years ahead were successful in business.

Maggie's girls were fiercely competitive and this often led to arguments.

'I'm doing the West End this week,' announced Sarah.

'I've already told Mrs O'Reilly that I'll be seeing her next week and she wants extra for her cats,' responded Grace.

'I'm not doing the East End. The Jones's have got a horrible, bad-tempered dog.'

The girls would go round to the back door and measure out the required milk with their dipper into whatever utensil had been left out. This was usually a tin milk billy but when the householder had forgotten to put out a vessel and came bleary-eyed to the door some strange containers were produced.

In Kaikoura town, times were even harder than on the outlying farms. The basic problem was unemployment.

Henare Tai, like his ancestors before him, had been a fisherman. But caught in a southerly 'buster', his fishing boat had been thrown on to a reef in South Bay as he was attempting to escape the storm by rounding the peninsula to seek shelter. His boat had been smashed to matchwood. Henare had been lucky to avoid drowning and escaped with several broken ribs and a chronic 'crook back'.

His boat had been uninsured – they were hard times for insurance companies too – and the cost of medical treatment had exhausted his meagre savings. He had nothing. With his bad back he was limited in the work he could do but had managed to get some 'relief' work which brought in a few shillings.

Pita, his nephew, who was staying with the Tais for a few weeks, had been lucky enough to get into a work camp. He had come out of it with, as he said, 'a few spare bob', and had taken Henare for a few beers at the local pub.

Henare had asked him about the work camp.

'The tucker was not too bad but we were housed in old army huts and they were diabolical. The wind blew through every crack and we had been issued with old army blankets that you could spit through. The main road through the camp was mud most of the time and you sank into it up to your ankles. You wouldn't believe it but some wag had put up a sign "Tory Street" and on the bunk house one that read: "No communists need apply". But there you are,' as he flipped a shilling on to the bar, 'we at least earned ourselves some pocket money. This is on me.'

Henare, a proud man, accepted the beer but felt uncomfortable that he was unable to return the shout.

'The work was a joke,' continued Pita. 'In the first few weeks we were building a golf course, for the nobs I suppose, plus-fours and all that carry-on. Well, we barrowed soil backwards and forwards all day. The old lags wanted to spin the job out and whenever the supervisor was some place else they would barrow the soil back again. Talk about put and take. When I first arrived I wondered what the hell was going on. It didn't seem to make much sense. But we were getting paid one pound eight shillings a week and that was on top of the grub we got.'

Henare put his beer down. 'You didn't do too badly then. I get only two quid a week on relief work, chipping weeds off the side of the road and such like, but I've got a family to keep. It just can't be done. It costs us a pound a week for rent and almost four shillings for coal for cooking and power. Another three shillings goes on milk and four shillings on time payment on the furniture. That leaves the missus with six shillings to buy food and meat and to clothe all of us. We don't eat fish now and I used to catch it.'

Pita shook his head, 'I suppose I'm lucky I'm not hitched and can move round a bit. We did some tree planting. That was pretty boring. I was waking up in the night, after I'd planted a few thousand, screaming: "Six paces, spade, plant, heel, six paces". Can't see the sense of planting so many. They're only pines, you know. They grow quicker than the native trees but still won't be ready for thirty or forty years. Christ, I'll be seventy then or else pushing up daisies. I can't see what use they'll be. Make one hell of a lot of matches,' as he struck a light and puffed the cigarette he had just rolled.

'Here, help yourself to the makings,' and he pushed his tobacco tin along the bar top to Henare. He accepted.

'Don't tell the missus, as she thinks I've given them up. I was reading in the paper the other day about a Maori rugby team that was supposed to be grubbing rushes. It was supposed to be a work relief scheme and they were getting paid as well as getting fit. Well, they got the money but didn't cut any rushes. Big stink up north about it and it even got to Parliament. Sir Apirana Ngata reckoned Maori should not be employed on these useless jobs but should be used to develop our own lands. We shouldn't have to beg for crumbs from the table. Ngata stuck to his guns but finally had to resign. I think he was right. Someone one day is going to make a packet out of those trees you've been planting and it won't be us – unless they're on our land.'

'You're right, uncle, we seem to be at the bottom of the ruck' (Pita played rugby for Marist). Rugby prospered during the Depression and he saw much of life, not as 'a rich tapestry', but as a rugby field. 'We don't seem to be seeing much of the bloody ball. You can't score unless you get the ball.'

'I also saw in the paper that even with the Depression they're still holding Waitangi Day celebrations. The report said we Maori, mind you they'd be mainly northern tribes, expressed our gratitude to "their Excellencies". For God's sake, we're living in the 1930s. I don't for the life of me see the need for someone representing the King to be poncing around in a fancy hat decorated with chook feathers. We're not a colony any more. What the hell do we need a viscount for?' Henare took another sip of his beer.

'You know he's not really such a bad guy, Henare. Didn't he come through here once? Knows quite a bit about farming and he did give us the cup for the rugby tests against the Aussies.'

'This article did say that he suggested a thirty per cent cut in his own salary and he draws on his own funds so that he can make all these tours. Remember when he was here he knew a fair bit about pigs. Apparently he has a farm back in England.'

'And speaking of two feet in the trough, I don't go much on this bloke Coates in the coalition government. You can't expect a decent performance from a team made up of blokes with different styles of play. Forbes, though, seems a good bloke. Played rugby as halfback for Canterbury, you know. A good runner with the ball and could kick with either foot. He'd make a good prime minister.'

They were hard times for the people of the Kaikoura coast but they survived. As a people they had become more resilient and appreciative of the good life their land could provide. The pakeha population was beginning to realise the truth, long known to the Maori, that they in turn owed something to the land.

Good times returned with the election of the Labour Government under Michael Joseph Savage in 1936. The world economy had revived in any case and perhaps the new Labour Party was lucky to be swept to power on the crest of the wave of economic revival.

In the United States the Depression had focused attention on man's earlier mistreatment of the environment, particularly in the dust bowl region and areas in the south such as the Tennessee Valley. There a new deal for the poor was seen to be linked with a betterment of the land, a 'grass-roots' approach, whereas the solution to poverty in New Zealand was seen more in a policy of social welfare. It was just a fortunate accident that prices for the farm commodities New Zealand produced rose on world markets and enabled the social engineering of the Labour Government to be paid for.

For Davey and Maggie in Kaikoura, higher prices for butter and cheese enabled them to put in a larger, all-electric milking shed. Davey was able to top-dress his pastures and renew fences. He was more fortunate than many other returned servicemen who had bought their farms at inflated prices after the war and had then found prices for farm products falling on a world market and the Depression coming upon them. Many saw their farms sold by the banks.

With the return to better times Davey bought himself the latest Ford V8 saying, 'To hell with the cost.' For their children, it meant a better education. There were more books available, they learnt to read better than their parents had. The chances of a university education came within the reach of even a working class family such as theirs. As Davey said, 'We can be proud of what Michael Joseph has done for this country even though much of his politics comes from Aussie trade unions. Of course he's Irish, you know.'

For Henare Tai, better times meant 'social security'. He was able to work a few hours a week at the fish-processing plant packing crayfish for the overseas market and also qualified, as a result of his crook back for a small disablity pension. His doctor's bills and medical expenses were paid by the state. He was happy enough, but never more so than when he managed to go out with one of the fishing boats for a day's fishing. As he wound the drum and the big groper came gasping to the surface his 'crook back' seemed to give him no trouble at all. As they headed back towards the Kaikoura Mountains and the fish-processing factory, Henare experienced an ache, nearer his heart than his back, that neither the sea nor the land were his in the way they had been for his ancestors.

As Pita had said when he last stayed with them, 'I've got a good job but I feel as though I'm sitting on the side line and not being asked to take part in the game. Bloody government does everything. It's like the coach telling you all the time how you should play the game. I'd like to make a break on me own.'

Pita soon had the chance to do his own thing and make a dab for the goal line. At the outbreak of World War II he was among the first to enlist in the newly formed Maori Battalion and was assigned to the company made up of mainly South Island Maori.

They played rugby in the searing heat and sand of the Western

Desert of North Africa, far from the cold blue seas and snowy mountains of the Kaikoura coast. Many of his fellow players survived the war and went on to play for All Black rugby teams as great as any in the past.

Pita Tai did not. Today, you will see his name not on any representative rugby team photograph but on the stone monument in the memorial gardens at Kaikoura as having given his life in World War II. His epitaph on the simple white cross in the military cemetery at Tobruk is the only other write-up he received for playing in the big game: Pvt Pita Tai, NZ 045963, Killed in Action, 3.5.40.

Chapter 6
Defending the Land

In 1940 New Zealand was again involved in a war in Europe. In August of that year the New Zealand War Cabinet approved the establishment of a Home Guard. Until the Japanese surprise attack on the United States naval base at Pearl Harbour on 8 November 1941, and the New Zealand declaration of war against Japan on the same day, membership of the Home Guard had been voluntary. It now became compulsory for men of military age not in the army and all men between the ages of forty-six and fifty. The original volunteers had no uniforms, only arm bands and an assortment of weapons, mainly shotguns, sporting .22 and .303 rifles and target rifles.

With the surrender of Singapore and the sinking of HMS *Prince of Wales* and *Repulse*, and the bombing of Darwin, New Zealanders had real fears of an imminent Japanese invasion. New Zealand's main army force was serving in the Middle East. Three young men, descendants of Moki, were serving in the Maori Battalion and over one hundred others from the Kaikoura district were serving overseas in army, navy or airforce. Meanwhile the defence of New Zealand had become critical and the army took control of the Home Guard. By 1942 the Home Guard in the thirty-three zones throughout the country had been issued with uniforms and boots. Major-General Young CB, CMG, DSO, a retired previous chief of the general staff was appointed to command the reorganised Home Guard.

Special New Zealand Army Order No. 261/1941
Operational Tasks: Throughout, training will be so arranged as to secure the continuous interest and enthusiasm of all members.

'This is just a bloody waste of time. Do you think that uniforms are going to make any difference? If Japs are going to come into the beach here do you think they'll be worried about how we look?' The speaker was Grant Adair, great-grandson of James Adair. He was the local trade union secretary of the clerical workers' union and was running true to form in being against most things. Flat feet had kept him out of the army.

'Mind you, the boots will come in handy, but we're going to look ridiculous in these old uniforms. And having to clean the brass buttons on this useless cap is the last straw. I've got black spots of Brasso all over it. How are you supposed to clean them?'

Davey O'Neill, as an old soldier, was expected to provide answers on a variety of military matters that perplexed his fellow Home Guardsmen. He would have much preferred serving overseas again but, although he volunteered, his gammy leg meant he had to make do with part-time service in the Home Guard.

From his haversack Davey produced a strip of metal with a slit down the centre .

'You're wasting your time trying to clean each button separately. Just slide them on this, bunch them up and then away you go with the Brasso and elbow grease.'

Grant snorted in disgust. 'And as the Japs wade ashore I can dazzle them with my brass buttons. An old uncle of mine told me when I was a boy that when he went to the Boer War, they wore fancy uniforms. He was in the cavalry, and their red and white jackets and brass buttons gave the Boers something to aim at. Later they changed over to khaki uniforms. I would think these are some of them they're dishing out to us. Why else would they smell so much of mothballs?'

'I don't think I can do mine up,' said fifty-year-old Henare Tai, fisherman and great-grandson of the warrior, Moki. He was a man of imposing proportions, perhaps fifteen or sixteen stone in weight but so tall he was well-proportioned, with a barrel chest and massive upper arm muscles developed from many hours of pulling in long lines and crayfish pots. He strained into his 'new' jacket but it served much the same purpose as a strait-jacket so that he stood with arms apart like a grey-headed gorilla. As he brought his arms together there was a minor explosion and the jacket parted down the back.

'Ah! That's the answer. Much better.' He flexed his muscles and winked at others of the platoon. Davey O'Neill again explained with a grin, 'In the army there are two sizes, too large and too small. And by the way, your cap, field service, that's your hat, you wear two fingers above your right eyebrow, not on the back of your head.'

'Well, they can stick their boots.' James Anderson, white-haired and bearded, of unknown age, but known to have been a shepherd on Winchester station for at least thirty years, was regarding the army-issue boots with some disapproval. He was peering intently at the sole which was an inch or two from his nose. 'These wouldna' last five minutes on rocky ground. I'll stick to me own. If I'm going to die for me country I'll at least want to be in a decent pair of boots.' He looked down at his own double leather, hobnail-studded boots. 'At least with these I'll be able to kick the bastards to death.'

'You know, it's all a matter of morale,' said the Reverend Michael Fearon, ordained minister of the Church of England, and vicar of St Stephen's in the East End of Kaikoura township. 'We will all feel much better if we are in proper uniforms.' It was unfortunate that as he said this he happened to be looking at the hunched-up form of Henare Tai, for whom the uniform, as much of it as he had been able to struggle into, was not doing a great deal for his morale. The Reverend Michael felt he should say something as he had been appointed by the commanding officer of the East Coast (South Island) Battalion as platoon officer of the Kaikoura group. He continued, 'You see, it's like this: my appointment as second lieutenant had to be printed in the New Zealand Gazette as a requirement of the Hague Convention. In the same way we have got to be in uniform because if we are captured not in uniform then we could be shot.'

'For crying out aloud. That's typical of a capitalistic system. We have got to follow the rules. Do you think the Russians on the Eastern Front are worrying about uniforms? They're going to be shot by the Germans whether they've got uniforms or not. At least our Russian brothers are more concerned about fighting than about uniforms and who are officers and who are not.' Grant Adair was a member of the Labour Party and rumoured to be a supporter of the Communist Party. He didn't much care if he was ruffling the Reverend Michael's feathers. To be fair, the Reverend Michael had at one time been going to make the army his career and had attended the army college at Duntroon in Australia and had graduated with the Sword of Merit. He was an accomplished horseman and a crack shot. He had not found life as a peacetime officer very rewarding. A little later he became a born-again Christian, and had gone back to college, been ordained and been posted as vicar to St Stephen's, Kaikoura. He was the only one of his platoon, assembled in the church hall to be issued with their 'new' uniforms, who cut anywhere near a soldierly figure. Davey O'Neill, in spite of three years' service in World War I and an MM for bravery, was perhaps still too much Irish at heart to accept military discipline, and that included wearing uniform. When he explained to the others the 'right' way of lacing up their new boots it was purely coincidental that his way was the approved army method. It just so happened it was the most effective way, and even old James Anderson agreed, although it was his own pair of boots he was lacing back on. Davey dressed for comfort and could never be persuaded to do up his top button, a dereliction of military duty which was later to earn him a run-in with army authority.

Second Lieutenant Fearon's platoon ('The Reverend Michael's Own' as locals in the town sometimes called it) was one of three which made up B Company based at Kaikoura. He had been selected as platoon commander by the battalion commander in Blenheim who had been guided in his selection by the army directive that 'qualifications for a commission are the power to lead and to inspire confidence and respect with mental alertness and a reasonable standard of physical fitness.' The Reverend Michael met all of these requirements reasonably well.

The commander of the Kaikoura-based company, with the rank of captain, was Thomas Browne, owner of Winchester station, and grandson of Captain John Browne. The Brownes had always enjoyed a military involvement although they had not been much good at it, and Thomas had joined a cavalry Territorial unit in the 1920s. Of the 'qualifications for a commission' in the army Home Guard directive, Thomas Browne seemed to satisfy none of the requirements although riding kept him at 'a reasonable standard of physical fitness'. He had been appointed by the battalion commander in Blenheim. They had both attended an expensive Anglican boarding school in Christchurch and played in the same polo team.

Special New Zealand Army Order No. 261/1941
Its general scope will be as follows:
(a) achievement of a high standard of weapon training and complete confidence in the use of weapons allotted.

At the first evening parade, held on Wednesday because on Tuesdays the parish hall was used by Mothers' Union members packing fruit cakes for the troops overseas, Second Lieutenant Fearon, as a starting point for more systematic training, read New Zealand Army Order No. 261. The defence of the country needed to be taken more seriously as the news from the Pacific was not encouraging, with the Japanese moving rapidly through the Dutch East Indies and into Australian New Guinea. Now, although New Zealand's situation in the South Pacific was becoming desperate it was not the New Zealand way, Maori or pakeha, to show any visible sign of enthusiasm for an official directive. In fact, quite the contrary, and before Second Lieutenant Michael had moved on to task (b) in the directive there was an outcry of protest. ' "Weapons allotted," ' shouted James Anderson, wagging his beard and at the same time holding aloft his weapon. 'I could spit further than this peashooter. It might be all right for bowling over rabbits but I don't think the Japs would let me get close enough. The government', James did not have a lot of time for governments, of any party, 'took my .303 hunting rifle and then "allotted" me this. I could hit a deer at 300 yards with my rifle. What do I do with this, say to the first Nip who comes ashore, "Here sit on this, and then pull the trigger"?'

All Second Lieutenant Michael could do was assure them that better weapons were promised.

'Ah, the glorious promises of the army,' sighed Davey O'Neill, 'it all comes back to me. We were promised more machine guns, more tanks, more artillery support, fewer mad charges "over the top." When it comes down to it lads, well, it will be up to us.'

'We have other weapons, you know,' continued Second Lieutenant Michael, 'the Molotov cocktails we made seemed pretty effective.' This was something of an exaggeration because although the mock tank they had attacked had been burned out their own casualties had been high with several nursing burns to assorted areas having to attend as out-patients at the local hospital.

The first batch of bombs they made had almost resulted in casualties to their fellow soldiers in the New Zealand expeditionary force overseas as the Mothers' Union ladies had parcelled up the shiny jam tins along with their soldered up tins of Christmas cake for dispatch to the 'boys overseas'. They had been located and recovered by the rightful owners before the calico-covered parcels had been posted. The jam-tin hand grenades, when tested by being flung from slit trenches dug in the beach, had an obviously lethal effect on the wooden 'Jap' replicas. The charge of three-inch nails had shredded the plywood. Their time lapse before explosion was, however, somewhat variable, from just seconds after having left the hand to a nail-biting wait of twenty minutes. Molotov cocktails were retained in the armoury but nail bombs were deemed too unpredictable. In the bomb department the platoon had one notable success which drew a commendation from the battalion commander East Coast (South Island).

Liam O'Hara had taken part in the revival of the whale hunting based at South Bay during World War I, which continued until the 1920s. He had become quite expert in handling explosives both for the harpoon gun and for the explosive killing lances. The lances had consisted of a hollow pipe into the end of which an explosive charge of gelignite was packed with an electrically fired detonator. Henare, although he didn't think much of those who used this diabolical device on whales, was perfectly happy to help use it against any Japanese invaders. They had tried out their version of the whale lance on a deserted section of beach.

Second Lieutenant Michael had put Liam O'Hara in charge of explosives and given him three stripes to put on his 'new' uniform. Liam had supervised the making of the jam-tin grenades and was a little put out when the project had been abandoned. He was determined the whale lance demonstration would be successful.

The battalion area commander from Blenheim, Major Jonathan North, had agreed to attend the demonstration. The Kaikoura platoon had taken up their positions in the sandbag-protected trenches they had dug as one of their earlier contributions to the war effort. When they had been dug it had seemed a complete waste of time as Japan, the third of the Axis Powers, had not yet entered the war. Now it was not beyond the realms of imagination that these trenches might have a use in addition to having provided elderly Home Guardsmen with some exercise.

Second Lieutenant Michael gave the order, 'Watch your front,' and the platoon adopted a warlike posture as they peered seawards over the sandbags. Liam O'Hara supervised the assembly of the whale lance. 'Right, warhead out,' and Corporal Henare pushed the first length of pipe forward over the sandbags.

'Right, Henare, now you keep feeding out the wires. For God's sake keep those bare ends away from the battery. James, you could take the battery further along the trench just to be on the safe side.'

Major North edged towards Second Lieutenant Michael.

'How safe is this weapon?'

'Well, when it was used on whales they had no problems but of course it hasn't been used like this before. But Sergeant O'Hara knows what he is doing.'

'Connect on another length,' said Sergeant O'Hara and Corporal Tai screwed on another length of pipe. The 'warhead' was now half-way across the beach and heading promisingly for the pile of boxes, much scarred and burnt from earlier attacks of Molotov cocktails and jam-tin bombs, which was the designated target, a recently landed boat-load of Japanese marines.

Davey O'Neill, who had already been ticked off by the battalion major for having his top button undone, lent on the sandbags and tried to disguise the fact that he was having a few quick puffs of a 'roll-your-own' whilst all eyes were on the snake-like object writhing across the beach. He wondered why the Japanese marines would still have been sitting in their landing craft or have had any further use for it. But other than his experience of Flanders mud in World War I he felt he was strictly a dry land soldier and not able to speak with any authority on beach landings. A continuous line of pipe with accompanying electrical wires now stretched from trenches to the 'Japanese landing craft'.

'Ready to fire, sir,' reported Sergeant Liam O'Hara, in the best army style but spoiling it rather by turning on Corporal Tai and shouting, 'For Chrissake, Henare, let go of the end. When we fire it it's going to kick like an army mule.'

'We're ready, sir,' reported Second Lieutenant Michael to even higher authority and Major North gave the riding crop he affected a flick. Second Lieutenant Michael nodded at Sergeant O'Hara who was holding the bare ends of the wires ready to touch them to his car battery.

'Stop,' screamed Second Lieutenant Fearon. 'It's floating.' Sure enough, with the incoming tide the 'enemy landing craft' of fire-blackened packing cases was floating out to sea. On this part of the coast, along this beach on a fine day there is only one line of breakers and the enemy vessel was rocking quietly just beyond the surf line. Corporal Henare Tai had fished along this beach and knew it well.

'It won't move much from there. Let's put on a few more lengths and we can still reach it.'

'You're on. You screw on a few more lengths this end and I'll go down the beach and straighten it out a bit.' Sergeant Liam O'Hara was not going to abandon the demonstration without a fight. 'The warhead end is waterproof, so just keep shoving it down the beach.'

Henare soon had his son Rewi dragging up more pipe from the reserve trench and he was frantically screwing extra lengths on. Rewi fed out matching lengths of electrical cable. Fortunately the 'Japanese landing craft' had not picked up a current and was still straight out from the beach.

Sergeant O'Hara came pounding back up the beach and hurled himself over the sandbags into the trench.

'You beaut, we're going to do it,' he said to Henare who was grinning ear to ear. He looked towards Second Lieutenant Fearon who was also smiling, took this as sufficient confirmation and plunged the bare wires on to the battery terminals.

The sea lifted, there was a muffled explosion and pieces of packing case rained down over a wide area of sea and a few shredded boards fluttered into the observation trench, strengthening the battalion commander's impression that this was 'the real thing'. This spectacle was accompanied by cheering and whistles from the trenches.

Major North was very impressed. 'Well, that seemed to go very well, congratulations.' It had been for him something of a baptism of fire. As a solicitor and city councillor he had been appointed more for his abilties in administration rather than any experiences of a military nature. The explosion he had just witnessed and the destruction convinced him that he had come very close to the realities of action.

Young Davey O'Neill shook his head in almost total disbelief. He turned to James Anderson and asked, 'How on earth are they going to know where the Japs are going to land to get that contraption into position and what in the name of all that's holy are the Japs supposed to be doing while all this is going on?'

James Anderson slowly wagged his head, adjusted his false teeth and declared, 'If they'd left me with me Lee Enfield I could have shot the lot of them before they had come closer than two hundred yards from landing. There's no need for all this nonsense. All we have to do is shoot the buggers.'

However Major North was satisfied and the Kaikoura platoon's company commander in due course received a letter of commendation for the considerable initiative shown.

The full extent of the success of the 'whale harpoon' venture went unknown to military authorities. The tremendous explosion of gelignite had killed a good number of kahawai, which Henare and his son Rewi gathered as they floated to the surface. After the official party of officers had left the beach some half-gs of beer were produced and the kahawai were barbecued whole on the beach.

Davey O'Neill, glass of beer in one hand and a fillet of barbecued kahawai in the other, conceded that there were some aspects of military service that compensated for the long hours of boredom and military discipline.

Special New Zealand Army Order No. 261/1941

(b) Sufficient physical training to ensure personnel maintenance and a reasonable standard of fitness for tasks allotted to them.

Since the 'phoney war' stage of Home Guarding, with the digging of trenches and the filling of sandbags, the Kaikoura platoon had not been required to do physical training. This changed with the arrival of Henare Tai's youngest son, Rewi into the platoon.

Rewi Tai was hoping to complete a degree at the University of Otago before being called up. He was required in the university vacations to work in an 'essential' industry or serve in the Home Guard or Civil Defence. He'd tried Civil Defence.

'Those guys were crazy, rushing around at night with stirrup pumps putting out imaginary incendiary bomb fires. Where the hell did they think the incendiaries would come from?'

He preferred the Home Guard. Coming home for a few hours, soldiering at weekends was no great hardship. He was studying physical education at university and backed up the Second Lieutenant in his endeavours to raise the level of physical fitness in his platoon. Although only nineteen, he enjoyed a certain level of respect in the platoon and the wider community of Kaikoura as he played representative rugby for New Zealand Universities and the Junior All Blacks. He had the platoon doing all manner of exercises to strengthen this or that set of undiscovered muscles. Old James Anderson and one or two others sat it out, considering a smoko at these times would contribute more to their overall fitness and well-being.

Rewi appreciated that fitness took many forms but he had this brought painfully home to him when old James Anderson consistently out-walked him when the platoon went into the back country on a goat-shooting expedition. James had suggested the outing as a means of getting some exercise and also for some small arms practice. Approval for the use of live ammunition had been obtained from battalion headquarters. Wild goats had multiplied alarmingly from the first few introduced by the early whalers and, as their shooting brought a bounty, it was hoped that the platoon's mess funds would be considerably augmented. The Second Lieutenant and old James Anderson each fired one shot for each goat they saw. Rewi seemed to catch up with old James just as the goat he had shot was tumbling off a slope or ledge down into the valley below. 'Get the tail off that one, lad,' and old James would be away again to bag another goat.

The total count for the day was eighty-seven goats, the Reverend and James shooting neck and neck throughout and ending in a draw with forty-three each. There was some debate about who from the other twenty-four members of the Kaikoura platoon had shot the other goat. It was agreed that whoever had shot it, it must have been an accident. Davey O'Neill had not taken part in view of his leg but did agree to man the base camp, to which he had transported sufficient half-gs of beer not to earn criticism from the hunters.

Special New Zealand Army Order No. 261/1941

(c) Foot drill and arms drill to include pride of bearing to facilitate handling of arms and to ensure movement with reasonable precision and alertness.

'Present arms. One, two, three; one, two, three, one. Move only on the one, pause on the two and three.'

Staff Sergeant Jack Ryan was permanent staff army based in Area 10 Christchurch. He had been sent to Kaikoura specifically to bring the Reverend Michael's platoon up to scratch on rifle drill. It was not that the platoon had been singled out for special treatment because of its lack of proficiency in this department but rather that the Officer Commanding Home Guard New Zealand, no less than Major-General

Young himself, would be calling at Kaikoura to inspect the Company of which their platoon was a part. They would form part of a fifty-strong guard of honour for the occasion. Hence the special instruction in presenting arms.

Staff Sergeant Ryan continued, 'Shout it out, one, two, three. Not loud enough, let me hear you. Lift the rifle on the first "one". Private Anderson, don't climb up it. Private Tai, it's not your girl friend, crash it on to your shoulder. Corporal Tai, the hand comes straight down to the side on the final "one", hold your gut in if it's getting in the road.'

Number 3 Platoon under the commmand of, now, Lieutenant Michael Fearon looked very smart and very professional. With the reorganisation of the Home Guard under Major-General Young had come an issue of battle dress and 'new' weapons. The platoon members were all equipped with .303 Lee Enfield rifles, some dating back to World War I, but the likes of Old James Anderson were more than satisfied to have, as he said, 'The best rifle ever made. Beats even the Martini; bit much woodwork, but that can easily be cut off to improve the balance and then you've got a first-class hunting rifle.' When he had appeared on parade with his rifle trimmed down to suit his requirements, Staff Sergeant Ryan nearly died as words, for once, failed him. Davey O'Neill also almost died, of laughter: he could imagine the repercussions throughout the army of someone treating army property in this way. Staff Sergeant Ryan was persuaded by Lieutenant Michael not to take it further until he had seen the results on the rifle range. There Old James Anderson scored maximum possible scores on 'grouping' and 'snap' shooting but was a little down on his target results, explaining he liked a target that was moving. For the purpose of uniformity of the honour guard a spare, intact, fully-wooded rifle was obtained so that Old James could take part. He wasn't very keen and could not make the connection between presenting arms and shooting Japs.

By June 1941 the number of New Zealanders under arms in the Home Guard exceeded 100,000. This expansion and the fact that wooden replicas of rifles had been replaced with the real thing and that some units were even receiving Bren machine guns was largely the work of Major-General Young. He was a no-nonsense soldier and as a previous chief-of-staff knew the way the army system worked and was able to play the system to give him the results he wanted for his Home

Guard. Early on he was aware of the problem of uniforms and as a gesture wore 'civvies' himself.

To say that the notice from Wellington that General Young was to visit Kaikoura on a tour of inspection caused a flap in Blenheim headquarters would be an understatement.

The battalion commander had arranged for the general to stay at Winchester with the Brownes.

He had been received there with all the ceremony due his rank. As the khaki-painted 1939 Chevrolet swung off the main highway and approached the impressive stone gateway leading into Winchester in a cloud of dust, Billy the rouseabout waved his hat from the main road paddock, one of the shepherds passed on the signal from the cow paddock and Julie, the maid, rushed from her lookout position in the attic, once Huia's bedroom, down the stairs to give warning to the Browne family.

Captain Thomas Browne was in his new issue battledress uniform and wearing his ED (Efficiency Decoration). This award was for length of service in the Territorial Army and was in no way a measure of the wearer's 'efficiency'. Captain Browne had ordered that for the Major-General's visit 'decorations shall be worn'. The very smart army driver who opened the passenger's door for the general was in full uniform, and as she came up to the salute and thrust out her chest, there was not exactly a whistle but an exhalation of breath from the assembled shepherds and shearers. Captain Browne glared towards them but his expression changed as Major-General Young stepped from the car in sports coat and grey slacks.

'Name's Young, beautiful property you have here.' And as Captain Browne seemed to have lost his voice, he added, 'Wouldn't have minded doing a bit of farming myself when I retired but they brought me back for this lark.'

Captain Browne, having recovered from the shock that the general neither looked nor spoke like one, introduced the members of his family. Mrs Browne had been toying with the idea of curtseying but didn't think it was quite the thing to someone in a sports jacket.

Formal dinner was served in the dining room, which had not changed much since the days of the first Captain Browne. The crossed lances were still above the fireplace, though the tiger skin had developed mange and had been burnt. Captain Browne had no dress uniform to wear but replaced his ED ribbon with the actual medal. Not much compared to a CB, CMG and a DSO and the old boy would be wearing his dress uniform. But Captain Browne was again disappointed as Major-General Young appeared for dinner in a double-breasted business suit that showed obvious signs of having travelled long distances in a suitcase.

Captain Browne got the conversation off to a military start by pointing to the Bengal lances and commenting, 'Afghan Wars, my grandfather you know, built this place.' That was the first and last topic of a military nature that was discussed over dinner. The general was more interested in sheep and horses but after dinner when the ladies had withdrawn and the port was being passed round he did relate one story of his World War I experiences. The topic had been raised by Captain Browne's son who had been invited to dinner from the neighbouring run he managed. He asked the general if he thought some of the Home Guard might be rather old to be effective in the event of a Japanese invasion.

'They'll do a good job,' was all the response he got from the general. 'But that reminds me of a fellow I met when I was inspecting front-line troops in France in the first do. Noticed this fellow who seemed old for a soldier or prematurely aged. Had him shifted back to a base job. Later came across him and asked if he liked his new duties. He did. I asked him his age. "Sixty, sir". Asked how he came to be at the war. He explained he was a widower with an only daughter of whom he was very fond. She became engaged to a young fellow who enlisted. The daughter was so upset that he agreed to give a false age, join up, and look after the girl's affianced. I told him that it was a fine gesture. I asked him how the young man was getting on. The old soldier replied, "Well, sir, it was like this, he was a very good cornetist and they kept him at home in the band!" '

The next day at the Kaikoura public domain, with most of the populace of the township looking on, Major-General Young inspected the guard of honour who performed very creditably. Some of the closer of those looking on were rather perplexed by the hissing sound the guard made as they went through the present arms. One wag reported that the general's driver didn't know whether it was her bosom deflating or a tyre on the general's car. Rewi Tai explained to some of his friends after the parade that the hisses enabled the fifty Home Guardsmen to keep in time so that it was: 'hiss, hiss, up; hiss, hiss, across; hiss, hiss, down.'

During the inspection of the honour guard Captain Browne feared the worst when the general stopped in front of Private Davey O'Neill. Davey's top button was undone as always. However, it was the colour of his MM ribbon that had caught the general's eye. He pointed at the ribbon. 'Where?' he asked and Davey replied, 'The Somme.' 'Well done, Private.'

Captain Browne was both relieved and proud when the inspection concluded. He then led his company in a march past and was rather disappointed that the general couldn't actually salute as he was again wearing his business suit, but now freshly ironed that morning by Julie.

After the parade was dismissed, tea and beer, with sausage rolls made by the Mothers' Union, were served in a large marquee erected on the domain, probably about where one of the larger of the Maori pa had been located before its destruction by Te Rauparaha and his northern raiders. Rewi Tai, remembering the stories of his people and his great-great-grandfather Moki, thought it strange that the Kaikoura coast should again be threatened by attack. As he shared a beer with Davey O'Neill he asked, 'What chance have we got if the Japs try to land here?'

'Well,' said Davey as he took a pull on his beer, 'we've got no idea where they might land, we've got nothing out there,' and he pointed, with his sausage roll, across the Kaikoura peninsula to the eastern horizon, 'except the American navy to stop them before they get here and if they land even opposite our beach trenches we wouldn't stop them for long, not long enough for our territorial troops to get here any road. No lad, if they decide to land then we'll give them a fair go but in the end we'll get bloody beaten. Look at Singapore; had some air cover, big guns, even if they were pointing the wrong way, and a Brit army and they were beaten in days. No, lad, we've as much hope of winning this one,' and he pointed to the ample frame of Captain Browne, 'as he has of going through the eye of the pro-bloody-verbial needle.'

Although Rewi Tai did not know it, around then, much the same question was being asked by another young man, serving in a destroyer, the *Yukiyama*, of the Imperial Japanese Navy. His name was Sub-Lieutenant Hiro Watanabe. He asked the question of his watch commander. A combined Japanese task force of cruisers and destroyers running the gauntlet through the narrow Tulagi Strait had surprised an

Allied force of about the same strength and had practically annihilated it. These waters would subsequently be known as 'Iron-bottom Sound' for the number of ships sunk there. Sub-Lieutenant Watanabe's destroyer and the others of the Japanese force were practically unscathed.

'Sir, with respect, after a victory such as this, surely, sir, we cannot be defeated?'

The lieutenant of the watch had replied, 'We have defeated them on land, our Zeros have cleared the skies and our Imperial Navy has sunk most of their warships. There is nothing to stop us taking control of the whole of the South Pacific. The war is practically won.'

 Both Sub-Lieutenant Watanabe's watch officer and Davey O'Neill were to be proved wrong, but that was still in the future. Back on the Kaikoura coast Major-General Young was discussing weapons with Sergeant Liam O'Hara, who, after the success of his whale lance, was explaining the possibilities of his latest invention.

'It's basically a backpack sprayer that we use for eradicating gorse, but I don't see why we couldn't fry Japs with it too. With the right spray adaptor we can shoot a flame up to 30 feet. I think we might get it a bit further and a bit hotter if we added some petrol to the kerosene.' The general made non-committal noises in the back of his throat; he was not well up on flame-throwers. 'Well, just keep up the good work, Sergeant, we need new ideas.'

'What about Bob Semple's tank, General, can we make enough of them here?'

'Well, just between me and you, Sergeant, that was dreamed up by a politician,' one, by the tone of the General's voice, of the opposite political persuasion to his own. 'We tested it out pretty thoroughly but it was almost a complete failure. Of course it will have some propaganda value. We had pictures taken of it that made it look mighty impressive. Might make the Japs decide to invade Australia before they take us on.'

'They built it on a bulldozer tractor, didn't they, Sir?'

'Yes. It was worth a go, but the corrugated steel they used as armour plating was far too heavy and the thing was much too slow. Positively ponderous. Remember the early ones on the Somme?' he asked Davey

O'Neill who had joined them. 'Well, Bob Semple's tank was even slower than those. Mind you if we got a few of them into position they could be used as pill-boxes. But since they mounted only a few guns, their fire-power was pretty pathetic.' The general realised that he was not doing much for morale. The Reverend Lieutenant Michael Fearon had already preached to him on its importance both to the Home Guard and the Kaikoura civilians. He hastily added, 'But we have over 100,000 well-armed men in the Home Guard now and new weapons are coming up all the time. We hope to issue a Bren gun to each Home Guard company and, as more become available, to each platoon. And the New Zealand-made Sten sub-machine-guns are starting to come to hand.'

Davey O'Neill looked over the top of his beer at the general and helped himself to another sausage roll. As an old 'dig' he had heard it all before.

Special New Zealand Army Order No. 261/1941
(d) Intimate knowledge of their own locality in order to take immediate advantage of tactical mistakes on the part of the enemy and to act as guides to reinforcing troops.

When the Reverend Lieutenant read this order out to his platoon there were hoots of derision.

'The only "tactical mistakes" we'll be able to take advantage of are those of our own officers,' declared Grant Adair. He'd used the same argument over the years in his union against the bosses. 'They'll make the mistakes and we'll be left to pick up the pieces.'

The Kaikoura company soon had an opportunity to put this order into effect. Training exercises were being devised all the time.

'Typical of managers,' sniffed Grant Adair. 'They sit on their backsides behind their desks dreaming up things for us to do. Most times when they don't work they blame us.'

Sometimes the Home Guard were used as the 'enemy' against territorial or regular army units. On this occasion the exercise had been planned from Area 10 army headquarters and involved the Kaikoura Home Guard company as defenders of a beach landing which they were required to contain until they could bring up regular army reinforcements.

No landing craft were available to land the 'enemy' and the operational plan required them to move into position by land and take up an attacking position on the beach just above high water.

A major from headquarters explained the exercise to Captain Browne and his three platoon officers.

'Your company will be in extended line on the lower slopes of the coastal hills, here. You will have some cover from the coastal bush. You will move forward to make contact with the beach invaders. Blank ammunition and grenade thunder flashes will be issued. The invading 'enemy' must not be allowed to move inland off the beach. As soon as you have made contact you will send runners to the Canterbury Rifle Company which will be positioned further south. Their transport will bring them up the Main Coast Road and they will take over from the Home Guard and launch a full-scale attack on the 'enemy'. Your runners will need to use their knowledge of local terrain to guide them into position. Are there any questions?'

Several occurred to Captain Browne but he did not voice them for fear the Major might think his knowledge of military tactics (he couldn't get that Gilbert and Sullivan refrain out of his mind) were a little less 'than a novice in a nunnery'. He finally stuttered out 'Nun… nery, none, sir.' However Lieutenant the Reverend Michael spoke up.

'What knowledge of the terrain will the invading forces have, sir?'

'Well, we can presume the Japs will have copies of our ordinance survey maps and so our chaps will have the same. They will be able to take advantage of any features of the terrain they can read off their maps.'

'Thank you, sir,' replied Michael. 'And what about fire power?'

'The Japs will have an advantage; we've got to accept that as a sad fact, so our chaps on the beach will have six Bren guns and I know your one hasn't arrived yet. So you will just have to keep up rifle fire and accept that you can't do much about the Brens except to keep your heads down. You can use whatever initiative you like to hold them on the beach but of course no live ammunition or grenades can be used.'

Lieutenant Michael returned to his platoon and explained the situation to his NCOs: Sergeant O'Hara, Corporal ('Corp' to his squad) Henare Tai and one-time Sergeant O'Neill MM who had recently and reluctantly been made lance-corporal.

'Would they like us to tie both hands behind our backs?' was Lance-Corporal O'Neill's comment when the exercise was explained. 'If it's Mikonui Bay, what relief features are they going to read off their maps and exploit? Well, they can't get round our right flank because the cliffs of Amuri Bluff will stop them. Left flank we're a bit exposed. I would suggest a Vickers machine-gun on that end of our line but we don't even have a Bren to put there.'

'I agree with you, Lance-Corporal, but what about this gully coming up off the beach where the stream comes out?' Lieutenant Michael pointed out the feature on the inch-to-the-mile map. 'They could follow that up and be completely screened from us until they were up in the hills. They're bound to attempt that one, it's straight out of the tactics handbook.' At military college the Reverend Michael had excelled at tactics. 'What do you suggest?'

'Well, another Vickers or a Bren gun would stop that one; if we had any, but I've got an idea that might work there,' suggested Sergeant O'Hara. Lieutenant Michael hoped it did not involve explosives but rather felt it would.

'What do you think, Henare?'

'Well, Rev., it's going to be a full moon.' Which the Rev. Lieutenant didn't know quite how to fit into the tactical plan.

'Will that favour us or them?'

'Sure as hell won't favour them, Rev. With a full moon and a spring tide, there won't be any room for people on that beach tonight. They'll be as wet as shags. It does seem to be a bit one-sided though, them with six machine-guns and us with none. I think we should look at evening things up a bit.'

'Well, we may be able to work something out, but we had better be moving up the hill as the 'enemy' are due to take up their positions on the beach at 1800 hours.'

By 1730 hours the antagonists were in place. Two platoons of the Canterbury Regiment were on the beach as 'enemy' and, stretched along the crest of the low coastal hills were the three defending platoons of B Company Kaikoura Home Guard. The massive Henare Tai, was also pondering the situation and how he might make use of the 'local knowledge' mentioned in the army order that the Reverend Michael had read to them. First consideration was that the tide was nearly at dead low. In fact, being a spring tide, it was much lower than normal so, at the moment, the 'invaders' had plenty of room. Army headquarters had briefed them on the times for high and low water, but as Henare watched them digging in, he realised they had not been told about the extra high spring tide. They were using their trenching tools to dig quite deep pits and the Bren gun teams at each end had provided themselves with empty sugar bags which they were filling with sand to give themselves the luxury of rests for their weapons. Henare had seen enough to have worked out a plan. He made his way sideways through the tangle of bush on the hill face until he came to his platoon commander and confirmed with him that come high tide at about midnight the 'enemy' would be flooded out and while they were coping with the exceptionally high tide, he and his youngest son Rewi would balance up the Bren gun situation. Lieutenant Michael considered that this displayed the 'initiative' required in the Major's briefing and told him to go ahead.

'Nothing too physical though, Henare.'

Sergeant O'Hara had at the same time been giving thought to the gully coming up off the beach and, as Lieutenant Michael had feared, had come up with an explosives solution. He too scrambled through the supplejack creepers and round tree trunks to confer with his platoon commander.

'Too dangerous, you could actually blow someone up if they decided to advance up the gully.'

The whistle went from further along their line as Staff Sergeant Ryan, who was acting as one of the observers and umpires for the exercise, signalled the start of the exercise. Almost simultaneously it was answered with a blast from the umpire attached to the invading forces.

'Check it out with the umpire. Explain that we could launch an immediate counter-attack down the gully to check if it's still clear and then make a quick withdrawal and while they're blazing away with the Brens they're bound to have there, we blow both sides and block it. When they launch their attack inland they will have to climb over the blockage and be exposed to our wished-for Bren.'

'We're working on the Bren situation, Sergeant, but your idea seems sound enough, and not too dangerous. I'll put it to our umpire. After all, there is always some element of danger in showing some "initiative", and "initiative" is what the Major asked for.'

Staff Sergeant Ryan gave his approval for the plan to block the gully, 'providing it's a small explosive charge.'

'Oh, just enough to nudge a few boulders down into the stream bed, practically nothing at all, Staff, you'll hardly hear it.' Sergeant Liam O'Hara did not explain that he had in mind about five sticks of gelignite each side. The Reverend Michael sent a runner to Captain Browne who was back at company headquarters, so far back it was nearly on the other side of the hill. As he was going to order an immediate sortie down the gully he hoped that any negative reply to his request to blow in the sides of the gully would arrive too late. They had been ordered to take any 'advantage of tactical mistakes' and as indecision was to be expected from Captain Browne, the Reverend Michael saw no reason why he should not take advantage of this.

Sergeant Liam O'Hara meanwhile had scrambled through the bush back to the main road where his truck was parked and transferred into his haversack as many sticks of gelignite as it would hold, together with the necessary detonators and fuses. Much of the coast, including the Kaikoura peninsula, was made up of limestone which was quarried, crushed and spread on local farms. Liam was responsible for the blasting at the Kaikoura quarry, hence his considerable skill with explosives and his ready access to them.

The Reverend Michael's platoon, with blood-curdling yells, charged down the gully leading to the beach. They were met as expected with bursts of Bren gun fire. The Reverend Michael signalled for his men to take cover as he was conscious of the umpire watching their every move and he did not want to sustain any 'casualties'. They sought the cover of the giant boulders in the gully and made their way slowly towards the beach keeping up a sporadic fire of blanks. Further back up the gully Sergeant Liam O'Hara was setting his charges into the banks of the gully. Once set to his satisfaction he rapid-fired three rounds, the pre-arranged signal, and the rest of the platoon quickly withdrew back up the gully. As they passed him he lit the very short fuses and scrambled back himself over the boulders and on to the terrace above.

The resulting explosion was highly spectacular and left the attackers on the beach with ringing ears. The umpire on the defenders' side had not been as well drilled as the rest of the company, who were getting quite seasoned to Sergeant O'Hara's explosions, and had covered their ears. He failed in this elementary precaution and was deafened for some time and could not really judge whether the explosion was just the 'nudge' he had sanctioned, or something much greater. The invaders on the beach had no warning at all and were all deafened, shocked and wondering whether they had come under either heavy mortar or artillery fire. It was about a hundred times bigger and louder than the thunderclap training fireworks they had previously experienced.

The full moon that had brilliantly lit the beach and allowed the defenders to locate accurately the dispositions of the invaders and in particular the location of the much-envied Bren guns, had disappeared behind thick overcast cloud. The attackers were now in pitch blackness and unable to see the results in the gully of the tremendous and inexplicable explosion. Its effect was exactly as Sergeant O'Hara had predicted; he was, of course, a professional. The upper end of the gully was filled with great boulders and any attacking force would now have to climb over these on to the terrace and be exposed to fire from the Kaikoura company. There were no casualties from this phase of the battle of the beach, except for minor bruising of some of the attackers from smaller stones flung a considerable distance by the explosion. It was not until some hours later that Staff Sergeant Ryan's hearing returned and he had recovered sufficiently to enter on his clipboard the results of phase one of the beach defence. He awarded the Kaikoura Home Guard side full marks for 'initiative'.

It was about midnight when Henare Tai emerged from the bush and stood, all six foot two inches of him, before his platoon officer, stark, staring naked. As the Reverend Michael was sitting he did not quite know where to look or whether to return the salute as Henare drew himself up and brought his hand up to his eyebrow with great gusto and announced, 'Ready to start, sir?' This surprised Staff Sergeant Ryan, who had edged closer to see in the dark if this apparition was really what he thought it was, but he was now beginning to expect surprises. Certainly, the staff-sergeant thought, he won't need any camouflage paint, as all he could see of Henare in the darkness was a perfect set of gleaming teeth.

Henare moved off through the bush like a shadow, along and down to the beach just beyond the 'enemy's' right flank. He disappeared into the darkness in a few strides.

Henare slipped into the sea well clear of the Bren emplacement and swam along the beach until he judged he was behind their positions. He skulled himself in until he heard voices.

'My bloody boots are full of water. Give me a hand to move these sandbags forward. Who gave us the info about the tides here? They're well above what they said would be high water and the tide is still coming in. We didn't come here to play sandcastles. Those weapon pits we dug are full of water.'

Henare heard another voice reply, slightly to his right, and guessed these would be the Bren gunners holding up the right end of the line.

'You've got nothing to complain about, I'm soaked up to me back-side. By the time we are due to launch an assault at dawn we're either going to be drowned or end up right out in the open on the top of the beach.'

If they had looked a bare yard or two behind them they would have seen a dark shape in a glowing phosphorescent mantle, like a chief's cloak, emerge from the gentle surf.

Henare thought to himself, 'As my people used to say, "Attack at dawn when you can just see the enemies' ankles".' He slithered forward, grasped the webbed ankle of the outer Bren gunner and pulled him back into the brimming weapon pit. His shout of surprise became a strangled gargle as he disappeared under water. His partner sat up but could see nothing. Suddenly a hand reached out of the blackness, grabbed him by the front of his battledress and yanked him on top of the first Bren gunner who was just coming up for air from the drowned weapon pit. He went down again under the weight of his companion and as they both came up spluttering, Henare launched forward, scooped up one, then another Bren gun, as many ammunition pouches as he could find by touch in the dark and scrambled down from the beach, across some swamp and into the cover of the bush on the lower slopes of the hill.

When, still naked and dripping, he presented himself before his platoon commander and the exercise umpire he was an impressive sight, draped with ammunition pouches and with a Bren gun in each hand. Staff Sergeant Ryan again ticked the 'initiative' column for the Home Guard and placed a corresponding cross against the regulars.

'Oh, and sir,' said Henare, 'they are attacking at dawn. That will be just after five o'clock.'

'500 hours,' muttered Staff Sergeant Ryan, and scored the Home Guard company again under the heading of 'intelligence of enemy'.

By this time the situation of the invading forces on the beach was uncomfortable, to say the least. All were wet and hungry, as the attack off the beach had originally been scheduled for mid-evening and no food was carried. They had been forced high on to the back beach by the incoming tide but were able to take cover again as the tide dropped in the early hours of the morning, but lying on wet sand in wet battledress

did nothing for what the Reverend Michael Fearon would have called their 'morale'. This suffered a further downturn when the loss of the Bren guns was reported.

The major commanding the 'invaders' was, as one of his platoon commanders said, 'on a rather short fuse'. This was not helped when the desultory rifle fire that had kept them pinned on the beach was joined by a long burst of Bren gun fire from the Home Guard lines. The major nearly burst his battledress.

'All officers and NCOs to me,' he rapped out to his company runner. 'At the double.'

This proved yet another 'tactical error' by the 'enemy' as both their left-flank Bren guns were manned by lance-corporals. The Brens, for those without local knowledge, would have seemed safe enough as the left flank of the 'invaders' was hard against the steep cliffs of the Amuri Bluff. What they didn't know was that the younger member of the Tai family had crayfished around these rocks on many occasions and knew that at least one of the natural caverns that develop in limestone, though narrow, went from one side of the bluff to the other. He had waited until the tide had gone down a little from high and made his way through the narrow crevice, not a large cavern, but sufficient for him to squeeze through, and had come out within sound, if not sight, of the Bren gunners of the left flank. Rewi had crawled, also stark naked, like his father, behind the rocks until he could hear the Bren gunners talking. They were as wet and disgruntled as their opposite numbers at the other end of the beach had been. Rewi had been awaiting his opportunity for almost an hour when he heard the runner pelting along the beach.

'All NCOs and officers to the major at the double.' And, to the lance-corporals, ' 'e's going to have someone's guts for gaiters.' The two corporals immediately set off along the beach, bent double, pounding along the wet sand and, Rewi hoped, without their machine guns. It was no lighter on the beach than in the tunnel that Rewi had come through but he knew by the sounds where the Brens would be set up. Within half-a-dozen strides he had gathered up both of them and as much ammunition as he could grope for in the dark. The tide was near dead low, which made his retreat through the sea tunnel so much easier.

He had to make two trips as he could not hold both machine-guns at once and force himself through the narrow, sea-made fissure in the rocks. As he emerged the second time and climbed up a stream valley leading to his company's positions in the hills, the faintest blush of pink was appearing above the sea on the eastern horizon.

'You beauty, these will even up the odds.' Sergeant O'Hara was ecstatic as he grasped the Brens and hugged them with a passion he usually reserved for gelignite. 'These will give us four for the gully.' Sergeant O'Hara was not familiar with the army manual that recommended the flank position for machine-guns. He proposed to the Reverend Michael, 'We'll kick them in the guts as they try to get out of the gully.' The Reverend Lieutenant, though deploring the language, agreed with the sentiment and ordered the Bren guns to the centre along with the other two 'liberated' by Rewi's father. These decisions were all made without reference to their company commander, Captain Browne, who was nominally directing the operations of the Kaikoura company from a headquarters position down the other side of the hill. The last communication the company runner had brought was that explosives should not be used in the gully. As no one within a ten-mile radius would now have any doubt that an explosion had taken place, the Reverend Lieutenant, who was in effect commanding the Kaikoura company, decided that if he sent a signal that they were 'preparing to defend our positions against dawn attack', it would be sufficient to keep Captain Browne beavering away in command headquarters and from making any rash decisions.

The attack from the beach came just as the first rays of the rising sun struck across a gentle sea and fingers of light grasped the coastal hills. As expected by Lieutenant Michael Fearon, the commander of the 'invading' force had recognised the cover offered by the gully to reach the sea terrace above the beach and had concentrated most of his attacking force there. Even when his troops, charging up the gully, came to the mass of boulders brought down by the enormous explosion of the previous evening, they did not associate the rock wall they now faced with the explosion and just accepted it as another 'cock-up' in map reading by headquarters and proceeded to clamber over the obstruction to the terrace above. As soon as they heaved themselves up and on to the flat ground of the terrace they were met by the massive fire of the four Bren machine-guns and much of the combined rifle fire of the Kaikoura company, who were stacked row behind row up the hillside.

'Just like being at a rugby game in the stand at Carisbrook,' shouted Rewi as he blazed away with the Bren gun he had claimed. The sound was deafening and a pall of cordite smoke hung in the early morning air over the beach. But as blanks were being used the attacking force continued to scramble up the gully and to move into the fringe of the bush. As they did so the Kaikoura platoons made a slow, orderly withdrawal to the crest of the hill where they occupied prepared positions and made ready to halt the 'enemy's' advance.

Before the second phase of the battle of the beach could start, the umpires' whistles, first one then the other, sounded and the troops of both sides collapsed in exhaustion. Captain Browne had moved up the hill to join his Home Guard on the crest and the major of the invading 'enemy' forces and the two umpires also moved up there for the debriefing on the first phase.

Staff Sergeant O'Ryan turned to the 'enemy' major.

'What reserves did you leave on the beach, Major?'

'The two Brens,' and he scowled at Captain Browne, who in all innocence was at a loss to account for the look he had received, 'and a handful of Three Platoon in case we were forced to retire.'

'Well, by our reckoning they're all you have left. The Brens and rapid rifle fire wiped your men out as they came up over the end of the gully.'

Rewi and Henare, each cradling a Bren machine-gun, had been close enough to overhear the judgement of the umpires, and Rewi winked at his father and had the last word, speaking in Maori, 'There's something in this local knowledge thing. I reckon the score is about thirty-nil to us.'

It was shortly to be game, set and match as the battle entered its second phase. The directive for the Home Guard that required the guardsmen to 'use their intimate knowledge of their own locality' also required them 'to act as guides to reinforcing troops'.

Henare Tai and Rewi, in view of their outstanding success with Bren gun acquisition and local knowledge, were deputised by Captain Browne to guide the other company of the Canterbury regiment, who were acting as 'reinforcing troops', to the Home Guard's position on the ridge top.

They went down the Main Coast Road in Henare's Model A Ford in a cloud of blue smoke, and soon came to the GM transports of the reinforcing troops.

'Doesn't take much "local knowledge" to bring them back along the main road. What about a bit of variation?' suggested Rewi. They agreed on a 'variation' that should further embarrass the 'enemy' beach force.

The captain of the reinforcing company fell in with the scheme readily enough. The plan was quite simple. It featured the same cave through the Amuri Bluff that Rewi had used earlier. Half of the relieving company would be led by Henare back to support the Kaikoura Home Guard company on the hill crest and the other half would be led by Rewi through the cave – the tide would be dropping again – and could attack the 'invaders' in the rear. It didn't work out quite like that as the umpires once again intervened and suggested that the 'enemy' invading force would have to disengage and withdraw as they were now faced by the Home Guard and the reinforcing half company in well-prepared defensive positions. They withdrew, again choosing to use the central gully. As it was now late afternoon, the tide was well out and the other half of the reinforcing company had dug in on the beach prior to launching their attack from the rear. The retreating 'enemy' streamed back on to the beach, sank to their knees in exhaustion and immediately came under a withering fire from their regimental comrades dug in lower down the beach.

The umpires' whistles again sounded. Rewi and Henare once more made sure they were handily placed for the debriefing. For the major of the 'enemy' forces it was mercifully brief.

'I fear, Major, your casualties for the day are twice the number of men you originally started with.'

Staff Sergeant O'Reilly of the regular army reflected that local knowledge and raw initiative seemed to have an edge over spit and polish.

The last two of the army orders, under general Order No. 261, that Lieutenant the Reverend Michael Fearon read to his platoon in those early days of training were the two that were to cause them to come in for some considerable derision from the good people of Kaikoura. The orders called for 'action patrols and observation posts' and for 'practice in rapid calling out and assumption of operational tasks particularly during hours of darkness.'

Henare Tai asked, 'What the h…, heavens does that mean, Rev? Why should we need practice in "calling out"? The Japs will know we are here without our "calling out".'

Lieutenant Fearon was above all things a patient man. 'Well "rapid calling out" means, I think, that we should practise turning out during the night in response to some threat so that we can do it rapidly.'

'I have to turn out twice each night now without any threat,' mumbled James Anderson.

'And what about the bit about "consumption of operational tasks"? What are we supposed to do about that?' asked Henare Tai.

'Well, they expect us in an emergency, I suppose that would be some sort of invasion, or sighting of enemy ships, or a submarine or something, in which case we "assume", that is we take over the role of the army. We are the first line of defence and have to go in straight away and do, well, whatever needs doing, until the proper, I mean regular, army arrives. It is important we get there as soon as possible, so there is a need for us to practise.'

The whole question of a 'rapid call-out' was raised again at company parade the following week and the officers and NCOs met after the parade to work out a training programme. Captain Browne opened up the discussion.

'Now we have the weapons, we have shown we can take on the Japs if they land anywhere along our coast but the problem is, how will we know when and where they have landed? It could be any time of night or day, probably night.'

The Reverend Lieutenant Fearon fell back on his army equivalent of the Bible, Special New Zealand Army Order No. 161/1941 and quoted Order (g) which called for 'patrols and observation posts'. 'We need round-the-clock observation so that the moment enemy landing craft, or whatever, are sighted, then we get a report back here at headquarters and we all turn out.'

'Easier said than done,' suggested Sergeant O'Hara. 'We don't have enough radios for patrols to be able to report back. We have practically two hundred miles of coast to watch: I don't see with our hundred or so men how we can do it.'

'I think horses would be the answer.' Captain Browne had also been calculating the distances involved if they were going to patrol the entire Kaikoura coast. 'If we had mounted patrols they could each cover a greater distance than foot patrols.'

Henare Tai, who did not much like horses, thought he should steer the discussion away from them.

'My grandfather was a whaler and they had much the same problem. All those miles of coast to watch and a whale might pop up anywhere. They had to be able to spot it, then away they would go in the whale boats.'

'Don't be daft, Henare, they just had to wait until the whales swam past.' Grant Adair could always be relied on to provide a negative viewpoint. 'Then they simply rowed out and harpooned them. Different altogether to Japs.'

'But don't you see,' continued Henare, 'they had to have lookouts and from these they could see each way for miles up and down the coast. We could set up lookouts on the top of the peninsula and on some of the coastal hills. We could use some of the original whale lookouts like O'Reilly's.' Grant Adair, as a union official, was well practised in attacking innovative ideas. 'The Japs are not likely to land in daylight. How can we see them at night?'

At this stage James Anderson joined in, as usual almost a full lap behind. 'I've ridden 'orses for most of me life and I'd bloody-sight rather ride than walk. If we gotta patrol then I be for riding.'

'You're not going to be rounding up Japs as if they were sheep, James. The horses would be just to get you out to your observation post.' Grant Adair could be quite reasonable when he was talking to one of what he would have called 'the working class'. 'But what we're not having is officers riding and the men walking. Might be all right for the Brits but we're not having it here.'

Captain Browne was looking somewhat put out and the Reverend Lieutenant Fearon thought he should placate him and try to establish an agreed plan.

'Well, with petrol rationing it would seem a very good idea for our observers, rather than going out to their observation posts by motor car, to ride out on horseback.'

Captain Browne straightened his shoulders and nodded. Lieutenant Fearon continued. 'I think Henare's suggestion of using the whaling lookouts is a grand idea. Now if we sight something suspicious: ships, submarines or, at the worst, landing barges, how do we signal that back here?'

'The whalers used code flags and different flags meant humpback, right or sperm whale, depending on what they had sighted.' Henare always had an interest in the whales although sightings were now rare.

Grant Adair could be relied on to seize on any obvious flaws in any proposal, unless it was for a wage increase for his clerical workers, and asked, 'How about at night? We couldn't see flags then.'

The opportunity was too good for Sergeant O'Hara who said just one word: 'Rockets'. Captain Browne had lost the drift of the discussion, so Sergeant O'Hara proceeded to explain.

'It's easy to make rockets: a bit of gun powder and a fuse, and you're away laughing.' Captain Browne was doing anything but, in fact he had turned quite pale.

'Before you load the gunpowder you mix in some chemicals that will give you colour: red, green or blue. Then you can signal with coloured rockets. A red rocket, for example, might be for sighting a Jap submarine. On most days they'd work in daylight too.'

Grant Adair was still not convinced and asked, 'What about the "rapid call-out"? How do we know we have to turn out? We can't stay awake all night waiting for a sky-rocket to go up.'

'We will just have to have a roster so some of the company can be manning the observation posts and back in Kaikoura there will be a headquarters group and another roster for those watching out for the sky-rockets.'

Thus a well-thought-out plan of action was forged. Lookout posts were selected as far north as the Wairau River, from whence over one hundred years before Te Rauparaha had launched his attack on the Kaikoura pa, to the Amuri Bluff in the south, through which just a few weeks ago Rewi Tai, great-great-grandson of Moki had led the Canterbury regulars against an 'enemy' landing. Where Rewi's great-grandfather Hone had looked out to sea to sight a possible right or humpback whale, members of Rewi's Kaikoura Home Guard company looked out day and night for a different enemy.

The Japanese Imperial Navy was sweeping all before it in the South Pacific. It was moving south into the Coral Sea north-east of Australia and an invasion fleet could any day move out of the mighty Japanese base of Rabaul. Once at sea there was nothing New Zealand and her allies could do to stop it before it arrived off the New Zealand coast. The main ports of Auckland, Wellington, Lyttelton and Dunedin had coastal

batteries and this would be known to the Japanese. For this reason, the New Zealand defence planners considered it unlikely the larger ports would be the invasion points. More likely, landings would be made in 'soft' areas with no defences and then the larger ports and cities would be taken from an encircling movement from the landward side, in much the way Singapore had been captured. It was considered unlikely that landings would be made on any part of the rocky Kaikoura coast except at the larger plains area and the sheltering peninsula of the township area. Here landing would be comparatively easy for the initial assault and once a bridgehead had been established, larger troopships could anchor in the bay. Elsewhere along the coast, there was no extensive plain where an invading force, once ashore, could get a foothold and manoeuvre.

Captain Browne had received secret orders from battalion headquarters in Blenheim of action for the local Home Guard to take in the event of a threatened enemy landing. If the enemy was permitted to land at Kaikoura and occupied the town it would make subsequent counter-attack by New Zealand regular forces almost impossible as there would be the risk of unacceptably high civilian casualties. The secret orders to Captain Browne were quite explicit:

New Zealand Army Order 2087
In the event of a positive sighting of an invading force, the commanding officer B Company (Kaikoura) Home Guard will, in collaboration with the Kaikoura Civic Authorities, action the total evacuation of civilians from Kaikoura township. Civilians will be evacuated initially at least ten miles inland. In addition the Home Guard will take all measures to:
1. Prevent the landing of the enemy
2. In the event of their landing to contain them within the landing bridgehead
3. Facilitate the arrival into the invasion zone of reinforcing regular army forces

The setting up of the lookouts and a system to achieve a 'rapid calling out' had been done most meticulously. Retired men such as Henare Tai and James Anderson, manned the lookouts during the week. They took out with them, on horseback, supplies for the week and quite enjoyed the peace and quiet of being away from home. At weekends they were relieved by the younger members of the Kaikoura Home Guard who were still holding down regular jobs. Headquarters in the parish hall of St Stephens was manned round the clock. The Reverend Lieutenant Michael Fearon did more than his share of duty there but he was able to fit in some of his own pastoral duties at the same time. The local telephone system, in particular the operator on the manual exchange, played a key role in ensuring that any sighting of enemy ships would result in the 'rapid call-out' of the local Home Guard company. A system of flags hoisted by those guardsmen manning the lookouts could be relayed along the coast, picked up by other guardsmen and some women volunteers in a house that had been built on the top of the peninsula to take advantage of a view both north and south along the coast, not very far from where one of the early Ngai Tahu pa had been. Rockets would be used at night. When on two practice occasions Sergeant O'Hara's rockets had been used, the result as the agreed signal was transmitted along the coast, was both spectacular and effective. In the event of a sighting of the enemy signalled by either flag or rocket, the watchers on the top of the peninsula would telephone the local exchange and the operator would put them through to Home Guard headquarters. Once headquarters had decided a call-out was warranted, the services of the local volunteer fire brigade would be enlisted and their siren would be sounded. This would bring out all members of the guard working or living in the Kaikoura town area. For those on farms in the outlying districts, the telephone operator had a list of numbers to contact with the message, 'Home Guard immediate call-out, now.' She had, for the several practices of the system, then added, 'This is a practice only.' On two successive weekends the guardsmen had been required to get themselves to the parish hall assembly point as quickly as possible by whatever means of transport was available. Bicycles, horses and, for those able to obtain petrol, motor cars, and a great variety of tractors, on these occasions moved *en masse* into Kaikoura through the one main street of the West End. For rapid transport to the reported enemy landing place, large farm trailers were towed behind some tractors. Up to twenty men were loaded into each trailer. Seated ten-a-side with upward-pointing rifles, newly issued battledress uniforms and tin hats, they looked as threatening as any motorised German grenadier unit.

The question of the wearing of uniforms had resulted in one of the fiercest of the Kaikoura company's discussions. Captain Browne would have liked to have been thought a disciplinarian, whose commands went unquestioned but many of his commands invited question as they were often quite absurd and old hands like 'Young' Davey O'Neill MM answered their commanding officer's more fanciful demands with a single word such as 'bullshit'. Even though a sheep man, Captain Browne understood the expression but was at a loss as to the appropriate military response. At that stage the Reverend Michael would tut-tut and, all smiles and sweet reason, would endeavour to pacify his commanding officer and a full-scale discussion would break out. This very democratic system of arriving at policy for the Kaikoura Home Guard did have some disadvantages in that those either with their own agenda, such as explosives in the case of Sergeant O'Hara, or with ability in manipulating people, such as Grant Adair, often obtained a result that did not sit happily with the rest of the company. The discussion over the wearing of uniforms and the 'rapid call-out' followed the usual pattern.

Daniel Doyle, who milked a hundred cows out near the Hapuku River, complained, 'I was hay-making that last Saturday we had a call-out. The missus came out to the paddock with the message. Right, I unhitch the baler, hook on the big trailer, and I'm orf like a scalded cat. I'm in Kaikoura in fifteen minutes. First thing Liam O'Hara says is "Where's ya uniform?" I keep me .303 on the tractor as we sometimes see a wild pig or goat, so I had that.'

Grant Adair felt obliged to support such an obviously worthy cause. He turned to Lieutenant Fearon and demanded, 'What is this man to do? He turns out in good time as required and now you penalise him for not wearing his uniform. Surely the main point of this exercise is to turn out as quickly as possible to meet any threat of invasion?' Grant was so eloquent one might have thought he was of Welsh rather than Irish extraction. His eloquence had quickened the blood of the local butcher, Clayton Jones, who was of Welsh descent.

'I was told the same, although I was first to arrive. As soon as the siren went off, I dropped my cleaver, grabbed my rifle from the back room, told the boy he was in charge, didn't even put on my coat but dashed down here. "Where's your uniform?" I'm asked. "To hell with my uniform," I reply. "I can kill Japs in this apron as well as I can butcher a pig".'

Captain Browne had been in his uniform an hour or two before the call-out, mainly because, unlike anyone else except the platoon commanders, he had known the call-out time. The problem of all his company being in uniform, or, rather, not being in uniform, had not entered his head. When the company had started to trickle into the assembly point in what they had been wearing at the time, he had naturally drawn their attention to their being 'improperly dressed'. He met with a furious response from the men and the Reverend Michael's attempt to pour oil on troubled waters was more like pouring petrol on a fire to put it out.

'You realise that under the Geneva, or it might have been the Hague Convention, we must wear uniforms if we are going to fight, otherwise…'

'Otherwise nothing,' seethed Grant Adair, 'The Japs don't keep to the rules; why should we? As I see it we've gotta stop them on the beach as quickly as possible. That's the whole point. If we stop to get properly dressed they'll be ashore, moving inland and we won't be able to stop 'em.'

The question of wearing uniform for an emergency turn-out was never fully resolved. Rather the question had been rephrased as to how much of the uniform should be worn. It was agreed that battledress tunics should be worn, and these could be kept with weapons where they would be easily accessible in the event of a turn-out. It was also agreed that battledress trousers would be optional. This drew applause and some lewd suggestions. Corporal James Shanahan, who was also in the volunteer fire brigade, gave a demonstration of how trousers could be left 'concertina'd' at night and stepped into straight out of bed.

The final decision on uniform wearing seemed reasonable, and this was the basis on which most decisions were made in the Kaikoura Home Guard. For a night turn-out, as most would have to get dressed anyway, it was agreed they might just as well put on uniform.

'If the Japs get down as far as this and it becomes the real thing then uniforms are not going to matter much anyway,' were Grant Adair's last words on the subject as they filed out of the parish hall after the evening's parade.

The real thing for the Kaikoura Home Guard and the people of the township, though they did not know it, was just a few miles off the east coast of the North Island and heading steadily and undetected towards the north-east of the South Island and the Kaikoura coast.

A month had gone by since the Kaikoura Home Guard's finest hour when they had successfully defended the beach at Mikonui. The moon was again full and it was a clear night with good visibility. James Anderson and Henare Tai were manning the lookout on a high bluff fifty miles north of the peninsula and township. It was after midnight so only one of them, James Anderson, was on duty, which consisted of occasionally sweeping the sea with the large army-issue binoculars and making innumerable cups of tea. There was a large seal colony below their lookout on the bluff and their antics kept James amused. They fished close in among the rocks and bull kelp and there was little chance of mistaking them for a ship or submarine.

'The real thing' was meanwhile only a mile or two off the Kaikoura coast and now turning in towards land with deadly intent, almost opposite the tin shed that was James and Henare's lookout.

The moon was still rising over the eastern horizon so that, although providing excellent illumination to see the approaching menace, it also meant that anything approaching the land was, as James Anderson later put it, 'coming at us out of the sun, but it was the moon, you understand, and all we could see were shapes and these sort of flickered about because of the reflections off the water.'

As they approached the shallower water off the coast, the humpback whale and her calf dived, swam further inshore then surfaced about a mile out. One hundred years ago humpback whales had been almost wiped out from the coast but, with protection, were now starting to return. James's scan with the binoculars caught the whale as she surfaced, a shiny black shape riding semi-submerged on a gently rolling silver-carpeted sea.

'Wake yourself, Henare,' screamed James, 'there's something out there.' He tried to keep the binoculars on the object and at the same time to reach across with his boot to kick the side of Henare's bunk. Henare, after humping himself over once, shot bolt upright in the bunk and cracked his head on the wooden slats of the one above.

'For God's sake, what's all the racket about?' groaned Henare as he grasped his head.

'Get over here and take a look at this. Looks like a Jap sub.' As he adjusted the binoculars, which were not night glasses, he let out a whoop. 'It's a sub all right, just surfaced, maybe two of them.' If he had been a whaler he might have recognised the typical plume of the humpback whales as they blew but in the moonlight their expelled breaths could have been mistaken for the superstructure of a submarine. 'Yes, there's a second one, they're probably refuelling or something.'

'Don't be daft, James. Let's have a shufti through those glasses.' The army-issue binoculars looked less bulky in Henare's massive hands. He altered the focus and swung them in an arc.

'About halfway between the inshore rocks and the horizon. No, further to your left,' directed James.

At this point the two whales sounded. All Henare saw was a blurred image of their humps slipping beneath the swell. The whales were head on so there was no way that Henare could have recognised the distinctive silhouette of their humps. Unlike the sperm whale they did not usually lift their tails out of the water when sounding.

The two objects Henare saw could have been the conning tower followed by the stern of a diving submarine.

'You're right. One submarine and probably two. What happens now?'

'Well, there's not a hell of a lot we can do about submarines but we are supposed to signal a sighting as they may be carrying out a recce for a general landing.'

Henare was using a shielded torch as he scrabbled around in one corner of the hut.

'Where the blazes are those rockets?'

'In the rucksack with our spare ammunition. I've got a note in my top pocket here of what colours to use.'

'I've got 'em.' Henare came back to the moonlight streaming through the hut window clutching four cylindrical brass tubes.

'Give us your torch so I can read the colour codes on me list. Here we are, "submarine sighting, colour green".'

'This one's got green paint on the nose, so I suppose this is it. Now we need, according to Sergeant O'Hara, a three-foot long stick to fit in here. Some of that drift wood'll do the trick. Now a bottle. Reminds me of the fifth of November. We used to take a Guy Fawkes round the town and buy bangers and sky-rockets with what we collected. There's an empty half-g over there.'

They pointed the rocket out to sea, set a match to the fuse and it 'whooshed' up with a very satisfactory, brilliantly glowing green tail. Sergeant O'Hara had been proud of the brilliant green he had created from a few pinches of garden fertilizer in the gunpowder but he did not see it for the good reason that he was in bed in Kaikoura township some fifty miles south and, even if he had been out of bed and watching he would not have seen a green tail. The rocket from the Home Guard lookout on the the hill above Waipapa Bay, thirty miles south of the 'submarine' sighting, which was intended to relay the original message south, was clearly... red.

It was never made clear exactly what went wrong at the Waipapa Bay lookout. Some said that the two Home Guardsmen were both colour-blind, others that in the moonlight the red marking on the nose cone would have looked green. Everyone however was quite sure of what happened next. As soon as the green rocket fired by James Anderson and Henare Tai was sighted by the watchers at Waipapa Bay they, with great expedition, shot their rocket into the air – a glorious and glowing red. They could not have been colour-blind because they immediately realised that their rocket was a different colour. It was this colour, red, that was picked up by Mrs Elizabeth Jones at the Kaikoura peninsula lookout and the sighting phoned through the local exchange to Home Guard headquarters. The Waipapa Bay lookouts, realising their mistake, tried to remedy things by firing the correct colour, green. This merely compounded their mistake.

As it was a weekend and university holidays, Rewi Tai was manning the telephone at Home Guard headquarters and immediately woke his duty officer, Lieutenant the Reverend Michael Fearon, with the report of a sighting of a red rocket.

'Are you sure they said "red"?'

'Yes, sir. I knew that red was for a number of enemy ships so I asked for confirmation. Definitely red.'

At this point the telephone rang again and was answered by Private Tai. 'Yes, yes, got that, "followed by green".' Private Tai looked grim as he hung up.

'Red followed by green, sir. The very worst...'

'Yes, I know, Rewi, "group of ships" followed by green: "including troop ships or landing craft". This is the very worst thing we feared. We've got to call the Company out as soon as possible. Get on to the local exchange and get them to put into effect an immediate call-out.

Phone Home Guard headquarters Blenheim so they can block them along the coast road to the north, although they're most probably heading for the peninsula here. Contact army headquarters Christchurch for immediate assistance. We will also have to evacuate the entire town. I'll phone Captain Browne and he can contact the mayor.'

The mayor, Andrew Adair, whose great-grandfather had been one of the many Adairs in later years to follow James from Donegal, had been on the town council for twenty years. Adairs had been on the council, and several had been mayors, since the 1860s, but never before had any of them had to make such a difficult decision as Andrew Adair now had to wrestle with after he had been woken by Captain Browne's call just before one o'clock that morning. He had turned out the other councillors and some of the council staff. With some he had considerable difficulty persuading them that he was sober and with others that the sightings were not yet another practice exercise by the Home Guard. He remembered seeing a news report of the attack on Pearl Harbour and after his sobriety and veracity had been called into question several times he started to use the phrase: 'This is not an exercise' and found it was even more effective if he repeated it: 'This is not an exercise'.

The possibility of the evacuation of Kaikoura township had been discussed with the army but only in the most general terms. It had been agreed that in the event of a landing on the peninsula, and it was the most feasible landing place for one hundred miles north and south, it made good sense for civilians in the town to be evacuated 'out of the firing line'. But there had been too little time for any sort of rehearsal for this event, even if the good citizens of Kaikoura township had believed that an enemy invasion was even remotely likely. It had certainly happened in Singapore but since then the Japanese had been dealt a set-back in the Coral Sea by the United States navy and it was certainly the opinion of the Kaikoura Irish that the 'slit-eyed bastards' would be stopped before they got as far as New Zealand. Captain Browne's faith in the Royal Navy had suffered a near mortal blow when both the *Repulse* and *Prince of Wales* had been sunk on the same day by Japanese bombers but he was still not prepared to place his trust in the ability of the United States navy to shield them. When he received from Lieutenant Reverend Fearon the report of the 'red followed by green' sighting he had little doubt that it was 'the real thing'. It was perhaps the conviction in his voice that persuaded the mayor it was not just another Home Guard exercise.

'Andrew, it's just not possible to evacuate the entire town, be reasonable.' John Abrahams, town clerk, looked round the council table for support.

'What alternative have we got? That invasion fleet can only be heading for the peninsula here. It's too rocky or the sea is too rough along the rest of the coast. If they had been heading for Christchurch they would have stayed further out to sea and our lookouts would not have seen them. Given that they are coming here then, if we are going to do anything to oppose them, we've got to get the civilians out of the way. Browne and his Home Guard may not be able to hold them up much but at least they'll have some chance if the civilians are not in the road. There's just no option. If the Japs land here and get into the town then all hell will break loose. If they are attacked then God knows what reprisals they'll take against our people here. There were all sorts of atrocities at Singapore after it surrendered.'

'It's going to be very difficult to evacuate the hospital and the old people's home. We just haven't got the transport.' Dr Wilson was the local doctor and a member of the council. Andrew Adair rubbed his eyes and looked up.

'You're right, it can't be done. We'll just have to take the risk and leave them there. What say you organise a large red cross for the hospital and shift the old people into there. Being on top of the peninsula it should be out of the direct line of fire if there's street fighting in the town.'

'What about the rest of the townspeople? How do we let them know what to do and get them to do it?' The town clerk was shaking his head and obviously believed it was a lost cause and evacuation of the town was just not possible. He turned, shrugged his shoulders again and looked expectantly at the mayor.

'We've a number of volunteers in civil defence and they will have to go round door to door and get everyone out into the streets. Those with motor cars can start taking people out as far as the Kowhai River bridge. Any buses and trucks can take more.'

'What about petrol?' Chris Kennedy owned the local garage. Chris, with his broad Scottish accent, did not warrant the label 'canny', but he was a careful businessman. 'I'll need coupons or some sort of authorisation before I can just give out petrol to every Tom, Dick and Harry.'

'Here's your authorisation,' and the mayor scribbled on a piece of notepaper. 'But if the Japs arrive here you won't get any authorisations from them.'

So an evacuation plan of sorts was stitched together. The doctor left to see to his responsibilities and other councillors and council staff left as they were briefed or used the telephone to put the evacuation into effect.

Meanwhile, fifty miles to the north the 'enemy' was following a great shoal of succulent krill which covered acres of the sea off the coast and they boiled to the surface as the two feeding humpback whales blew bubbles to concentrate them, rose beneath them and gulped great mouthfuls of the krill which they strained through their baleen plates. The mother and her daughter, having taken their fill, turned back towards the shallower water closer to the rocky shoreline. It was then that both Henare and James saw them again but this time on an angle as they headed towards the shore and more clearly as they blew. The moonlight turned their spouts into columns of silver that seemed to be drawn back magically into a burnished sea.

Henare immediately recognised the spout as that of a humpback.

'Well, I haven't seen one of those for years.'

James had not seen the whales spout. Henare handed him the glasses. He brought the two black, silvery shapes into focus.

'Cheeky buggers, those two subs are sitting out there again.'

'You stupid berk. They're not subs. They're a humpback and her calf.' Henare could see this even with the naked eye. 'See their humps as they go down, they're… ' Henare broke off as he realised what they had done. 'Christ Almighty, we'll have the entire New Zealand navy here soon – all three of them – to sink two humpbacks.'

Meanwhile in the township the evacuation had started.

It was now just after a quarter past one in the morning. Not a good time to be woken and told to get yourself ten miles inland. Many had been woken by the fire siren calling out the Home Guard but had turned over again in their beds only to be woken an hour later by the civil defence wardens knocking on their doors.

The warden knocked on Mrs Agnes McKillock's front door. Jessie was a university student but was home for the vacation. She did her best to explain to Mrs McKillock the need for the evacuation but was not very successful. Jessie had found the sight of Mrs McKillock, when she eventually came to the door, rather daunting, her hair in curlers and her nightgown being of a cut and size that reminded Jessie of the Bell tents she had slept in at Girl Guide camps.

'No chit of a girl is going to tell me to get out of my house. If you're right and the Nips are coming I'll face them here.' Jessie bit her top lip and felt a little sorry for the Japanese invaders. 'What they do to me they'll do just the same if I'm ten miles away and at least here I've got me home comforts. I'm not budging. I've kept the hubby's twelve-gauge that he used for duck shooting. The first Nip that shows his slit-eyed face in this doorway won't have a face.' Jessie decided that Mrs McKillock would have to take her chances, and her chance of survival seemed somewhat better than the first Nip who darkened her doorway. She went back down the front path. The garden looked unreal in the moonlight and she could smell Mrs McKillock's old-fashioned roses. What would happen to this, and them all, when the fighting started? Her grandfather was in the Home Guard. He lived with them and had already turned out when the siren had sounded. He's too old to be having to do this, she thought, as she went up the path to knock on yet another door. Here she was more successful. A young woman answered the door and her husband appeared behind her. He must have been in an occupation, perhaps the cheese factory, that exempted him from military service. They had two very young children and the wife was prepared to flee on the spot. As Jessie returned down the other side of the street she noticed they were already on the move. As they pushed both a pram and a sulky, and had bundles under their arms, she thought they looked like pictures in the newspapers of refugees fleeing before the German blitzkrieg. The moonlight captured the moment in stark black and white.

Within the hour the streets were thronged. All manner of vehicles were being pressed into service: bicycles, prams, even wheelbarrows. Some of the 'refugees' were intent on travelling light, and quickly. Others trudged along with what looked like all their worldly goods on their backs, determined that at least some of their most precious possessions would not fall into Japanese hands. Those with motor cars were running a shuttle service out to the Kowhai bridge and then back for another load. Several Newmans' tour buses were in town overnight and these had been pressed into service. Some of the Home Guard called out earlier from the outlying farm districts had arrived by tractor and now their tractors were being turned about to take trailer-loads of the Kaikoura citizenry out of the danger zone.

The Kaikoura Home Guard company had taken up their defensive positions. Number One Platoon was dug in along the beach in the East End of the town, overlooking Kaikoura Bay, from whence over a hundred years before Te Rauparaha had driven ashore in his war canoes to attack the Ngai Tahu. Hone Tai, cousin of Henare, and also a descendant of Moki, remembered the history of his people and shivered as he grasped his rifle, scanned the bay, and hoped that Kaikoura town would not suffer the same fate at the hands of the invader as his people's pa had, one hundred years before. Above the beach trenches, Lieutenant Reverend Michael's platoon was ready to provide covering fire for Number One Platoon below on the beach or, as they had an excellent view of the coast to the north and the local shoreline, to redeploy wherever the main attack came. Number Three Platoon was at the ready outside headquarters in the church hall, prepared to move off by tractor and trailer if the invaders landed further along the coast, although this was considered unlikely. Sergeant O'Hara had wanted to lay some of his gelignite 'whale bombs' on the beach but the Reverend Michael had persuaded him that they could be put to better use mining the fishery buildings around the 'new' wharf (the 'old' wharf was the site of the early whaling station and now little used). He pointed out that if these buildings could be levelled then it would deny the enemy cover and provide an improved field of fire for the Home Guard defenders. Sergeant O'Hara was able to assure the Reverend Michael that 'not a stick will be left upright, sir. Just give the word and I'll blow the lot to kingdom come, if you'll excuse the expression, sir. I'll mine the wharf too, sir. I'd like to hold firing that one until we have some customers actually on it.' As a man of the cloth, the Reverend Michael had some qualms about this; he thought there should be some limits to how far one should go in killing the enemy even in God's name. Particularly difficult in the First World War, he thought, where the Germans had also enlisted God on their side. However, he thought as he shrugged his shoulders, the Japs by and large aren't Christians and deserve what they get, or is 'an eye for an eye' a bit too Old Testament?

'Right you are, Sergeant, but make a careful note where you lay your charges. We may have to take them up ourselves.'

This premonition of the Reverend Michael was about to bear fruit as some fifty miles north along the coast, Corporal Henare Tai and James Anderson thought of ways, other than magical, of turning two Japanese submarines back into a humpback whale and her calf. Henare exclaimed, 'We've got to get on the blower back to Kaikoura or all hell will break loose. Come on, we'll have to go down to the coast road and ride back to Barney O'Reilly's place. He's got a phone there. We may even be able to get a feed of crayfish while we're there.' Henare picked up a saddle and bridle in one enormous hand and kicked open the corrugated-iron door of the hut.

James Anderson prepared to follow him. 'They'll realise soon enough that it's not an invasion. Won't hurt Browne to have to get off his fat backside. They've been tucked up in their beds while we've been out here roughing it and going without.' The pile of empty beer bottles he passed as he staggered out the door after Henare gave the lie to James Anderson's complaint, but he continued muttering as he pulled up the girth strap on his saddle.

The ride down the hill to the coast road was not easy. There was a little-used track through the coastal bush. Two in the morning was not the best of times to be slipping and sliding down it. The full moon was of some assistance. Once they hit the coastal road they were able to break into a canter.

In the East End of Kaikoura by 2.30 that morning there was little sign of life. A black Labrador left by its departing family howled to the moon. A blackout had been in force for much of the war but there had always been the occasional glint of light as a door was opened or a blind adjusted; now there was not a glimmer.

Quite suddenly there was a blaze of light on the top of the peninsula. Captain Browne, who was doing the rounds of his platoons, was with the Reverend Michael's Own at the time.

'What the bloody blazes are they playing at? Sorry, Lieutenant, but those lights will be seen miles out to sea.'

'I believe, sir, it is the hospital.'

At this stage the hospital was lit even more brilliantly by a spot light and figures could be seen erecting a banner of some sort on the roof.

'Those idiots are giving the Japs a beacon to steer by. It'll be like a moth to a candle. Switch it off.'

Those on the roof had little chance of hearing him and continued to erect their banner. It was a very large red cross.

The Reverend Michael could always be relied upon for a reasonable explanation. 'They've obviously not been able to evacuate the hospital and are making sure the Japs know what it is, sir. They're letting them know it's a "safe zone".'

'Safe zone my ar… aunt. They didn't bother about the red cross on hospital ships after Singapore and are not going to observe the niceties of war against us. They've had it all their own way from the time they took on China.' Captain Browne took breath with great difficulty. 'Send a runner and tell them I order them to put out those lights – now! Tell them they can switch them on again when we are dead on the beach.'

Most of the populace had been evacuated. A few, Like Mrs McKillock, old or obstinate, or both, had been left. Some like Mrs McKillock were preparing to meet the Japanese invaders head on; others had plans to conceal themselves.

Whereas in the town all was quiet, ten miles away at the upper Kowhai bridge there was chaos. There was no way of knowing how many from the town had been taken there, probably a thousand, but many had chosen to go to relatives and friends on neighbouring farms. There was no shelter and no food, although the river provided water. It was not the ideal place to be, even in summer, at three in the morning. Mayor Andrew Adair had come out on the last bus from Kaikoura and attempted to reassure the 'refugees'.

'We are better off here. It looks as if the Japs are going to land at Kaikoura, or close to it. If we'd stayed we would have made any defence impossible.'

'But how long will we have to stay here? We've two small chidren and we've brought no food except a bottle of milk.'

'My husband's on medication for his heart and we didn't bring his pills.'

'I was running a shuttle with the car and my wife and kids came out on one of the tractor trailers and I haven't seen them since.'

The mayor listened and reassured but there was little he could do. By three-thirty there had been no sound of gunfire from Kaikoura and the 'refugees' were huddled in disconsolate bundles along the river's stony banks.

Some had heard the approaching growl of the GM trucks but for those who had had managed to doze off, mainly those who had the forethought to have brought blankets, it came as a surprise as truck after truck turned off the main road from the south and turned on to the shingle Kowhai bridge road. In turn, they swung off the road on to the shingle river bed in a herringbone pattern ready to head back down the road to Kaikoura. As each truck stopped, the tail-board was dropped and troops of the Canterbury Regiment jumped down, stretched themselves, and checked their weapons. Andrew Adair hurried halfway along the convoy to where a group of officers was gathering.

An officer with a crown and pip on the shoulders of his battledress stepped forward from the group and introduced himself.

'Lieutenant-Colonel Webb, commanding the Canterbury Regiment.'

Andrew explained about the sighting and the resulting evacuation.

'You've done a grand job, Andrew. What's the situation now in the town?'

'Nothing had happened when we left and we have not heard any gunfire so presumably they've not landed yet.'

'Right. The quicker we get in there and dig in the better. We will want to know if there have been further sightings of the enemy force. This could be a diversion to draw us away from Christchurch and the enemy flotilla may be making a feint here. We've got to stay on our toes and be prepared no matter which side of the scrum they come round'.

The colonel was obviously a rugby player and as he gave a string of orders and the troops piled back into the trucks and they roared off down the road in a cloud of dust and as the soldiers shouted out and waved to the Kaikoura 'refugees', Andrew thought they looked for all the world like a rugby team heading off for an away match. If the Japanese are preparing to land in strength, Andrew thought, not many of them will be returning from the 'game' alive. As he watched the convoy turn off the shingle road, and the accompanying dust cloud die as the convoy headed along the main coastal road for the township, he wondered whether they would arrive at the town before the enemy flotilla had succeeded in landing troops. Would the Japs, he thought, stand off and bombard first or rely on stealth and creep in on landing craft? Not much chance of concealment with this moon, he concluded.

The 'enemy flotilla' was in fact now directly off the Kaikoura coast still following, sieving and swallowing thousands of a broad patch of krill. As the whales surfaced the sea turned to fire as the water cascaded phosphorescent off their satin backs. The lookouts in the Reverend

Michael's platoon did have night glasses and although sightings of whales were now rare, compared to the thousands of humpbacks that must have journeyed along this coast on their long migration from tropic to Antarctic seas before the whalers annihilated them, they had no trouble identifying them as whales. It was confirmed when the mother playfully rolled over and extended a great knobbly fin fifteen feet out of the water slapping it down on the silvered sea. Their report to the Reverend Michael, by runner, stated: 'Sperm whales sighted 0330.' The report, although not entirely accurate regarding the type of whale, was sufficient to cause Lieutenant Michael to feel an immediate pang of doubt which in turn caused a sinking feeling in his stomach. At that moment the telephone was ringing at Home Guard head-quarters in the church hall.

Private Rewi Tai took the call from his father Corporal Henare Tai. 'We're calling from Barney O'Reilly's at Waiuku. That sub sighting rocket, well, it wasn't a sub. It was two humpbacks.'

'Hold on Dad, we got a red rocket from Waipapa. That's for a number of enemy ships. The whole town's gone bush. What's this about whales?'

'We shot off a green. That's for a sub, but there wasn't a sub, only a humpback with a calf. They looked like subs the first time we saw them but I'm telling you now they was whales.'

'Well, we got a red and a green rocket from Waipapa lookout. That's for the whole works and Captain Browne has evacuated the entire town. We'll have the regular bloody army from down south rolling in at any time now.'

'Look, we're sorry, son, but you better start undoing it all. I repeat, no Japs, just two whales. Over to you. James and me are going to have a feed of crayfish while we're here.'

As Rewi hung up his field phone, the link phone rang and Lieu-tenant the Reverend Michael informed him of the sighting of the 'sperm' whales and expresseed his fears concerning the accuracy of the Japanese flotilla sighting.

'Sir, I'm up to here with bloody whales, sorry, sir. I don't care what sort they are but all I know is that the sighting from Corporal Tai's post was incorrect, and they also saw whales. What they saw at Waipapa that made them fire a red and a green I haven't the faintest idea, probably a school of porpoises. You've got to excuse me now, sir, but

I'd better get in touch with Captain Browne.'

The convoy with some 600 troops of the Canterbury Regiment pulled up as it approached the Kaikoura peninsula and the troops debussed and formed up by platoons along the beach. It was not very far perhaps from where, several hundred years before, the Ngai Tahu had disputed possession of the coast with the original Ngati Mamoe tribe. As there was still no sound of firing from the township they assumed the enemy had not yet landed but they proceeded cautiously in open order in a long skirmish line with the right flank anchored on the beachline. As they advanced into the outskirts of the town they used standard street fighting tactics and 'cleared' each house before making a dash for the next. All were empty. Until they came to Mrs Agnes McKillock's cottage.

As the trooper opened the front door Agnes fired both barrels, an outcome to be expected if both fingers are on the triggers at the same time. The blast sent Agnes backwards over her chair in a flurry of nightwear and legs of such monstrous proportions that any thoughts of ravishment by an invading enemy would have been immediately extinguished. The trooper did not lose his head, Agnes's aim having been a little high, but a number 4 shot had caught him on his brow and catapulted him in a heap at the feet of his section corporal. He was the only casualty of the 'invasion'.

However, it could be said that Captain Browne was also a casualty of the débâcle. He was a proud man and to have to explain the nature of the mistaken sighting first to Lieutenant-Colonel Webb of the Canterbury Regiment and then to Mayor Andrew Adair was a soul-searing experience. But the reaction of these men was nothing to the scorn heaped on him and the Home Guard by the rank and file of the Kaikoura citizenry. His response to the almost daily heckling, of which he and the Home Guard were the butt, that it was a useful exercise for 'the real thing', was poor defence against the string of whale and Jonah jokes.

The Kaikoura Home Guard were never called upon to defend their coast against a real invasion, but neither did every soldier on active service get to to fire a shot in anger at a real enemy. As the Reverend Lieutenant Michael Fearon said at the end of the war, 'Perhaps "they also serve who only stand and wait".' In spite of Davey O'Neill's doubt that the war could be won by such bumblers as themselves and Sub-

Lieutenant Hiro Watanabe's confidence in the final outcome of superior Japanese bravery and strategy, Japan on 15 August 1945 agreed to an unconditional surrender.

The two atomic bombs that ended the war also, in a paradoxical way, ushered in an era of peace. The Cold War came to an end as the wall between East and West Berlin toppled. Based on wartime developments, intercontinental planes became larger and faster. For young people OE was as much part of growing up as the pimples of adolescence. To study the natural environment, before it vanished for ever, and particularly things still 'green', young and old travelled to the far ends of the earth to look with awe at orang-utans in Sabah, erupting volcanoes in Alaska, gorillas in Zaire and… whales in New Zealand.

The Kaikoura coast was about to experience an invasion of people greater than at any other time in its history. Into the Pacific Ocean after 1871 a trickle of Europeans had followed the *William and Anne*, the first whaler 'to burst into that silent sea'. Now a cosmopolitan army of tourists flooded into the Kaikoura coast – the Whale Coast. They travelled from the far corners of the world, not to hunt the right, humpback and sperm whales for their bone and oil, but simply – to watch.

Chapter 7
Land-based Whale Watching

Moki of the Kati Kuri subtribe of the Ngai Tahu tribe would have been astounded to have seen his great-great-great-granddaughter Harata Tai confidently handling the wheel of the 45-seater twin-jet Hamilton catamaran *Wawahia* as it bucked into the gentle southerly swell and headed south-east into deep water. Harata was taking the same route that her ancestor Moki had paddled over one hundred and fifty years before when he had set out on his unsuccessful journey to seek assistance for his subtribe from the paramount chief at Kaiapoi against the impending attack by Te Rauparaha.

Harata's Whale Watch craft had been tractor-launched at South Bay and now, as it cleared the limestone reefs, she opened the throttles and the catamaran stood up on its twin hulls and the foam surged froth-white from its twin jets.

It was from this same South Bay, close to a plaque set on an upstanding rock, commemorating their courage, that turn-of-the-century whalers, with the revival of the industry, had set out in pursuit of whales with high-speed motor boats and bow-mounted harpoon guns. The whale watchers heading out on Harata's boat would grudgingly have conceded their courage but, as one, would have abhorred their butchery of the whales.

The whale watchers had arrived by bus in South Bay from the Kaikoura depot, strangely enough located in the Kaikoura railway station, Whale Way station to the locals. The only passenger trains coming through the town are a daily two-way link between Picton and Christchurch, so the railway station is little used. The little station had seldom before seen the number of people, now from all over the world, who queue for Whale Watch bookings or wait when sailings are cancelled as a result of rough seas.

On arrival at South Bay they had boarded the catamaran by way of the stern steps on the launching trailer before the tractor gently backed the craft, with its full load of whale watchers into the channel, a natural cleft in the water-worn limestone, which had been enlarged to take the latest and largest of the Whale Watch boats. As the twin hulls slid into the water the colours were dazzling: the light blue of the sea and the deep yellow hull with Maori curved spiral patterns along the side, a deep blue observation cabin and enclosed flying bridge, where Harata stood. The brilliance of the colours was accentuated by the white of the limestone reefs and the flashing, wheeling, screeching gulls in the foreground. In the background the still snowcapped peaks of the Kaikoura mountains stood sentinel.

Moki would have recognised the fern-like pattern on the sides of the great catamaran, as it was much the same as the carved decorations ornamenting the Kaikoura war canoes he knew, and the whale motif near the stern. The words 'Whale Watch', however, even if translated into Maori, would have been beyond his comprehension. He would not have understood that world opinion, in most countries anyway, was now opposed to the hunting of the whale, many of which, such as the great blue, had been hunted almost to extinction. Even the two hulls of the catamaran would not have seemed remarkable to him as many of the Maori canoes of his time were twin-hulled.

Moki would, however, certainly have been amazed that so many people had travelled from all over the world just to see the whales. The *Wawahia* and her sister ship *Uruaro*, smaller, but still carrying thirty passengers and powered by triple 250 horsepower outboard motors, could each make four trips a day, weather permitting, to the deeps off the coast so that the watchers might catch a glimpse of the whales surfacing and sounding. These large, purpose-built boats were a far cry from the small converted fishing-type boats that the Ngai Tahu had first used to convey tourists when they were establishing whale-watching on the coast.

These were not the right and humpbacks that the whalers had hunted so cruelly, but sperm whales seeking giant squid and groper in the deep sea canyons along the coast. The Kaikoura Deep was a southern branch of the Hikurangi Trough off the North Island of New Zealand and its depths of more than a thousand metres provided the favoured food of the sperm whales. These were young bulls who would spend some years feeding here, bulking up and growing to almost twenty metres before leaving their bachelor pad and bountiful larder and setting out for tropical waters to take on adult responsibilities.

Moki had known by the set of the waves, the tides and the moon when and where to catch fish. He would have been astounded at the sophisticated sonar equipment used to locate the whales as they hunted along the sea canyons for squid. Harata kept the big catamaran heading straight into the swell coming up with the southerly breeze and the twin jets discharged a double track behind. The jet engines Moki would have understood, in principle anyway, if it had been explained to him that they propelled themselves in the same way as the octopus and squid he used to catch moved themselves backwards, by sucking in and blowing out a jet of water.

Harata eased off the throttles as the sounder got a fix on a whale and the catamaran rolled in the gentle swell. The watchers waited, perhaps for an hour if the whale had just sounded. Suddenly the sea rose and boiled up and the black knobbly head and back broke surface and, with an explosive burst of fish-smelling spray, the whale blew, not straight up but slightly to the side. Definitely, as Harata had predicted, a sperm whale.

Most of the tourists were standing. Some gazed silently in awe, some Japanese girls screamed, an American attempted a not very convincing 'thar she blows', a Scot in the same row muttered under his breath, 'we not be hunting them now'. Cameras clicked and flashed and some saw the spectacle only through the lens of a video camera. Harata kept the catamaran about fifty metres from the whale as it regularly blew to recharge with oxygen its tons of blood for another dive into the depths. She kept up her commentary.

'This is Hoon. "Hoon" is Kiwi English for a tearaway young fellow. He's been hanging about here for a few years now and is a bit of a show-off. Has been known to come up tail first. We can recognise them by their flukes – that's their tail. Some are notched, some droopy and so on. Earlier in the season we can hear the humpbacks singing on the hydrophones.'

The whale gave a final snort, the back arched and then the tail rose slowly. Applause from the Japanese girls. Ever so slowly the great, muscle-rippling bulk slid straight down, aiming for some dark cavern a thousand metres below. A smooth circle of water remained momentarily on the surface to mark the 'footprint' of the whale.

Harata opened the throttles on the twin jets and the catamaran gathered way. The corkscrew rocking in the southerly swell whilst waiting had caused two of the Malaysian women to be sick and they hung over the side. Harata scanned the sounder and followed the image of a whale along a deep water canyon as it herded squid before it. After two more whales were sighted and duly watched, Harata swung the cat towards the Kaikoura peninsula and opened the throttles. Several others besides the Malaysians were feeling a little queasy and were pleased enough to be heading back to firm land and the comfort of hotel, camping ground hut or camper van.

The old wooden Pier Hotel had become a popular watering hole for those tourists who had been whale watching or who were waiting for the weather to break so they could set out. Just across the road was the restored Fyffe House built by the first of the Kaikoura shore whalers. It was here back in the 1860s that James Adair, fresh from the gold-fields to take up land at Kaikoura, had called for supplies. In front of Fyffe House whales had been dragged out of the water and flensed.

The tourists enjoyed the historical aura of the place and also appreciated the conviviality of the old-style public bar. Some of the crew of the Whale Watch boats also regularly dropped in. Harata came through the doors into the bar and joined her two cousins, Tui Martin and Liam O'Neill, and Liam's friend Patrick Adair.

Tui and Liam, like herself, had Maori blood. Though proud of her Maori roots, Harata had never been able completely to accept and identify with her Maori heritage. Her parents had died when she was young and she had been brought up by her aunt in the pakeha manner. Though she spoke some Maori it was very much a second language. She both admired her cousin Tui and was a little envious of how self-confident she was in her Maoriness – she had mana. Tui could trace her ancestry back many generations. Her family tree going back a mere 150 years included Moana, the wife of Moki. Tui had the same proud features, the high cheek-bones, the almost hooked nose, the flashing eyes and out-thrust chin, but above all else the relationship was evident in the dark lustrous auburn hair. Tui had attended one of the new kohanga reo schools where she had learnt Maori and had absorbed Maori traditions from an early age. Her father was pakeha but her mother was of the Ngai Tahu tribe. She was an ardent activist and she seemed to spend most of her time espousing a variety of Maori causes and attending protest meetings in various parts of the country. As Queen Elizabeth, who had earlier in the week flown in to New Zealand, would be in Christchurch later in the month, Tui was heading down there to take part in yet another protest.

Patrick Adair, the fourth member of 'the club', had a dairy farm on the plain just out of town, and regularly joined the group after he had completed milking on a Friday evening. His dairy farm had once been his grandfather's and was one of the original blocks broken in by the early Irish. Patrick was Harata's boyfriend. She had just moved out to live with him on his dairy farm and he hoped to be able to talk her into marriage. Patrick felt that her cousin Tui was too fiery by half and they generally did not see eye to eye, in fact most of their encounters were toe-to-toe slugging matches. Their regular Friday night arguments generally centred on the question of land. Their viewpoints were polar opposites: Patrick, like his Irish forebears who had come from Donegal landless, was proud to be the owner of land; Tui's people had lost theirs and she was ready to fight for them to get it back.

When Harata arrived, pulled up a chair, and accepted a beer the conversation was general chat but then they got on to the Queen's visit and that started Tui off.

'The Queen can get stuffed as far as I'm concerned,' declared Tui.

Harata and Liam exchanged glances and waited for Patrick to take up his shillelagh. As they expected, Patrick immediately took up the challenge.

'Look, I'm of Irish descent, Tui, and my people didn't have much love for the English but what are you beefing about? The government this week has given the Tainui Maori 170 million dollars in compensation for pinching their land and the Queen, while she's here, will sign an apology for the English starting the Land Wars against them. What more do you want? Or are you only happy when you are nursing a grudge?'

'Which question would you like me to answer first?' Tui had taken a sociology degree at Canterbury University, Patrick had been among the fifty per cent in his year who had failed the national school certificate in English. Tui used words as a duellist uses a rapier; Patrick chopped away as if he was using a slasher against a gorse hedge.

'Whata ngarongaro he tangata, toitu he whenua.' Tui used Maori to rile Patrick. She succeeded.

'Come off it, Tui, give us a fair shake. You know I don't know Maori.'

'Why the hell should I have to translate for you? Maori should be the official language of this country. You were talking about going whitebaiting at the mouth of the Cow-tra River before. Not only you but most people in Kaikoura say it that way. That is an insult to my people. It's got nothing to do with your bloody cows, it's the Ka-hu-ta-ra River. For God's sake, get Kai Ko-u-ra right too,' Tui thrust her face into Patrick's and almost spat out the words. 'Its not Kai-kor-ra.'

Patrick took shelter behind the jug of beer they were sharing, for which he was paying. Tui, except for occasional part-time jobs, was on the dole and managed beer and 'cigs' for herself but considered 'shouting' a luxury she could ill-afford.

'Come off your high horse, you haven't explained what you are beefing about. What's your problem?'

Tui drew a deep breath. 'Right, I'll translate. It means: "Man disappears but the land remains". The land is everything to us.' 'And the sea too, and what is in it,' interrupted Harata, who had been content until then to stay out of the conflict and listen from the sideline.

Patrick tossed his head in exasperation. 'But the Waitangi Tribunal is looking at your claims and you should get Crown Land in compensation for what was taken from you. You've got to be realistic and move into the twenty-first century and not keep harping back to the past.' Patrick thought it time he drank some of his own beer.

'We are not harking back,' countered Tui, 'but we must know the history of our Maori people so that we can use their values to determine our future. We've previously been pushed around or looked after by a benevolent government and told what is good for us. We must now stand on our own two feet. What we want is tino rangatiratanga, Maori sovereignty.'

'You pig-headed woman, can't you see you've got that now, at least at tribal level.' Patrick poured himself another beer and appealed to Harata as he continued.

The Kaikoura Ngai Tahu have tribal control in a tribal way of the whales, haven't they, Harata? In taking tourists out to see them by boat anyway. You've local control over a local resource – the whales. You've got control where it counts. You've got to be reasonable, Tui. The government has to retain the power to make laws for all New Zealanders, whether they're pakeha, like me, or Maori, like you. We're all New Zealanders.'

The fourth member of the Friday night social club had, like Harata, kept out of the fray, but now decided to join the action. Liam O'Neill was just twenty-two and in his final year of an engineering degree at the University of Canterbury. He often came home to Kaikoura for the weekend. He was the grandson of Davey O'Neill, who had died only a few years previously, well into his nineties. Liam's great-great-grandfather had married Huia of the Ngai Tahu, so there was both Irish and Maori blood in his veins. He had inherited no aggressive tendencies from either side of his family. He was a very quiet, even shy, young man.

'I don't agree with either of you,' said Liam in the quietest of voices. 'You want to put the clock back, Tui, and suggest that before 1840 there was some sort of Maori nation. I don't think there ever was. Every tribe was a kingdom to itself, often having to go to war to survive. We here in the South Island considered that the South Island belonged to us through ahi kaa.' He looked at Patrick, 'Means "those who kept the fires burning". So although we were attacked and defeated by Te Rauparaha, his people didn't stay long enough to "keep their fires burning" over a period of time and stake a claim to the land.'

Tui disagreed. 'But some of the tribes did agree to form a federation before the Treaty of Waitangi was signed with the British and anyway, if we can't be ruled by our own chiefs there's no reason why we can't have separate Maori health and education systems.' Tui had been too long out of the discussion to hold back now. 'The present system of government in New Zealand disadvantages Maori.' Tui launched into her well-rehearsed spiel. 'Three-quarters of Maori males and 85 per cent of Maori women receive an income below $20,000. Two-thirds of Maori aged over fifteen have no educational qualifications.'

'Put a sock in it, Tui.' Patrick was becoming riled, 'We've heard you spouting those statistics before. Anyway, in a poor year for butter fat I'd earn less than that. Climb down off your soapbox and be real. The tribes can do a lot of these things already. In education they've their Maori language nests, "hangi reos", or whatever they are. You've done it yourselves with whale-watching and you are now going to be into fishing in a big way. The tribes can do this sort of thing at local level.'

Harata nodded in agreement but did not intend to enter the fray and poured herself another beer from Patrick's jug. Liam, still quietly, but firmly, carried on the discussion.

'And that's where I disagree with you too, Patrick. Do you really believe, Tui, and you too, Patrick, that the tribes could work together? Look at the outcry from some of the northern tribes when the Ngai Tahu did so well in getting fish quotas. Are the Ngai Tahu going to get one metre of timber or man-made fibre board out of the Kaiangaroa pine forests if the government returns that land to the North Island tribes? No, not a chance, once they get their hands on those trees.'

'You, Liam, are just putting forward materialistic issues,' replied Tui. 'There's also the need to recognise the spiritual source of tribal taonga, that's "property", Patrick.' This was also one of Harata's hobby-horses and she could not resist chipping in.

'That's exactly what we are doing with the whales. We've got to look after whales and our land for those coming after us so that they are still there in the future.'

'Just what I said to you, Tui, you are going to get your land back, or the equivalent.' Patrick noted that she was again filling her glass from his jug. All take and no give, he thought. 'What's your gripe then?'

'I'm not really complaining but it's taking so long to get our land back. I'll be pushing up daisies before we see it.'

'Another thought,' and it was now Patrick's turn to be difficult, 'why the hell should you get your land back anyway? Our people who came from Ireland were a bit more fortunate in that their families in Donegal rented some scraps of land and most of them were able to hold on to their farms during the famine, but what about the Catholic Irish who were evicted by English landlords? Do you think they could put the clock back now and go back and say, "Could we please have our land back, kind sirs?" Like hell they could.' Patrick was becoming a little steamed up and swallowed several quick draughts to dampen the fire.

'Your mentioning the Irish,' nodded Liam, 'reminds me of another aspect of tribalism. You know our Irish forebears, perhaps even more so the Catholic Irish, were pretty tribal. They stuck together, didn't mix much, and looked after their own. There were some real stink-up rows on the Kaikoura council and on some of the school boards between the rival factions. All part of the local scene then. Do you remember our grandparents, Patrick, talking about the "micks"? If they'd had their way you never would have been called Patrick. But I think we in New

Zealand have moved past that sort of society. Do we want to be going back to a tribal society? How would it work in your vision of Maori self-rule, Tui? Would you be giving all our Ngai Tahu cousins the top jobs, as seems to be happening in most countries in Africa? Tribalism is the scourge of Africa. Look at Rwanda. One tribe massacring another. They take it in turns.'

Tui had no thought of giving anything away. 'But a form of regional sovereignty would work. I think some of the Indian tribes in the United States have separate local states.'

Liam smiled, 'You want the South African word for that sort of separate development? It's "apartheid". Great idea, we should try it! You may prefer the American term which is "reservations". Do we really want separate racial groups in New Zealand? Perhaps you'd like to go in for a little bit of redistribution of people, as well as land, to tidy things up a bit. We could send City Maori back to their rural iwi. The Serbs called that "racial cleansing". Sounds rather fun.'

'You're just going to extremes, Liam.'

'Coming from you, Tui,' Patrick rejoined, 'that's the pot calling the kettle black.'

Tui was usually quite proud to be labelled an 'extremist'. Now she tried to keep her cool and reason with Liam.

'We should scrap our present system of government and legal system. Just because they worked in England doesn't mean they're the best system for New Zealand. We should go back to some of our Maori ways of providing justice. For example, rather than concentrating on punishing the criminal we should make sure the victim is paid back what they lost.'

'Here we go on compensation again,' groaned Patrick. 'You're just looking for another hand-out. Anything your lot gets free comes out of the New Zealand tax payer's pocket. Speaking of who pays,' Patrick drained his glass, 'the next jug is on you.'

Tui, jug in hand, marched across to the bar for a refill. Liam found himself admiring her long auburn hair that, hanging loose, came almost to her backside, which Liam thought undulated engagingly in her tight blue jeans. That's enough, cool it, thought Liam, you don't want to be grabbing any tigress by the tail, or any other part of her anatomy. An argument most Friday nights in the pub is one thing but a more serious interest in Tui could only result in altercations every night of the week.

No, it's not on. A great looker but to get closer to her would be like playing with dynamite.

Liam decided, on her return, to launch one final attack which, if successful, should sufficiently sour their relationship to keep him safe if, inadvertently, in a weak moment, he made a pass at her. He had known her at university but only casually as a cousin from Kaikoura. He had chosen not to associate himself with the group of Maori activists Tui hung out with. They all seemed to have half-baked ideas in Liam's opinion. As an engineer he was amused at one of Tui's group who had tried to cut down a tree of some significance as a protest but had used a chainsaw that was much too small for the task and botched the job. Hope to God they never get to rule the country or they'd screw that up too, he thought.

As she returned to their table with a full jug he stood, which he knew she hated almost as much as if a male opened a door for her. She glared at him as she slammed the jug down, the froth spilling over.

'Thanks, Tui.' Liam was stalking his prey with some caution. 'I've been thinking about what you were saying and you were right about our present system of law and government. It is rather confrontational. The issues always seem to be presented in black and white: if a Labour politician says one thing you can bet National policy will be the absolute opposite.'

Tui seemed mollified by Liam's more reasonable viewpoint.

'Yes, sure, the Maori way is based more on consensus and co-operation. On most issues we would hold a hui. You can stop bloody grinning, Patrick, you know damn well that means a 'meeting', and everyone has a say. Our Maori people today would be better off if we went back to the way we governed ourselves before the Treaty of Waitangi.'

Tui was taking the bait nicely, thought Liam. He used some Maori he remembered from his grandmother: 'He wahine, he whenua ngaro ai te tangata' to placate Tui, and then translated to keep Patrick quiet: ' "Women and land are the reasons why men die" I suppose you've got to get the land back first?' asked Liam, the angler gently twitching the fly.

'Yes, you're right, Liam, some of our claims have already been upheld by the Waitangi Tribunal and, as I said before, the others are just a matter of time.' Tui, if Liam had been sea fishing, was about to swallow hook, line and sinker.

Liam prepared to strike and reel her in. 'What rights would you have had in the good old days to have reclaimed land lost to your tribe by conquest? Was there anything in Maori law which enabled land conquered and occupied by one tribe to be reclaimed at a later time by its original owners?' Tui was trying to marshall her thoughts but he kept up the barrage of questions.

'If Te Rauparaha had "lit his fires", stayed in occupation of Kaikoura longer, after he had attacked and massacred our ancestors, was there any way under Maori law the Ngai Tahu could have regained that land? Perhaps you could have asked Te Rauparaha's Ngati Toa people for compensation? What compensation did our Ngai Tahu people who came back twisted and bent from captivity at Kapiti receive? Nothing.'

Tui was, with difficulty, trying to keep her temper in check.

Liam went on. 'There's still bad blood between our Ngai Tahu and the Ngati Toa.'

'You're wrong, Liam,' interrupted Tui. 'We don't continue to harbour any grudges against the Ngati Toa. You can sling off all you like but our iwi has tried to heal the wounds of Te Rauparaha's raids. I'll give you one example. The great-granddaughter of Chief Taiaroa of our southern cousins married a great-grandson of Te Rauparaha. Sure, it was an arranged marriage.' Tui stifled a giggle. 'The story goes that she couldn't swim and they put the two of them together on an island in Lake Ellesmere until there was a successful proposal. You may well laugh, Liam, but that was back in the 1920s, and there have been lots of other intermarriages.'

'We're not talking about marriages of convenience, Tui.' Liam was not to be sidetracked.

'You're quite prepared, Tui, to accept pakeha law, and favourable rulings from the Waitangi Tribunal, if it means you get the land back, but at the same time you want to scrap pakeha law. That's one hell of a balancing act.'

'Liam, I don't want to fight with you. You are almost of our whanau and certainly of our Kaikoura hapu. Our strength is to maintain and re-establish these links of our Maori heritage, and reinforce our bonds within our iwi.' Tui was again quoting from one of her press releases. 'Once we have re-established our economic base with land or sea-based ventures then political power will follow for our Maori people.'

Liam spoke quietly. 'I am as proud of my Maori heritage as you,

Tui.' Liam was no longer just point-scoring but desperately serious. 'You know when Captain Hobson said at the signing of your Treaty of Waitangi "Iwi tahi tatou", he used the word "tatou" which means "us and you together". This, for me, is the way it has got to be. We're not one homogeneous people but we can be one nation. We are too small a country to have some form of dual government.' Liam held up his hand and Tui held her peace. 'Way back there was conflict between Maori tribes, there was rivalry and competition for resources of land and sea when the Europeans arrived. My Irish forebears didn't see eye to eye with the English squattocracy of the big sheep stations. Roman Catholics and Protestants regarded each other with suspicion and sometimes open enmity. But through good times and bad, floods and snowstorms, wars and peace, they each made their contribution so that we have the nation we have today.

'The lesson we can both see mirrored in the Whale Coast, Tui, is that our nation has not been created by one group of people on its own, but from the magic that is created from the relationship between us. I would like to see us continue along that path.'

As Harata and Patrick clapped, Tui lent across the table, held Liam by his shoulders and solemnly rubbed her nose first on one side of his nose then on the other. Liam froze in his seat. Tui lent back, regarded Liam and shook her head.

'We'll make a Maori of you yet, boy. I'm proud of you.' She brushed tears from her eyes. 'Too much bloody smoke in here. I'm off for an early night. Our group's heading for Christchurch at first light.' She made for the door.

Liam realised that he had made a serious tactical error in taking a hard line with someone like Tui. Rather than turning her off he seemed to have turned her on. He again couldn't help admiring her auburn hair or the snug fit of her jeans as she waved, tossed her head, and went through the door. Pity about her politics.

Tui, from the time when, as a little tot of four, she had been taken by her mother to the kohanga reo, was destined to be active in the Maori rights cause. On the other hand her pakeha father, John Martin, had never intended to get himself caught up in the legal complexities of Maori land claims. He was the eldest son of a Canterbury farming family whose forebears had come out in 1850, on one of the First Four Ships, to the new Church of England colony. He had attended, as a boarder, a Church of England boys' school in Christchurch, Christ's College, which was even more English than all but the most exclusive of English public schools. He had always wanted to be a lawyer. He won a scholarship to the University of Canterbury and graduated in law and was later admitted to the bar.

John and his family moved in circles in which they had little opportunity to meet Maori people. There were, admittedly, fewer of them in the south of New Zealand. The depredations of Te Rauparaha, some 150 years ago, had contributed to this. Perhaps John's family had not made sufficient effort, but at any rate the coming of Miro into his, and his family's life, had been something of a culture shock.

He had met, Miro, Tui's mother, when his school and Te Wai Pounamu College, a Church of England school for Maori girls, had presented to parents a joint musical concert. A drawback of single-sex schools is a chronic shortage of the opposite sex, particularly when it came to putting on dramatic productions and musicals. John was a very gifted musician and if he had not been so determined to follow law, could have become a concert pianist. He accompanied the Maori girls' choir when they sang Po Kare Kare Ana and Miro sang the solo part. John thought the song somewhat trite but had been enthralled by the rich, warm, contralto voice of Miro. He had never heard such a thrilling sound, such purity of tone but with a husky sensuality that sent shivers up his spine. It was not so much 'love at first sight' as 'love from her first note'. The shock of her voice at the first rehearsal had caused him to look away from his music and when he had dragged his eyes back from the Maori girl with her cascading black hair with auburn high-lights reflecting the stage lights he completely lost his place and stopped playing. Miro continued unperturbed and unaccompanied with unerr-ing pitch and time. She smiled as the last haunting note still hung in the air, and John thought it was more for him rather than at him for his stopping. The Maori singing teacher conducting Miro's group, turned towards John and said 'Great. We'll do it that way: the solo unaccompanied.' John felt foolish and after the rehearsal sought out Miro and stammered out his apology. From close up, John was even more impressed by this beautiful Maori girl with the waterfall of hair. When she eventually looked up from an embarrassed gaze at the floor, her brown eyes were as deep and exciting to John as the dark pools of the West Coast streams where he had fished for brown trout. Miro later told Tui that at first sight she had not been greatly impressed by this gangling youth in his black and white striped tie and blazer. Her upbringing had been Maori and she was suspicious of this young man with, as she put it to Tui, 'A posh way of speaking, more like a Pom than a Kiwi.' She also lacked his confidence and on the final night of the concert, found difficulty, when he sought her out afterwards, in sustaining a conversation, until they got on to music and found they had a shared passion. They started with the Beatles then Bizet through the classics and found common ground all the way. Miro was pleased that John was an admirer of Dame Kiri Te Kanawa – 'those songs of the Auvergne were really cool'- and of the Maori bass the late Inia Te Wiata – 'he really knew how to sing Gershwin'. John was in fact displaying the keen legal mind that was to take him to the top of his profession and had selected evidence of his love of music, that he knew would count in his favour with Miro in any verdict on his suitability as a suitor. Although his approach was deliberately calculating and he thought he could handle any relationship at an intellectual level, his strategy fell apart when Miro eventually smiled. She had the full lips and perfect teeth of her people – John analysed it that far and then, as he also later told his daughter, Tui, 'That's when all reason left me and I started to love your mother.' As both were boarders there were few opportunities for them to meet while they were still at school.

Miro had been encouraged by her parents to sit first School Certificate, and then try for the University Entrance examination. Only a small percentage of Maori girls, for a variety of social and economic reasons, gained this qualification but Miro was successful and was able to go on to graduate in nursing from the Christchurch Polytechnic. John was at the same time pursuing his legal studies. They saw each other regularly and both assumed they would marry when they had completed their studies. Some of their friends were living together but neither of their families would have approved of this and what their family thought was important to each of them.

At the same age Tui had lived with one lover, had stormed out, got involved with another 'no-hoper' (according to her mother) and had shocked her mother further by discussing with her the pros and cons of having a baby so that she could qualify for a domestic purposes benefit and thus keep up her almost full-time protest activities. To her mother's remonstrances Tui had replied, 'You and Dad were real squares.

These days you do your own thing. The days of the dominance of one sex and one race are over, Mum.'

Tui, from an early age, had engaged in vigorous debate with her father and he encouraged her to question everything. The discussions they had were always no-holds-barred free-for-alls. The only rule her father laid down was that she was not to hide behind her fluency in Maori. If she used Maori then he expected her to translate. This rule was generally adhered to by Tui, except when she made asides to her mother and they would both collapse in laughter. John considered it wiser if he did not know what these exchanges were about.

When Tui was nineteen and still at university, her father had made an important decision. He made up his mind that it might be less stressful, and life certainly more tranquil, if he joined his daughter's cause rather than continuing to oppose her. He decided he would represent the Ngai Tahu in their land claims. As he said, 'If you can't beat them, join them.'

His decision had finally been made after a particularly lively altercation. Tui had started it, as usual all smiles and sweetness.

'That guy was convicted for burglary, I see, Dad,' Tui commented as she looked up from the paper.

'Yes, pretty open and shut, identified coming out in broad daylight carrying a video recorder. First offence, so he'll get only a few months, may qualify for probation.'

'Bit tough, Dad, don't you think? Wasn't really his fault.'

'Oh, come on, Tui, he was clearly identified. We've just got to make a stand about these property thefts.'

'You pakeha are pretty hot on property, aren't you? People don't matter as much.'

'He had a fair trial. You can't make anything racist out of this just because he was a Maori.'

'My bloody oath I can. Says here he was unemployed, on the dole. He's on the bloody dole because Maori find it more difficult to get jobs than pakeha. What sort of life is it scratching along on the dole with no prospects of an effing job?

'Don't swear, Tui, it does nothing for your argument. Granted if they're twiddling their thumbs on the dole they're more likely to get into trouble. But I don't accept that as an excuse for wrongdoing. I thought the government was going to introduce work schemes whereby the fit unemployed would be required to work for the dole. That would at least give them some self-respect.'

'Self-respect bullshit. Your pakeha government is not going to do anything. At the Kaikoura marae we're already using the money coming in from whale-watching to provide jobs. If we get our own land back and access to other resources we're capable of looking after our own people, and don't need a patronising government to tell us what to do. We're pushing out the waka for the next generation. Your pakeha laws are shit-hot on property theft, what about land theft?'

'I am prepared to continue this discussion, Tui, but it ceases with the next obscenity. I do not use that word and will not have you use it in this house. Freedom of speech also carries with it some respect for the rights and sensibilities of others you know.'

'Okay, Dad, you're not in court now. But you've got to admit the Maori in general, and Mum's tribe in particular, were pretty shabbily treated in some of those early land deals. They were ripped off. The pakeha settlers were after land at any price. Well, not at any price because they didn't pay much, or anything, for most of it.'

'You're just generalising. Let's have a specific example, girl.'

'You're on. Year: 1859. Month: March. Day: 29th. That specific enough for you? On that date Chief Kaikoura Whakatau and the Maori people of Kaikoura sold to James McKay, representing the Crown, over two and a half million acres, from Cape Campbell in the north to the Hurunui River in the south along the coast and back to the inland Kaikoura ranges for the paltry sum of two hundred pounds. Specific enough for you, Dad? You're a lawyer, surely you can see that it was daylight robbery. James MacKay pretended he had to hurry off to Lyttelton to catch a ship just to speed up their acceptance. Oh, no. They weren't pinching a video recorder; they got two million acres of land.'

'Well,' conceded her father, 'that doesn't seem entirely fair but some of the land has remained in Maori ownership. That strip along the beach by the railway yards in Kaikoura township from where they run the whale watch I believe is still in Maori hands. They're using the railway station as a booking office for whale watching, aren't they?'

'Oh, yes, the pakeha's generosity was really touching. Out of the two and a half million acres, they set aside 5,566 acres – now there's a good specific figure for you. It's one I won't forget – use your new calculator and work out what percentage that was of what had been all – all, theirs.'

'But surely they were left with the reserves of land that they wanted?'

'Sure, some were the areas where they were actually living. Like Kaikoura Whakatau, the chief at that time, who was living at Mikonui, so four or five hundred acres were reserved there. But MacKay was still putting it across them in that he admitted later that from the pakeha point of view it was all pretty "worthless and useless" land. I've looked at this very closely, Dad, and if it's not actual theft then it must be at least fraud. Do you realise that as far as I can gather twenty-four of the twenty-six signing the deed of purchase did so with a mark or cross? Only Chief Kaikoura Whakatau and my ancestor Renata te Whiringa signed their full name. James MacKay probably wrote down the names of the others and told them where to put a cross. Do you think they really knew what they were signing away for ever?'

It was about this stage of the 'discussion' that John Martin decided that his daughter might have a case, a case he would sooner prosecute than defend. Tui took his silence to mean he had still to be convinced and resumed the attack.

'I suppose it was just sharp business practice and a case of not the buyer, but the seller, beware. It's like this guy you've just helped put away, he stole a lousy video recorder worth a measly few hundred dollars while the white collar pakeha crims, sorry, investors, are beating the taxman by shipping their millions off to a Cook Islands tax haven. It's still one law…'

'Hold on, daughter, I might be persuaded to come round to your point of view. Fraud is criminal deceit and an offence in law and through the Waitangi Tribunal it should now be possible to set some of these injustices to rights.' This time Tui remained silent. 'And,' continued her father, 'I might be prepared to interest myself in some of these land claims. But get one thing straight. I will not condone your sort of pointless direct action. That will achieve nothing except engendering ill will. And I want no truck with your ideas on Maori sovereignty. If you want a result you've got to stick to existing laws. I'll give you a hand on this, partly for the sake of your mother and her Ngai Tahu people, but I will do it according to and within the law. Any other way is a prescription for disaster.'

Tui had, for once, the good sense to remain silent. The deal was sealed as she gave him a hug and a kiss.

The topic was not brought up again until the three of them were attending the Sunday morning service in the Anglican Cathedral in Cathedral Square, Christchurch. Miro, in her own quiet way was even more strong-willed than her daughter and had insisted that Tui, in spite of her radical tendencies, followed in her steps by being true both to her Maori heritage and her Christian upbringing.

At the end of the service, as the last of the red-cassocked choir boys disappeared through the south transept and the congregation filed out, Miro moved towards the recently installed Maori tukutuku panels on the north wall. The warm, earthy colours of the yellow, red ochre, brown and black of the weaving contrasted with the coldness of the marble memorials and tiles on either side along the rest of the wall. Miro continued to look at the panels but addressed both John and Tui.

'This is our future. This is the way we need to go.' She read the inscription on the rimu board beside the panels. Tui provided the translation for her father: 'What is the most important thing in life? It is people, people, people.'

Miro continued, 'Both of you remember that land is not everything. Look at the tukutuku panels. Here is the balance that we are seeking. The panels on each side, the darker roimata, these are the tears by which we remember our ancestors but we do not stay in the past. The centre two panels are much brighter, full of joy, and the 'steps' of the tukutuku lead us up to heaven. So to preserve a balance and retain our mana we remember and honour our roots in the past but we go forward with trust and hope.'

Tui and her father looked across Miro at each other, and, for once, were in agreement.

In the next few days they would need all their trust and hope. The Kaikoura coast, and as far south as Christchurch city, was about to suffer a catastrophe greater than it had ever experienced in living memory. The great flood and snow storm of the 1860s, the disastrous floods that had swept through the township in recent years were as nothing compared to the forces of destruction that were about to rack the coast and vastly change its appearance. The transformation of the coast would make the works of man look insignificant. Man had certainly changed the appearance of the land, scratched the surface, by accident or design, particularly over the past 150 years, with roads and rail, farms and cities and unplanned ugly scars of erosion. The township of Kaikoura had grown from a Maori village and whaling station and now stretched from the old wharf where whales had once been dragged ashore, through East and West Ends along the bay and was now straggling north along the main road and rail line. The township, which for a hundred years had just ticked over based on its fishing and dairying industries and an influx of holiday-makers in the summer, was now booming. Restaurants and motels were springing up to cater for the tourist whale watchers coming to the coast in an increasing flood. Additional tourist ventures, such as swimming with the dolphins, had started.

The Japanese tourists knew and respected earthquakes, but the British, Europeans and Australians laughed and joked, albeit in a forced, nervous way, about 'the shaky isles'. They were all about to witness at first hand the threat posed to life and property from a land balanced astride two moving crustal plates of the fiery Pacific rim. Some of the tourists would not live to relate their experiences.

Some warning of the impending disaster, it was realised only in hindsight, had been signalled for some months before by the renewed activity of the volcanic cone, Ruapehu, in the central North Island. It had erupted violently several times, throwing up ash which had been distributed widely.

At 6.30am in Christchurch, on the day after she had attended church with her parents, Tui rolled over in bed and realised it was getting light. Some light at any rate was penetrating the grime on the window and the tatty grey lace curtain. She screwed up her face and remembered this was not the spick and span home of her mother.

Her parents lived in one of the fashionable suburbs of Christchurch in a valley of the Port Hills. Tui shared a flat in Kaikoura with one of the Maori guides working for Whale Watch but when she came to Christchurch, generally on a protest mission, she preferred to stay overnight with her activist friends in a run-down backpackers' hotel in what had once been a 'gentleman's residence' on the western side of the city, not far from Cathedral Square.

At the same time, in Kaikoura, as great earth forces built up explosive

243

pressures, Helen O'Donnell had turned on her bedside lamp and was sitting up in bed drinking the cuppa that James had brought her before he had gone out to milk the cows. He had brought the cows in and had just started milking. It was almost 6.35am.

John and Miro's house in Christchurch was part way up the Heathcote Valley just above the road tunnel that linked Christchurch with its port of Lyttelton. This was the same valley that over 150 years before Ngai Tahu warriors had run down, hurrying to return to their village at Kaiapoi to defend it against the war party of Te Rauparaha. Then in the 1850s Captain John Browne, his wife Elizabeth and their family had come down the Bridle Path through the valley to take up pastoral land in Kaikoura.

Rising steeply from the back door of Tui's parents' house, to around 650 metres, the Port Hills provided shelter from the prevailing easterly wind. It was an idyllic setting for their two-storey brick veneer house. The microclimate in the valley was almost subtropical and most plants flourished. A scarlet bougainvillea was in full flower across the veranda.

In the earth's crust below, forces of unimaginable power were building up to a crisis point.

At 6.35am neither Tui's father nor her mother was awake. They usually had the radio-clock beside their bed set to come on for the 7am news. This Monday morning they would be woken before the news, for the last time in this house.

Harata was skipper on the first of the early morning whale watch vessels due to leave South Bay at 6.30am, if the seas stayed down. She had been awake at five. Patrick had also been awake early and they had, to their mutual satisfaction, filled in the twenty minutes or so of spare time before they needed to get out of bed, he to milk 'the old girls' and she to repeat her spiel on whales. Harata lay back on the bed with her long dark hair spilling over her breasts and shouted out to Patrick who, in the contest they had just engaged in, had won the right to first shower: 'A big fat American woman asked me, "Dear, why are they called sperm whales?" I told her, "Lady, they've got balls that weigh half a ton, that's why they're called 'sperm' whales." I'm sure the silly cow believed me.'

Patrick came in, drying his hair, 'Speaking of cows, I could do with a hand with milking tonight.'

'You've got it, lover boy, but you can rustle up the meal. You can make a stew and we'll just need to heat it when we come in from milking. But now I have to dash. Can't keep the whales and the customers waiting.'

It took her only about a quarter of an hour in her Daihatsu hatchback to cross the Kaikoura flat and the gentle swell of the landward end of the peninsula. She arrived at the whale boats in South Bay well before the bus with the tourists from the township depot. The sea was flat, the sky a sullen grey, and there was as yet no wind, neither from the land nor from the sea. Even the sea terns were silent. The Kaikoura mountains still had snow on their peaks. Harata shivered but was not cold. The ghosts of my ancestors, she thought. We'll have to watch the weather today, something is brewing, either a scorcher from the nor'west or a southerly buster. Either way seas are going to get rough before the end of the day. She pulled on her life-jacket.

Almost thirty tourists boarded the *Wawahia* by way of the stern steps. The twin-hulled jet boat was launched by the tractor and was heading out to sea on the stroke of 6.30. As they left the limestone reefs behind Harata shivered again and thought it strange that no sea birds wheeled, dipped and screamed around the boat as it arrowed out. Except for the roar of the twin jets, the morning was strangely quiet and seemed to be holding its breath.

The unusual absence of the sea terns reminded Harata of a story one of her fishermen uncles had told her. He had lived in Oaro, a few miles south of Kaikoura, and the few Maori who lived there and the holiday bach owners had been plagued with wild cats. Her uncle had obtained some strychnine rat poison and had used this to rid them of the cats. He was out fishing some time later and as he was baiting hooks on his longlines, the sea gulls were stealing his fish baits. He still had the strychnine in his oilskin jacket pocket and smeared some on the pile of bait. He watched as some of the gulls wheeled in and snatched the baits. Nothing happened and the birds swung across to another boat that was fishing the groper hole. Suddenly the birds just fell out of the sky and splashed in the sea around the other boat. The other fisherman up-anchored and raced for shore. When Harata's uncle spoke to him later the fishermen said, 'I ran into a pocket of bad air, the bloody seagulls were dropping all around me. I got the hell out of it.' I had better not tell the passengers that story, thought Harata.

Strange too that there seemed to be no swell, the sea seemed lifeless. The dolphins that usually picked up the boat about here had not appeared. Going to be a stinker of a storm, thought Harata, hope we get this lot back to shore before it breaks or they'll spew everywhere. The tourists were unaware of these omens and awaited their arrival in whale waters with quiet anticipation. They would not arrive. It was almost 6.35am.

After
Land Uplifted

At 6.35am one hundred miles due east from Christchurch the motor vessel *Gale*, on her return trip from the Chatham Islands, gave an enormous shudder as if she had struck some underwater obstruction. For a moment the bow rose and the waterline was exposed and then she fell back into the sea.

The crew tumbled out of their bunks and headed topside expecting to find they had been rammed by another boat or had hit a dozing whale. They grasped the rail and looked over a flat and empty sea. Nothing. 'Like a painted ship upon a painted ocean.'

They looked up to the bridge but Captain Johnston was just as perplexed. He consulted his charts but already knew there were no reefs in this part of the Chatham Rise. The bottom was some hundreds of fathoms below.

The shock wave that had struck the *Gale* had originated from the enormous release of energy from the conflict of two great earth plates: in the centre of the North Island, below the smoking vent of the volcanic cone of Ruapehu, the Indian Plate was thrusting over the Pacific Plate and deep under the Southern fiords of the South Island the Pacific Plate was winning the titanic battle and was riding over the Indian Plate. The gigantic forces thus generated by the flexing and buckling of the earth's crust caused a sudden release of pent-up pressure in one of the crustal faults, the Pegasus Bay Fault, which continued north along the Kaikoura coast. It was faults such as this that had created the deep undersea chasms into which the sperm whales dived.

The sudden movement between up-thrust and down-warped blocks was the cause of the shock wave that had struck the *Gale*. It was measured on seismographs around the world at over 7.5 on the Richter scale. The local seismograph recording pens swung wildly on recorders near the centre of the earthquake then off the drum and recording ceased.

The energy released by the displacement along the Kaikoura Trench was the equivalent of all the explosives used in World War II. The immediate effect on the fish and whales in the trench was as if a series of depth charges had been fired: most were either stunned or killed.

The shock wave travelled at a speed of three kilometres a second. Most of the force was directed north and south: north to the national capital, Wellington, and south to the regional capital, Christchurch. Neither would escape lightly.

The sideways force was not as great but it came out of the sea at Kaikoura at over 7500 kilometres an hour and slammed into the peninsula. The limestone cliffs disintegrated and shattered rock fell in a pall of dust into the sea at its base.

The force ripped across the Kaikoura plain, realigning the landscape. James O'Donnell had built a modern, fortunately wooden, house on his dairy farm. The original blue gum trees, planted by his grandfather, provided shelter to the south. In front of the trees his wife had planted her rose garden. As the earthquake shock wave struck the cowshed the noise was deafening. The water tank was flung off its stand and the water seemed to explode out of it as it fell. James was knocked to the ground still holding the milking cups he had been about to fasten. He remained stuck to the concrete floor as the aftershocks continued and said afterwards, 'It felt as if I was in a vacuum that was sucking me down, and at the same time I could feel the concrete base of the shed moving under me.' He was luckier than another dairy farmer further inland who had just finished his milking and was herding his cows back out when the ground opened up beneath him. He fell spread-eagled and watched incredulously as a huge crack grew under him. He stretched himself to avoid being sucked down. Less fortunate was a cow just in front of him that disappeared as the earth opened and then closed.

A cow toppled alongside James and was kicking desperately to regain her feet. James took a blow in the ribs from a hoof but otherwise escaped unscathed. Pipes had burst and milk at first sprayed in all directions but ceased as the power failed. It was pandemonium in the cowshed as cows bellowed, staggered to their feet and kicked to release themselves from the milking cups. The shock caused their bowels to open and the shed was awash in milk and cow dung. They backed, pivoted, slipped and slid, forced their way out of the shed and stampeded into the house paddock. It would be some hours before James was able to round them up and several days before they again let down their milk.

James's impressions of the quake were confused. He remembered as he lay in the cowshed seeing his house jump into the air. 'I swear I saw the foundations and daylight underneath and it came down in a cloud of dust. The brick chimneys just seemed to collapse on themselves. The blue gums swayed about and then appeared to walk. I tell you, it was unreal.'

As the quake sped inland and he was able to pick himself up, James found that the cowshed had moved almost seven metres from where it originally stood. One row of blue gums had moved towards the cowshed but the row near the house had moved into the space vacated by the roses. The roses were now where the path from the cowshed to the house had been.

James's wife, Helen, had been in the kitchen. She remarked afterwards that the fridge-freezer had suddenly danced across the room towards her. 'It was almost like a do-se-do in square dancing.' As it toppled she was thrown to the floor alongside it. Everything came off the walls and the freezer cabinet saved her from being crushed under the old wooden dresser as it toppled. She was cut as the windows shattered into the room. The microwave oven she remembered seeing in mid-air and the hot water cylinder had suddenly appeared out of its cupboard, as she said, 'like a jack-in-the-box' before crashing to the floor. Pipes had burst and the kitchen floor was under water. As the worst of the shaking subsided she managed to force open the back door, in time to see the family car rolling down to the front gate. Bellowing cows were stampeding from the direction of the cowshed. Helen wondered if James was safe.

Cracks were opening and closing in the front lawn and the aftershocks, as she looked inland to the mountains, were still causing the plain to roll, as she said later to James, 'like a sea in a storm, so much for "solid" land. I swear the mountains also moved.' She remembered reading when she was at school that Cortés had described how the Andes danced during an earthquake.

James was still trying to calm the cows. His dogs were useless and he realised they had acted strangely even before the quake hit and were now in their kennels from which came the occasional mournful howl.

Helen was so shocked she just continued to stand on the front lawn and stare at what had been a new house. The chimneys had all collapsed and windows were glassless. The entire house had a drunken lean in the direction of the earthquake shockwaves but its wooden framing had flexed and twisted without collapsing. Helen didn't realise it at the time but they were much better off than many others in the rural areas of Kaikoura and infinitely better off than those in the cities of Wellington and Christchurch.

She realised in speaking later to other women in the district that they had escaped lightly. One woman from a nearby farm had just got out of bed and had sat on the toilet when the bowl was suddenly whisked from under her and out of the house. She was unhurt but understandably shaken. A local drainlayer later capitalised on the event by advertising in the *Kaikoura Star*: 'Our work will withstand an earthquake'.

Helen was still dazedly regarding their rearranged farm when her father-in-law's Toyota ute bumped its way up the drive, which now boasted a set of speed humps that it had not had five minutes before. As he climbed rather carefully out of the ute, Helen dashed into his arms. Over her shoulder he looked across to the sagging house and the rearranged landscape of shelter belts and cowshed.

'There, there, lass. Was a bit of a shake, wasn't it?'

Helen looked back at the house with its walls leaning in all directions, and began to giggle.

'What is it, lass?'

'Looks like the crooked house of the crooked old lady.'

'Well I'll say this, the war was never like this.'

James at this stage came up from the home paddock having given up on the milking, the cows, and 'those bloody dogs'.

'You know, they must have heard it coming because they were on their way out of the cow yard before it arrived. Made straight for their kennels and the buggers are still there.' James's main concern seemed to be for his cows and dogs but Helen felt he had also been anxious about her as he gave her a hug and kiss in front of his father, a most unusual occurrence. But as she thought later, this was a time of strange occurrences.

One had occured at the local sawmill. The saw doctor had started work early so that the big circular saws would be sharpened ready for the first shift. He was working on one of the giant two-metre diameter blades when the earth moved. He in a split second found himself trapped under several heavy blades. In answer to his cries, sawmillers coming in to work lifted them off, four men to a blade, one at a time, until he was freed. The saw doctor came out alive but with a badly lacerated thigh.

In the township of Kaikoura most of the older wooden buildings were still intact but, like James's farm house, leaning askew, pointing the direction the shockwave had taken. In the local shops everything on stands or on walls was now a chaotic mess on the floor. It was at least fortunate that the quake had struck before the shops were open, or the casualties would have been higher. The local chemist, after picking himself up after being thrown from his bed, negotiated the twisted wooden stairs and regarded with disbelief the mixture of pills and potions on the dispensary floor. He smelt a heady and explosive mix of ether, eucalyptus oil, methylated spirits and goodness knows what else. He remembered reading somewhere that the fires that had practically destroyed Napier after its big earthquake had started in a chemist shop. He also remembered that in those days medicines had often been sealed with sealing wax and every chemist shop had a lit gas jet, which had probably ignited the explosive cocktail mixed by the big quake. He looked down at his shaking hands. 'Well, we don't have gas jets these days but it might be a good idea not to light a cigarette.' As the aftershocks continued, he picked his way through overthrown display stands and cosmetics and the broken glass of the front window and joined the uninjured occupants who also lived over their shops, and tourists from the hotel who had sought comparative safety in the middle of the main street.

They would not enjoy their apparent safety for long. Tangaroa had not taken kindly to what the earth had done and had already mustered his forces to exact utu. That humankind would suffer was of little concern to the sea god.

People in the township had already been injured and some were dead. Concrete and brick buildings, those that had seemed the most substantial, were the worst affected. Façades and cornices on some of the older concrete buildings had tumbled down. At the Empire Hotel some guests had been in the foyer about to board an early tour bus and had rushed outside at the first tremor. The main shock had knocked them to the pavement. The concrete parapet had crashed through the veranda and crushed them. Their death cries, muted by the masonry and choked by the cloud of dust, mingled with the screams of those who had gained the shelter of the bus. They too may have thought themselves safe as the aftershocks lessened and became more widely spaced. They too may have been thankful to be on land, even though it was wobbling like a jelly, but few of them would have remembered that the sea was but a stone's throw away, or would normally have been. The sea had retreated several hundred yards. Tangaroa was assembling his forces before launching a counter-attack on the land.

At sea at exactly 6.35am the shock wave hit the whale watchers. They were the nearest human beings to the epicentre of the earthquake. The marine trench they had been crossing had suddenly dropped between parallel faults in the earth's crust and their jet boat reacted just like an aeroplane that had hit an air pocket. The boat was left hanging in the air as the sea beneath fell away. The twin jets raced sucking on air, not water, and the boat fell back, fortunately on an even keel, into the trough opened up by the earthquake. The impact was like a bus hitting a brick wall and the cries of the passengers were stifled as they had the air knocked out of them. Then shouting erupted in a dozen languages. Harata had fallen heavily across the instrument panel and, from the pain in her chest, thought she had suffered some broken ribs. She groped for the PA microphone and it fortunately seemed still alive.

'Okay, folks, just a little earthquake, I think.' Harata didn't just think it; she could see the pall of dust over the Kaikoura peninsula and plain and, even out as far as they were, she had heard the roar coming from the land. I knew Tangaroa was brewing up something. That sullen, lead-grey sea as we came out meant he was sulking and about to spring something. A southerly buster perhaps, but who would have thought an earthquake? What happens next?

'Just a bit of a bump, folks. We'll come round and check if anyone's injured but just keep your seats and make sure you have your life-jackets fastened.' Harata's calm instructions belied her feeling of panic. Is it over? Do we stay or return to land? They don't seem to be doing too well, as she again looked towards the land. The dust cloud still remained but the earth had stopped its writhing. She used her binoculars and could clearly see the rails of the train line to the south of Kaikoura buckled up in the air with the sleepers still pegged to them. The approaches to all the bridges, road and rail, seemed to have gone, although the bridges themselves seemed intact. This is serious, she thought, we'd better head back.

At that moment a whale broke the surface almost beside them. But from the expanse of pale stomach it exposed it was obviously upside down and either dead or concussed. The effect on the tourists was disastrous. After the initial intake of breath as it broke surface there was a gasp of horror as they realised the magnitude of the earthquake shock. The gasps became whispers as they sought to reassure each other. Harata realised they were close to mindless panic.

'Remain seated. We are returning to shore. We get a lot of these earthquakes.' Not like this little beauty, she thought. 'After the first jolt we may get a few little shakes until things settle down. There's nothing to worry about now. We'll have you ashore in a few minutes. With a bit of luck,' she added under her breath.

Just as she spoke, the trough they had been in began to fill and to build higher and higher. It rose fifteen or twenty metres, carrying the jet boat up with it. Afterwards she described it as, 'like going up in the lift in a multistorey building.' Harata was very, very frightened. Never had she experienced anything like this. The jet boat was now on the crest of an enormous wave, not breaking, more like a giant swell, but there was only the one. Harata could see for miles, across an otherwise flat sea and over the peninsula and plain, on what seemed to her to be eye-level with the Kaikoura mountains. She turned the jet down the back slope of the monster wave and like a surfboard rider they rode it safely down into the trough. As they turned for shore Harata saw the monster wave smash against the white cliffs. The peninsula seemed much higher but she assumed this was the effect of a low tide. The spray blotted out the mountains behind. She recalled the story passed down in their family from a whaler ancestor that in the 1860s a giant tidal wave, as they called them then, had raced up Akaroa Harbour. Harata remembered that the story had it that their ancestor's whale ship lifted seven metres.

The tsunami had raced at great speed towards the coast. Tangaroa was going to make the land pay dearly for its shameless insolence. First in the giant wave's path had stood the limestone cliffs and at their base and along the beach was the township of Kaikoura. Its people were picking themselves up and wondering that they had survived the quake.

Most of the older buildings of the township had collapsed. The

Anglican church was no more than a heap of stone under a cloud of dust. The cross off the spire had been flung some distance away and was stuck upside down in the front lawn. The wooden Sunday School hall that had been the headquarters fifty years before for the Kaikoura Home Guard was bravely still standing, although one wall bulged as if about to burst. Most of the older wooden cottages had also escaped great damage and had simply bent to the shockwave. The more modern bungalows had fared less well. The brick veneer walls had been pulled away from the wooden frames and collapsed outwards. The house frames stood, bent over as if to hide their state of undress. There was the occasional wall which for no obvious reason remained standing. The concrete fire station, built in the 20s, had fallen in on the fire engines, before they had driven out through the doors and, fortunately, even before they had been manned. Buildings that had been built since the 1970s to new earthquake specifications had withstood the shake well. But in Christchurch the buildings were taller and it had been traditional to build in stone and brick.

Within a split second of lifting the motor vessel *Gale* and the whale watch jet boat out of the water, the shockwave smashed against the high volcanic rock cliffs of Banks Peninsula and then struck the city of Christchurch. The seismograph in the Christchurch observatory went crazy as the shock with a five-metre lateral and two-metre vertical movement struck the city. The seismogragph needle swung wildly over the drum and flung red ink on the mounting and nearby wall.

The stone-clad cathedral in the central square of the city suffered badly. The entire upper spire toppled and crashed on to the paving below. In earlier, lesser, earthquakes the spire had suffered minor damage and the fallen original cast-iron cross had never been put up again. But this was much worse. The bells rang of their own accord in discordant peals and two of the largest crashed down from the bell tower. The stone walls cracked and toppled outwards. The limestone pillars of the nave were found afterwards to have been displaced and tilted but the wooden roof structure of matai and totara hardwood had held them from toppling. The recently completed Visitors' Centre, alongside the cathedral, designed according to the latest building codes, was comparatively unscathed except for a few cracks in its plate-glass windows. The noise was appalling: the rumble of the earth tremors, the madly tolling bells, the crash of falling stone.

It was the noise that woke Tui. The backpackers' hotel where she was staying had been in its heyday a fine mansion but had never been designed to withstand an earthquake. The quake shook the hotel, as Tui recounted later, 'like a Rottweiler dog shaking a mouse.' The old wooden building did not fall but was gutted. The solid plaster interior walls and ceilings slumped off and every brick chimney was demolished.

Tui said later that as she woke clinging to her mattress it was moving with a see-sawing, twisting motion. Her bed careered across the floor and crashed into that of the other woman in the room. Plaster covered them both.

'Everything was white. We were fortunate to have been on the third floor. We were scared but unhurt. Our pillows and bedheads had saved us from the falling lumps of plaster. We must have looked like snowmen.'

The brick, terracotta pipe-capped chimneys had crashed through the roof as if it were tissue paper, plunged through the third-floor landing and flattened and buried a bed in the room beneath. A friend of Tui's had moments before been flung out of the bed by the quake.

Another friend on the same floor as Tui was less fortunate. He had staggered from his room, blinded with dust, on to the landing and pitched through the jagged hole in the floor left by the chimney. He fell two floors below on to the broken bricks of the chimney. His skull was fractured, as were his ribs and both legs.

Unlike Tui, her parents had received no warning. The previous day it had rained and the clay hillside above and behind their house was wet and slippery. With the first massive impact of the quake the bond between yellow clay and underlying solid rock was broken and half the hillside was poised to slide into the valley below. Everything of brick on the house was now in a heap about it and the framework stood bare. Tui's father and mother had woken with the noise and shaking of the first shock and were just picking their way across the kitchen, which was strewn with broken glass and crockery, when there was a strong aftershock and the clay on the hillside above them moved. All of the houses on their side of the valley were buried in a sea of mud. Many of the householders were later dug out with little injury.

As for Tui's parents, the mud slide struck the rear of the house, broke off the wooden wall studs and the tile roof fell on them. This was buried in further mud slips as the aftershocks continued. Even the aftershocks were of a higher magnitude than severe earthquakes of the past.

On the opposite side of the valley the causeway approach to the Lyttelton road tunnel had also slipped into the valley and the mouth of the tunnel stood agape as if in surprise at no longer having an entry road. All the approaches had slipped away. A large truck transporting a container had dropped out of the open mouth of the tunnel and both truck and container had tumbled into the valley.

Tui and her room-mate managed to climb down the very much askew wooden stairs to the second floor. They hardly needed to use the second set of stairs to the ground floor as either it had come up or the second floor had dropped. Whichever, they were able to jump comfortably to the lower floor. They gave what first aid they could to Ken, who had earlier taken the most direct route from the top floor. He was obviously in need of urgent medical treatment, but when Tui ventured out the front door of the hostel she realised that there was no hope of obtaining an ambulance.

Cars parked outside in the street were at all sorts of crazy angles and some had been tipped on their sides. One further down the street had slipped sideways into a fissure that had opened up in the roadway. Those outside concrete or brick buildings were half buried under rubble. Water mains had been ruptured and were shooting fountains high into the air. Many people, mainly in nightwear, were congregating in the middle of the road. They obviously felt safer away from buildings of any kind.

As Tui looked to the south-east across the city she could see a great cloud of dust, beginning to settle, but many plumes of smoke were rising as if buildings were on fire. She learned only afterwards that wood-burning stoves had been flung in all directions by the quake, spilling burning embers that had ignited several hundred homes.

It was not until early afternoon that Tui flagged down a Land Rover that was doing duty as an emergency ambulance and they managed to get Ken to hospital. Even the newly built public hospital had suffered damage, not structural, but beds had been flung about, injuring patients, and anything movable, such as sterilizers, had been flung, with all of their contents, on to the floor.

In speaking to nurses, Tui learned that there had been some strange accidents caused by the quake. A taxi-driver had been brought in severely injured when the approach to a bridge over the Avon suddenly disappeared and his car nosedived into the river. A passenger plane landing at Christchurch airport had its landing wheels wrenched off when a fissure opened up across the tarmac. It skidded to a halt on its nose and belly and some passengers had been brought into the hospital with minor injuries.

The hospitals had first to cope with injuries to their own staff and patients and it was fortunate that few casualties came in at first as most major roads were impassable either with collapsed buildings or fissures across them. Where high-pressure water pipes had burst many roads collapsed as the jets of water undermined them. Princess Margaret Hospital looked a sorry sight. It was a modern building but had been veneered in brick and the outer walls had simply fallen off. The ferro-concrete frame, although looking rather odd with service wiring and pipes exposed, had been little affected and the hospital, after staff had cleaned up equipment that had been thrown everywhere, was soon operational again. Power had been cut off throughout the city but the hospitals were able to use their emergency generators.

Tui remained at the public hospital in the city centre and assisted the nurses in whatever way she could. While they had a quick cup of tea she listened with some of the nurses to the radio news. Reports were coming in from other centres. It would seem that of the cities, Wellington and Christchurch had been hardest hit. The report was on the devastation that had occurred in Wellington. Most of the modern high-rise buildings had been little affected. But all had shed their glass into the streets below. The recently completed Museum of New Zealand had also lost some glass but, as expected, absorbed the movement and had not been damaged. But the surrounding reclaimed land had liquefacted and the museum was now apparently an island in Wellington harbour. This rather amused Tui. 'They'll have to hire dinghies to get people out to it.'

However the report also said that a tsunami had been generated at the time of the quake but no details were available. Tui gasped as she realised that if there had been a tsunami and the epicentre was close to Kaikoura then… Tui visualised the little town of Kaikoura on the beach at the foot of the peninsula hill and extending along the beach ridge to the north. What chance would they have against a tsunami? None.

One of the nurses saw her shocked face and moved across to console her.

'What's the matter, Tui?'

'My mother's people come from Kaikoura. They could have been wiped out in that tsunami. The whole town is only a metre or so above sea level. They wouldn't have stood a chance.'

What Tui didn't realise was that right then, closer to hand at Cashmere, her mother and father were fighting for their lives, buried beneath their fallen roof and several metres of yellow clay.

Tui wept, not yet for her parents, but for her Ngai Tahu people of Kaikoura. For a thousand years, she thought, my people have bravely struggled and overcome adversities: the terrible hardships of the long voyage of our ancestors to Aotearoa, their trials in adapting to a new environment, the wars against other tribes, the land struggles with the pakeha, the present endeavour seeking self-determination. Throughout, we have retained our mana and our respect for the land and the sea. Now both Tangaroa and Tane have turned against my people and so has the Christian God who promised them salvation. How could such a terrible thing happen? Io or Almighty God, how could you let this happen? Tui collapsed against the wall, her face in her hands.

The ward charge nurse moved over to her side to console her. In spite of her grief Tui noticed and appreciated the aroha offered by the other woman. Tui's thoughts returned to the Kaikoura coast. Such beauty: never anything, anywhere in the world as beautiful as the blue sky, rain-washed, the seas rolling in from a thousand miles, the savage splendour of the rocky coast, the serenity of the bays around the peninsula with their blue, blue sea and achingly white limestone reefs. Swimming in rock pools at Kaikoura on a calm day in the swirling bull kelp. The tang of salt water, so clean, so fresh, so free. No wonder my ancestors depicted the swirling seaweed in their carvings. I can still remember ducking my head under the crisp, cool water and seeing the green-grey butterfish lazily rolling under the surface kelp and sucking at the white underside clumps of barnacles.

Tui came back to the reality of the hospital ward and the tender pressure on her shoulders of the ward nurse still holding her.

'Could an earthquake and tsunami sweep all that away?' In a small voice she asked the question aloud. Although fearful of the truth, Tui had one glimmer of hope as she realised that the recently built Ngai Tahu marae at Kaikoura was near the old pa site on the higher ground of the peninsula. But how high had the tsunami been and what were the effects of the earthquake? Kaikoura was Tui's spiritual home: her Ngai Tahu tribe were the tangata whenua. The thought of the destruction there and the loss of the last pitiful remnants of a proud hapu of the Ngai Tahu was all too much for Tui. The charge nurse guided her firmly to a spare bed and Tui curled upon it in a foetal ball, her head between her hands as she sobbed. She wept for those of her people at Kaikoura who had surely now set foot on the path of the thousands from which no traveller returns. She intoned the opening lines of an old lament:

Kaore te aroha ngau kino	Alas a bitter pain
i roto ra,	which gnaws within,
Ki te waka o Kaikoura	For the canoe of Kaikoura
i pakaru	which was wrecked,
Ki te hoa ka riro.	For the friend who has gone.

Tui drifted off into an uneasy sleep. She saw the swirling seas off the rocky promontory of Te Rerenga Wairua, where the Tasman and Pacific oceans battled for supremacy. She tossed on the confused surface. Kahawai leaped, thrown by strings of silver beads. Rangi wept. She saw her mother waving and heard the wailing. Her Ngai Tahu people of Kaikoura stood on the beach of the Twilight Sands as their time on earth ran out.

Tui was still in a tormented sleep when the first casualties reached the hospital from the terrible sequence of events set in motion at Lyttelton Harbour by the earthquake.

From the time the earthquake shock struck Christchurch, a haze of dust and smoke from burning buildings had hung over the city. But at the same time a pall of smoke arose from behind the Port Hills in the vicinity of Lyttelton Harbour. It grew higher and the east wind spread its inky blackness over Christchurch city. As Tui said when she woke to see it, 'Like a puraku, a shroud for the dead.'

It was only much later in early evening when the casualties started to be brought in that Tui learnt what had happened. The terrible events renewed her anxieties for her Kaikoura people. They, being closer to the epicentre, would have been worse affected, if that were possible, she thought.

Tui was able to piece together by talking to the least injured of the casualties the sequence of events that had occurred at Lyttelton. Many people were dead and most of the casualties were suffering from terrible burns. Tui, with no experience of working in a casualty department, was visibly shaken by the sight of some of the badly burnt. The mutilation of limbs and the clothing melted on to skin were bad enough, but some had their faces dissolved away and, though still alive, were puppet mockeries of human beings. What distressed Tui most was that so little could be done for the badly burnt except to relieve their suffering with painkilling injections.

Tui had initially helped with the unloading of casualties as they arrived in an assortment of vehicles. These had managed to negotiate the scarred but passable old hill road, as the tunnel to Lyttelton Harbour and its approaches had been badly damaged. As the number of casualties thinned Tui attempted to console some of the less seriously injured.

One of these was Captain John Erskine who had retired to live in Lyttelton after many years spent on coastal ships. He occupied a weatherboard house high on the hill above the centre of town. That his house was wooden-framed and clad saved him from the worst effects of the quake shockwave, and that he was high up, from the disastrous events that followed. He had slight abrasions and was suffering from shock from what he had witnessed from his sitting room with its view over the inner harbour and oil storage tanks.

'I hadn't slept well and was up early,' he told Tui. 'Had me porridge and had just put me feet up and was having a cup of tea and looking across, as I usually do, at the port below. Not many ships, other than Russian trawlers, in the inner harbour these days. All these container ships you know, me dear. The sun was just up and streaming up the outer harbour. Promised to be a grand day. The inner harbour was still in shadow. Well, next thing I'm thrown out of my rocker on to the floor. Pictures, everything, the lot comes down. The old brass sextant nearly brained me. Well, I knew it was a quake. But bigger than I'd known in sixty years. Terrible roaring sound and the whole house groaned. There was a screeching sound too and I suppose that was the nails pulling as the timbers twisted.' Tui gave him a sip of water. She patted his hand and he seemed eager to continue his story. Tui almost giggled as she thought of the lines from the 'The Rime of the Ancient Mariner': 'He holds him with his skinny hand… He holds him with his glittering eye'. The ancient mariner with his long, grey beard – short, well-trimmed and naval actually, grinned Tui – continued:

'Well, I've weathered some storms in me time but this shook me to me back teeth. I couldn't prise meself off the deck at first and had just got back into me rocker when it happened. I had a ring-side seat but it was terrible – awful.

'The big tanks across at the oil storage were at all sorts of angles and looked like the apples they used to float in a tub at the fairs when I was a boy. You could see oil had spilt from them but there was no fire and the containing wall would have kept the spillage in. But then something else happened and all hell broke loose.

'I didn't see it arrive but it must have come up the harbour at a hundred knots. I never thought I'd see a wave that size in Lyttelton Harbour. Although once down at the pub an old mate off the *Rangatira* – beautiful ship – ' Tui sensed he had slipped away to another, better, time. His eyes went glassy but he started up again:

'It was as high as a three-storey house. Well, it went clean over the driver's cabin of the container crane.' Captain Erskine for some time just stared, and drew a deep breath as he remembered the events earlier that day. Tui almost forgot her own nagging fears for Kaikoura as she looked at the frail, white-bearded old fellow. He had earlier told her he had no relations still alive and many of his old friends living at the lower level of Lyttelton were now, he feared, dead.

Tui wondered about her own parents. They should be safe enough. They are high enough and on this side of the hill. In reality both lay buried beneath the mud flow and the remains of their house. Both were still alive.

Tui thought how unfair it was that an old man, with no family to care whether he lived or died should be spared, when so many younger men, women and children had died in what had happened at Lyttelton.

'Well, that wall of water, it hit the oil tanks with a smack I can tell you. I could hear the "whoof" right up there, reminded me of a bloke winded in a fist fight, all the air knocked out.'

'The 'ancient mariner', thought Tui, is away again.

'The tanks just fell apart as the wave hit them. Nothing could stand up to that force. Remember a chief-engineer of mine, great fellow, a Scot, well-educated you know. Ah, now what was his name? Bound to have been Mac something. Ah, my memory. Couldn't find me teeth the other day, found I'd already put 'em in.' Tui was prepared for a considerable wait before the narrative resumed.

Kaikoura again returned to her thoughts. If a force so much greater and a wave so much higher had hit Kaikoura, what would be left? Some may be safe on top of the peninsula, but would they have had any warning or time to reach higher ground? After all, she thought, the town is built on a beach. Even the farms on the flat inland of the town would be engulfed by a tsunami of this size. What of Harata? And James? What of all their Ngai Tahu cousins? We've all got to take the path of the thousands and leave this world but will there be sufficient of my people left to take Maoritanga on into another century? Will there be enough left with the toto of the ancestors to remember and honour them?

'Peter Angus, wasn't a Mac at all.' Captain Erskine was obviously delighted to have dredged up the right name from the murky depths of his memory. Tui assumed the narrative was about to resume. 'And listens like a three years' child,' Tui thought, 'The Mariner hath his will.' Tui again suppressed a giggle, but an icy shiver went down her back; her feelings were closer to fear than laughter.

'I can remember him saying, it's like yesterday, no trouble remembering what happened forty year ago, that a wave of 30 feet would exert a pressure of 2 tons a square yard. Damned if I know what that would be in these new-fangled measurements, but it would be a hell of a wallop. Well, that wave sure knocked the living daylights out of them tanks. All I could see was a wall of water at the end of the harbour. Governors Bay at the head of the harbour must have been completely under it. Well, the worst thing was, this was awful, the steel of the tanks, all jumbled up and twisted, must have scraped and caused a spark.' The old man sucked in a deep breath and Tui wondered if he was ever going to breathe again.

'Boomf! It was the biggest bang I've ever heard.' This time Tui interrupted the narrative.

'Be back in a moment, love. They've got the radio on and there'll be another news bulletin.' Tui headed for the nurses' office. The time pips went and then the news came on. Tui was appalled at the news from Wellington.

Some of the major motorways had been tossed off their supporting piers. There had been numerous casualties when vehicles on the roads had nosedived off. Fortunately in the early morning, when the quake struck, traffic was not at its peak. Wellington was still completely isolated as all land routes had been severed. Slips blocked the main coastal roads to the north. There was criticism of the lack, due to government restructuring of the Ministry of Works, of heavy earth-moving equipment within the Wellington area. The airport was out of action as the runways were ridged and cracked. Reports seemed to indicate that the Hutt Valley was even worse hit than Wellington as there had apparently been some local movement along the old fault line that ran between the two cities. The news was dominated by reports of the Wellington damage. Even Christchurch's situation was reported only briefly. Of the fate of provincial towns there was nothing. Tui was left to wonder about the plight of Kaikoura.

One of the house surgeons bustled in just as the news bulletin recapped on the almost total isolation of the capital city with all major rail and road services cut.

'Transport here has been the problem too. Some casualties we've lost because they've been lying out there and we haven't been able to get them in. And sod to them,' this directed at a helicopter which flew over low, almost at window level, a cameraman in the doorway. A shot of the hospital was obviously required for a news item on the quake casualties.

'What have you got against helicopters?' enquired Tui.

'Not a thing against helicopters. We could certainly use more of them to bring in casualties, particularly the burn cases from over the hill. The trouble is, the television news people have grabbed some of them which we could certainly use. It's bloody ridiculous – they want to film the news almost before and certainly as it is happening. Same thing happened, I believe, at Kobe in Japan during their big quake. Camera-men and reporters flooding in but not basic supplies – including medical materials, like blood. We're already running short of some blood types. Helicopters could bring it in. But perhaps the public would sooner see pretty pictures on their tellies. If they want pretty pictures they could come in here and film some of the burn casualties.' He grabbed a bundle of records and barged out into the corridor.

Obviously an angry young man, thought Tui, but she was sympa-thetic when she thought of the ward out there, overcrowded with burn casualties. I'm sure I could do something over there to help get the casualties out to Christchurch. She resolved to try to get transport to take her to the port.

The news ended. Tui went back along the ward chatting to the burn patients who were fit enough. Most were wrapped up like Egyptian mummies and were not much interested in talking. She arrived back at the bed of Captain Erskine. He seemed to be dozing. She patted his hand and the bright blue eyes immediately flew open, the result of long years of watch-keeping, guessed Tui. He opened his mouth once or twice but nothing came out and then he croaked: 'And who would you be, young lady?'

'You were telling me about the big wave that hit Lyttelton.'

'Was I? Don't remember but I'll never forget that wave. Smashed all the petrol tanks, you know. Then they burst into flames. Then we caught the backwash of the wave. Back it came. But this time of course instead of white foam on top, they had blazing tops. I thought I was seeing things. Flames streaming out behind like a battle pennant. The black smoke just billowing up. And of course back it come through Lyttelton that had already been hit by the quake and the tidal wave. People in the water who had been swimming were set alight. It was appalling. I didn't want to watch. They were my friends, some of them, who were being burned alive. I could see them down below me. I couldn't look at it any more, it was awful, awful.'

Tui was shocked by his account and as the old man croaked on she thought, I've got to try to get some information on what happened along the coast to the north. Road and rail links are out but there must be some way of reaching Kaikoura. I suppose I had better also check up on Mum and Dad. They'll be wanting to hear from me too. She reflected that she might have perished in the backpackers' hotel. Was it just this morning?

The old man licked his lips. Tui gave him another sip of water. He had slumped down in his bed but struggled to sit up and once again plunged into his narrative, his voice slower and weaker. Tui wondered whether she should try to stop him from continuing but on he went, blue eyes staring and tormented. Tui remembered again her high school English teacher declaiming, 'God save thee, ancient Mariner!/From the fiends, that plague thee thus!'

Captain Erskine was certainly plagued by the sights he had seen. He stared into space and continued.

'The yachts in the marina had been torn from their moorings by the big wave and as they rose up on the blazing wave one after another, it'd be those with a bit of wood on them, they burst into flames. They were burning all over the harbour. Some people had been living aboard and they must have survived the first big wave. I saw two of them get their dinghy into the water but then up they went on the return wave and they were surrounded by fire. I didn't see what happened to them but I hope it was quick. Where they were was just blotted out by rolling black clouds as the oil burned.' Tui grasped his hand and the old man closed his eyes and shook his head. As he began again Tui could hardly hear his voice.

'During the war I saw ships burn but this was worse. There was nothing we could do for the poor devils down there in the port. I went out into the garden and was going to see if I could lend a hand to pull out some of the survivors from the terrible fires down there. But I must have taken a knock. I remember reaching the garden gate. And that was it. Must have passed out 'cause I don't remember too much until I came to in here.'

Tui realised that the reliving of what he had witnessed had drained the old man. Perhaps she should not have been so ready to hear his story. It must have been horrible. From the lower part of Lyttelton around the port few could have survived the holocaust. Those that had been brought badly burnt into Christchurch Hospital had been those cast up on higher ground and left stranded as the big wave and its fiery crest receded.

Tui settled the old man down and comforted him. She found herself also starting to doze off as the old man fell into a troubled sleep. She shook herself into wakefulness. Come on, old girl. Things to do. First check on Mum and Dad, then see if I can get across the hill to Lyttelton and then find some way of getting to Kaikoura. Shen went down to the hospital foyer and it was only when she tried a telephone and found it dead that the reality of the situation struck her: Of course everything's out, there's no power. The lights, the radio, the hospital's on emergency power. Well, where they are Mum and Dad should be safe.

As she came out of the main entrance to the hospital, a helicopter was landing across the road in Hagley Park. Another load of badly burnt casualties from Lyttelton, she thought. Bingo, why not cadge a ride? They'll be going back empty.

She raced across the road, hurdled the park fence and headed for the helicopter. Hospital orderlies were pushing stretchers and Tui looked away as she passed them. The sweet sickening smell of roasted flesh as they passed her almost made her retch.

The rotors increased in speed as Tui ducked under them and waved her hands at the pilot. He opened the door.

She gestured at herself, pointed and shouted 'Lyttelton'.

The pilot nodded and Tui scrambled aboard. They lifted above the plane trees of the park, banked and headed for the Port Hills. Tui noticed the raw yellow scars on the outer slopes of the hills and that some houses had been carried away and some partially buried in the slips. She tried to pick out her parents' house but was unable to locate it as the light, although still only late afternoon was dimmed by the smoke from Lyttelton. Greasy smoke from the oil tank conflagration, although diminished, was still rising from the port and this, together with the smoke and dust over Christchurch city, was producing a spectacular afternoon sunset. Torengitanga o te ra, the disappearance of the sun, thought Tui. She, even as a little girl, had always thought in both Maori and English. But this bloody helicopter is making so much noise I can barely hear myself think in any language. After listening to the terrible story of the old mariner she couldn't get the Coleridge she had learnt at school out of her mind, 'All in a hot and copper sky,/The bloody sun…/No bigger than the moon.' In a few moments the sun will drop behind the Alps and it will be dark. Tui wondered that all this could have happened in one day.

As the helicopter flew towards the Port Hills ahead, in the gathering gloom in the Heathcote valley some volunteer workers had made a start on rescue operations. Already they had dug out many who had been buried in the landslides. Most were uninjured but some had died of suffocation. They had started to dig around the collapsed roof of Tui's parent's house. They had made good use of the services of an excited, tail-wagging black labrador who thought locating the victims under the yellow clay great fun. He was even prepared to help with the digging and burrowed away wherever he sensed someone was buried. The tail every so often would back out of a hole and a yellow-capped nose would seek the approval of the rescue party as they urged him to 'seek'. No one had been prepared for an emergency of these proportions and while Civil Defence had taken overall charge, it was largely up to local communities to improvise rescue operations and provide neighbour support.

Tui's parents had been shielded from the full weight of the clay by the collapse of the roof, which had saved them by providing both protection and vital air. Once they had heard voices and the frenzied barking of a dog they had called out and the rescuers were able to dig their way under the remains of the roof and drag them out. Tui's mother they hauled out easily. The black labrador went almost berserk at this stage and was more nuisance than help. Tui's father presented something of a problem as his leg was trapped and broken under a roof beam. Once this had been lifted and held by rescuers they were able to slide him out. He was obviously in very great pain but managed a wan smile as the dog, now ecstatic, licked his face.

Tui crossed the Port Hills just above Rapaki Bay. She could still make out Te Upoko o Kuri, the dog's head rock, that looks down on Rapaki. In ancient times the chief of her Rapaki cousins had flung down his flax waist-mat here and claimed the valley.

The helicopter swung over Lyttelton harbour. Tui could see floating debris of all sorts. As they swung in towards the port itself, the blackened, burnt-out hulls of pleasure boats and the large freight containers were easily recognisable. They came in to land on Cashin Quay, avoiding a tipped-over and tangled container crane. Tui was astounded to see a large container ship, which must have weighed tens of thousands of tonnes, parked high and dry on top of the quay. It had been lifted on the tsunami wave and let down almost unmarked on to the concrete quay as the sea subsided.

The conflagration that had been sparked either by the oil tanks scraping together as they were buckled and twisted by the tsunami or by the shorting of broken power lines was dying down as the more volatile fuels burnt out. The outer harbour was oil-covered with only patches still burning, although from the few less-damaged tanks orange tongues of flame still flickered and black smoke spiralled up against the back drop of the Port Hills. The Lyttelton volunteer fire brigade had bravely tried to fight the fires within the inner harbour area but the water mains had been ruptured and their efforts to pump sea water were frustrated by constant blockages caused by debris.

The hardwood piles of the wharves had been blackened by the oil fire although the concrete superstructure had been little damaged. The inner harbour was covered not only with oil but with all manner of flotsam, blackened and for the most part unrecognisable. Except, Tui thought it rather odd, a large white refrigerator bobbing along as it was taken out by the tide.

Tui, as she walked along the waterfront towards what had been the town centre, was astounded by the damage. In fact she thought the lower part of the town where the tsunami had hit was not so much damaged as obliterated.

Above the wharves all was ruin. Houses, shops and hotels in the lower town had probably all been weakened by the initial shockwave and then been swept away by the tsunami. Only the foundations, like gravestones, commemorated where buildings had stood. The blazing red sun setting over the hills at the end of the harbour painted both the wreckage of the town and the still-standing buildings a bloody crimson. The scene reminded Tui of the surrealism of a Salvador Dali painting.

Tui had visited Rapaki and the port of Lyttelton often and knew them well. Both the Royal Hotel and the Mitre and the main area of shops along Norwich Quay had been swept away. Where they had been was a collection of flotsam and jetsam, on a grand scale, including giant pine logs and some railway petrol wagons from the cargo wharf below. The fine old buildings, mainly brick, of the last century, such as the two-storey old Harbour Board building had just vanished. Not even the bricks remained.

On the port side of Sumner Road, parallel with the shoreline, just above the main street, the buildings had also been swept away. On the higher side most of the buildings remained intact although the watch-maker's old brick building had collapsed, the result of the quake, and not the tsunami. Tui assumed that this part of the town was above the ten metres mentioned in the news as the height of the tsunami.

The road tunnel entrance was on about the same level as Sumner Road and the tsunami had been just high enough for some of the wash to surge into the tunnel. Tui learned afterwards that cars and trucks caught in the tunnel had been smashed by the initial impact of the wave and several had been disgorged at the other end. Of those caught in the tunnel there had been no survivors, but fortunately traffic had been light at that early hour.

There was little first aid work that Tui could help with. The burn casualties had been evacuated to Christchurch by helicopter. The Harbour Light Theatre, which stood on the higher side of London Street and had been only slightly damaged by the initial quake was being used as a mortuary and Tui had briefly looked in there to see if she could assist. 'We're through the worst of it,' a St John's ambulance volunteer assured her. 'We're down to a trickle now. Mainly burnt bodies that they're fishing out of the harbour. They'll be turning up for some time. Identification is the problem but we are managing fine, thank you.'

Tui decided that she owed herself a beer or something stronger to bolster her sagging spirits and headed one street up to the Duke of Wellington, which had been her favourite watering hole when she visited Lyttelton. She hoped it was still standing…

Tui recognised him immediately when she entered the bar. She had clambered in over a pile of concrete rubble that had been a façade, part of a modernisation project. The original weatherboarding underneath was still intact although most windows were broken. The bar which was now operating must have been picked up off the floor. It seemed to Tui that most of the survivors from the upper town must have been in the bar. The majority had injuries of some sort. There was standing room only.

He was at the bar, a beer in one hand, the other being used to embellish the account he was giving. Tui pushed through to the bar and finally got in her order: 'DB Draught, a handle will do.'

'Sorry, lady, the tanks in the cellar were all knocked for six. No draught. But some bottles weren't broken and we have plenty of tinnies. A lager do?'

Tui took her lager with her as she shouldered her way through the crowd, all of whom seemed to be retelling, at the top of their voices, their experiences in the quake.

The man she had recognised was a distant Ngai Tahu cousin from Rapaki. They had met on several occasions over the years at family weddings and funerals. As a girl she had had a crush on Hemi Tira-katene. Later whenever she was in Christchurch she would phone him and they had gone out together a few times. He was a very talented sportsman and played golf on a very low handicap. Tui did not admit to him that she could play at all and had been content to act as his caddie. She had to smile when she recalled their golf outings. There she was, a committed feminist, an activist fighting for the rights of Maori women, meekly pushing his trundler or in tournaments actually carrying his bag. Mind you, she grinned, as she looked along the bar at him, he is marvellously handsome. Tall, well-built, with the neck of a front-row forward and black curly hair. With a moko he could be one of our ancestor chiefs. Tui had also been out fishing with him. He held some of the fish quota recently assigned under the Waitangi Treaty settlement to the Ngai Tahu people and fished out of the port of Lyttelton. She had admired his supreme self-assurance when at sea: The way he balanced himself as the swell lifted the boat and the deftness and strength as he brought in the longline and the big hapuku. He was as one with the sea, like our fishermen ancestors, thought Tui; he should have children to carry on the the Ngai Tahu traditions. She was not in the habit of blushing. Feminists and Maori activists don't blush, she told herself, but as she caught Hemi's eye she felt a certain warmth come to her face.

'Kia ora, Tui. Am I glad to see you.' Hemi gave her a bear-hug that took the wind out of her.

'Careful of my lager, may be the last one left. Well, you are looking none the worse for the quake.'

'What are you doing this side of the hill? You weren't here when the wave hit, eh?'

Tui brought him up to date on her movements.

'Thought I might be able to help with the burn casualties. What a terrible thing to happen. The people in the lower part of the town didn't have a chance. You're lucky to have escaped but I suppose your boat got burned with the rest?'

'The sea might be a bit of a bastard but it looks after me. When the quake hit I was miles out to sea. I felt a bit of a bump at the time but nothing much. Just like coming off the top of a wave and coming down with a whack into the trough. Thought it was just a freak wave. Wasn't until I was coming back in up the harbour, eh, and the oil slick and all the rubbish was coming out with the tide that I realised something pretty awful had happened. Mind you, it was all over before I got back.

But although the sea was flat then it was pretty hairy coming up the harbour. There were containers bobbing everywhere. If I'd hit one of them it would have been curtains. Mind you, there were as many pine logs and they were harder to see. A lot of the pleasure boats from the moorings had been torched but many had not sunk and they were drifting out with the tide too. I just missed what I thought was a black submarine when I realised it was one of the railway petrol tankers. It won't be safe to fish out there for months. Lots of burnt bodies. Pulled a few in with my gaff but couldn't do much as I was flat out steering round the rubbish.'

'So your boat is okay, Hemi?' Tui, though genuinely pleased to see Hemi and to know that he was safe, had still, gnawing away in the back of her mind, concern for her relatives in Kaikoura. She had the germ of an idea. After all, they were Hemi's people too.

Road and rail links to Kaikoura were cut: bridges were down, slips would take weeks to clear and Tui knew that along the narrow coast road rocky outcrops would have come crashing down. But why not, thought Tui, use the ancient route taken by our ancestors – by sea. Our ancestor Moki had come that way, from Kaikoura, when he had visited Kaiapoi and after his capture by Te Rauparaha had been taken back that way en route to Te Rauparaha's stronghold on Kapiti Island. In Hemi's fishing boat it would be a breeze, we could do it in a day. I must find out what has happened to my people.

'We must find out what has happened to our people at Kaikoura,' Tui now said aloud and focused her large brown eyes at full aperture on Hemi. Hemi feared nothing, he was the proud descendant of warriors and whether at sea, on the rugby field or on the golf course he was unyielding. But when it came to brown eyes, particularly Tui's, Hemi was like a fat and thirsty pigeon coming to the trap.

'There's no way you – we – could get to Kaikoura.' Hemi had hardly said it when he realised that the noose of the pigeon trap was set. 'Except by sea. And how, my friend, do you propose to go by sea, eh?'

Tui said nothing but opened her eyes another f-stop and smiled. Her smile was the water which lured the thirsty pigeon to put its neck in the noose.

Hemi felt it tighten round his neck. 'Oh, I see – my boat, I suppose?'

'Well, they are your people too and we owe it to them to find out what has happened. There's been no news and the quake and the tidal wave could have been worse there. When can we start?'

'You don't waste any time, do you? I'd need to put some extra fuel on board and in normal circumstances inform the harbour authorities where I was going, but I don't suppose they'd be much interested at the moment. But, I'm not going anywhere until I've had another beer. Same for you?'

The barman was still able to meet the demand but was down to one brand – take it or leave it. No one argued and the mood became even more festive. The warm glow was heightened when in the increasing gloom (even in the undamaged parts of the town power was still out) the barman lit up an old kerosene pressure lamp. Its comforting roar was drowned out in the rising buzz of conversation.

'You rustle up enough grub and tinnies for a day or two and I'll meet you down at the fish wharf in about half an hour.'

As they emerged from the pub, Tui and Hemi were suddenly confronted with the sober realities of their situation. It was pitch dark. There were no street lights. They had no torch. It was only with considerable difficulty that they managed to scramble over the pile of rubble outside the hotel. Tui realised how terribly tired she was. Hemi was suddenly aware that he had set out fishing at four that morning and he could hardly keep his eyes open. He realised that even if they had succeeded in getting down to the fishing wharf it would have been foolhardy to find their way out of the harbour dodging the debris.

Hemi thought they could flag down one of the many cars that seemed to be moving about in the upper town, their headlights cutting swathes of light in the darkness. There was no sign of his own car which he had parked on the fish wharf that morning and he wondered whether, if he located it in the mud of the harbour bottom, it would be worth salvaging. They flagged down a car that seemed to be heading towards Rapaki but the driver assured them the road was still impassable. Hemi took Tui by the hand, not Tui's style to allow this, but at that moment she thought, I don't care a hoot. If he carried me I wouldn't give a damn.

They stumbled up the hill to the home of a Rapaki family, cousins of Hemi, and were warmly welcomed. They refused the offer of food but not makeshift beds. Tui dropped her jeans, remembered struggling out of her sweater, but nothing more until she awoke with the sun streaming in. The smoke had given her a bad taste in her mouth.

Tui, after breakfast, did the rounds of the remaining food shops. She had some difficulty in obtaining even the most basic food supplies for their journey and had to exercise all her wiles to extract a pack of tinnies from the barman at The Grand. She thought it fortunate that there was at least beer if no running water in the port. Whilst at the hotel she had tried again to phone her parents but the lines were still out.

Going down to the fish wharf was still hazardous. Tui tripped and stumbled over debris of every description and when she arrived she found she had been more successful than Hemi. He had been unable to locate any diesel fuel. A few hours before thousands of gallons at the tank farm had gone up in smoke and the diesel tank at the fish wharf had been ruptured. As he explained to Tui, 'There was just no diesel so I decided we'd switch to petrol. Quite a good outboard motor was jammed in the wreckage of the boat shed. Fired at first pull. So I went up the hill to see a cobber who had a few 40-gallon drums of petrol. Made a hell of a racket rolling a drum down here. We'll swing it on board. I've still got one full diesel tank and when we finish that we can hang the outboard out the back.'

'Do you think we can make it?'

'For sure, no sweat, we'll make it. If the worst happens I've a sail I sometimes hoist when I'm longlining. Weather looks okay. Only thing I'm really worried about is that I've got only one bunk. If we're going to be partners in this trip you might have some ideas there.' Tui swung a round-armer but Hemi had boxed at school and weaved out of range.

The inner harbour was surprisingly clear of debris. The outward-flowing night tide had done a good job. But when they went through the moles and into the outer harbour Hemi was called on constantly to alter course to avoid a variety of floating hazards. The giant pine logs which had just yesterday been neatly stacked on the wharf were the greatest threat as they floated low in the water and were difficult to sight. Tui stood in the bow in America's Cup style and indicated with out-thrust arm changes of direction to avoid these objects. Some of the 'objects' had been human beings but were now shrunken, blackened flotsam. All Tui could do was signal to Hemi to avoid them.

As they passed the Heads, Hemi spun the wheel, the boat heeled, and they headed north.

'We're on our way, girl.'

Tui made a mental note to put him right on the 'girl' sometime, but this wasn't the time.

'How long will it take us?'

'If we go in a straight line, it's roughly 100 miles to Kaikoura. This tub cruises best at about 5 knots. So, theoretically, about 20 hours. Mind you, I don't know what sort of speed we can do when we switch to the outboard. But barring mishaps, I would say we could be off Kaikoura peninsula at about five or six tomorrow morning.'

Tui was enjoying the journey. It was a perfect day, a few clouds on the south-west horizon, but otherwise a brilliant blue sky and only the gentlest of swells as they plodded across Pegasus Bay, the coast in sight.

They lunched well on what Tui had been able to glean in Lyttelton. The cans of beer had been put over the stern in a landing net and came up cold and refreshing. Tui was still anxious about the fate of the Kaikoura coast and her people and felt a little guilty that she should be enjoying the company of Hemi so much. He was so assured in all he did. When, at about 8 o'clock, the diesel started to cough and finally cut out, he lifted the outboard on to the stern, gave the fuel line a few pumps, used the manual start and they were under way again.

The sunset was again spectacular. To the north-west they could see the Kaikoura coastal mountains. There were still patches of snow on the higher peaks and these glowed pink then purple as the last rays of the sun reached across from the Main Divide. Tui was content to sit and soak it all in. She sat with Hemi in the stern and she placed her hand on his as he steered, using the tiller on the outboard.

'We both had a pretty rough day yesterday. I suggest we each take a four-hour watch, naval-style, so that the other can get a bit of shut-eye. You remember the problem I mentioned about there being only the one bunk. You might recall you got a bit toey when I didn't offer to share it with you.'

Tui lifted her hand off the tiller and caught Hemi just above his eye.

'Okay, it'll be a bit of a squash, but if you insist.' He held his head and groaned.

Tui leant across the tiller and kissed him. Hemi stopped groaning and transferred his hand to her back. In this way they continued for some time. When they both looked up, the coast was directly astern, and they were heading in the general direction of South America.

'Got to keep our minds on the job, girl.'

'I am not a girl.' This time she administered a sideways kick to his nearer ankle.

Hemi looked at her long and hard. She was wearing her own jeans but one of his shirts, much too large and unbuttoned.

'No, undoubtedly you're not. You can take the first watch until midnight and I'll get some kip. See you then. Don't go to sleep or we'll be on the rocks. Remember, just keep the Southern Cross where it is now and you'll be on the right heading. If you need more fuel just lock off the tiller while you fill up the tank.'

'Aye, aye, Cap'n. Any further orders? I'll have a cup of Milo when you come up at midnight. Sweet dreams. If we're sinking I'll give you a call.'

Hemi kissed her and she did not seem to mind. In fact she made no attempt to end it and Hemi pulled away as he felt the boat start to yaw. If he didn't watch it they could zig-zag all the way to Kaikoura. He looked back at her as he was about to go below and grinned when he saw their wandering course traced by the phosphorescent wake.

Tui enjoyed being alone. The outboard was noisy but after a time she was no longer aware of it and she was automatically making the small adjustments on the tiller necessary to correct their course as they slid from swell to swell. She recalled the events of the day before.

I'm probably sailing right above the fault line that caused it all. A thousand metres down there's a great chasm and at any moment the floor of that chasm could move and within minutes, hundreds, perhaps thousands, of people could die. But then this coast was created by such movements and we are just insignificant specks of life. We think we have control of our lives, but really we are just adapting to the power of nature. We learn how to go with them, the sea, the tides, and not oppose them. But going with the tide doesn't give us the right to sit back and do nothing – to drift. We can change things for the better. We can do positive things like preventing so many of our Maori sisters dying of lung cancer. We've got to exert ourselves:

| He moana pukepuke | A choppy sea |
| e ekengia e te waka | can be navigated |

Tui realised she had been sitting on the hard thwart for almost two hours and stood up and stretched. My bum's bloody sore. She grinned, that's what we've got to do as a people: get off our backsides and take charge of our destiny.

She looked up the coast in the direction of Kaikoura. Her people were now spread widely but many had still been at Kaikoura. Were they still there or had they been swept away? Tui looked at the sea, phosphorescent with myriad plankton. She thought again of the ancient mariner who had witnessed the disaster at Lyttelton Harbour: 'And a thousand thousand slimy things/Lived on; and so did I.' Could I bear to go on living if Kaikoura has been destroyed? She peered towards the land but they were too far out to see any effects on the coast of earthquake or tsunami.

Would life be worth living? Then she thought of Hemi sleeping in the cabin. She decided that life might have something to offer. He and she were of the same blood, Ngai Tahu. She had a duty to conceive children if some of their people were to live through into the next century.

Mm, she mused, perhaps not such an unpleasant duty. She saw Hemi again, legs braced, bare-chested, the sea spray flying as he pulled in the longline.

She was startled, and a little embarrassed at her secret thoughts, when Hemi suddenly materialised in front of her with a steaming mug of Milo.

'Okay, your turn for a snooze. I didn't sleep much. For straight-line sailing we seem to be wandering quite a bit. Doing a bit of tacking, were you?'

'I was doing a bit of thinking and had to make a few corrections but you might note that we are now bang on course. How are we going for time?'

'Well, it's a bit dark but my radar, which is rather primitive, shows that we are past Motunau. There was a blip on the radar screen which could have been the island there. It's hard to believe that 150 years ago, Te Rauparaha and his war canoes came this way too.'

Tui looked towards the coast although it was too dark to see. 'You ever thought there would be more of us Ngai Tahu today if he had not come south? We may find when we come to Kaikoura that there are even fewer of us.' Tears rolled down her cheeks. She still held the tiller. Hemi sat beside her, helped her steer and also thought it his duty to console her. Kissing her seemed the most effective way. The end result was much the same as from their previous embrace, except that now the distance east to Chile or Peru this time was increasing as they headed shoreward at a steady 5 knots for the rocky coast.

Hemi's sea sense again saved them as he realised their course left something to be desired. They came round in a gentle curve and the Southern Cross again twinkled over their stern.

'Off to bed' – he almost said 'girl' but corrected himself – 'wench, before, between the two of us, we wreck the boat.'

Tui was very much in two minds: she wanted to stay with Hemi but the previous day had taken its toll and she was desperately tired. She collapsed into the still-warm bunk and cuddled the pillow and breathed in the male smell of Hemi.

The cloud to the south heralded a change to a southerly wind. Not like the southerly buster that Moki had encountered in his fishing canoe as he had made his ill-fated journey to Kaiapoi. This was just a steady, gentle breeze.

Hemi hoisted the sail he sometimes used when longlining, cut the outboard motor and set his homemade self-steering system.

He realised that as they approached Kaikoura Tui's fears for her people were growing. Again he felt he had a duty to try to console her. In such a situation, he thought, one must also continue to be practical and keep in touch with the realities of the situation. So whilst enjoying his spell of the watch in the bunk he had worked out that with a little adaptation and co-operation two could fit in it. He was sure it would work although he had some doubts as to the extent of Tui's co-operation.

His doubts were completely unfounded. Tui, although not awake, had been dreaming of similar arrangements, and when he slid in alongside her, welcomed him, literally with open arms. They soon came to a mutual agreement as to the best way of conserving the small space they had available. Hemi apologetically whispered in her ear, 'Sorry, the only rubbers I have on board are my gumboots.' Tui was quite pleased to hear this as she had earlier decided that such a splendid example of Maori manhood should have children and in her not so much headstrong as practical way, had decided that she was the most suitable woman to bear them. 'We two are now one,' she giggled, 'not much chance of anything else in this bunk. We must remain together. He totara wahi rua he kai na te ahi (a totara tree split in two is food for the fire). Hemi did not have Tui's command of Maori but as he had been so warmly received, he guessed that what she said was complimentary.

It was an hour or so later that Hemi sensed a slight change in the motion of the boat and thought that they might be approaching too close to the shore. 'Sorry, Tui, but I must go up top and see where we are.' Hemi extricated himself from the embrace of Tui and the bunk with a great deal more difficulty than he had slid in several hours before. Naked, he emerged on deck and surveyed the horizon. The first glimmer of the dawn was reaching out across the sea to capture the land. The boat was close to the rocky coast, closer than Hemi had intended, but, he smiled; the risk was worth it.

The breeze from the south was now fitful and he took down the sail and, although he hated the noise, restarted the outboard motor.

He was soon joined by Tui, also naked. As they stood close together looking towards the coast, its features were gradually revealed in the dawn light. Had the boat been a Maori canoe, it might have been a scene dating back a thousand years.

Hemi pointed to a small island, painted white by sea birds, 'There's Rangi Inu Wai. We're not far from Kaikoura and you can just about make out the peninsula ahead.'

Tui had far from forgotten her concern for her people at Kaikoura but her immediate thoughts were still with Hemi who held her so closely. 'If we married, Hemi, you wouldn't beat me, would you?' Tui looked up at him with an impish grin.

'Why on earth do you ask a question like that? I haven't asked you to marry me yet, you shameless naked woman. The sea is peaceful and the dawn beautiful, why ask that now?'

'Well, that island we're just passing is called Barney's Rock by the locals. Barney Reilly was one of the old-time whalers. He was married to one of our Ngai Tahu women. When he came back from Kaikoura drunk she used to banish him to the island until he was sober. But he used to beat her and the story goes one day he clouted her over the head with a tea-tray and she died. That's why I asked you if you would beat me.'

'As I told you last night there are some things I don't carry on the boat. But if I had a tea-tray on board now I would surely clobber you with it.' He gave her backside a stinging slap instead. That broke the spell: the magic of the Whale Coast, another Eden. Hemi took the tiller while Tui went below and dressed. She then took over the tiller and Hemi went below. She could see the coast more clearly now and it certainly looked different, but in some way she could not place. When

Hemi came back up top she asked him, 'Is it low tide? The island and the rocks look higher out of the water than I remember them. The landmarks are familiar enough but somehow they look different.'

'Yes, you're right, but strangely enough it is closer to high tide than low at this hour. I have never seen the tide so low, even with a spring tide. Look at the kelp, it seems to be hanging way out of the water.

They left the rocky coastline behind as they crossed South Bay and headed to round Kaikoura peninsula. Hemi pointed towards the beach.

'Coast looks unchanged here by the earthquake, but look up the Kowhai river bed above the lagoon at its mouth, at least one span of the road bridge is down.'

The outboard chose that moment to splutter and die. No amount of coaxing and swearing by Hemi as he pulled the starting rope would induce it to fire. 'Plug fouled, I suppose. We're out of diesel too so I'll have to hoist the sail. That's a nor'wester starting to blow now so we'll have to tack out to sea to give us some sea room.'

 When they had been closer to the coast Tui thought that so far the damage to the Whale Coast had not been as great as she had feared. It looked as if the damage to holiday cottages and the whale watch base in South Bay may not have been too bad but it was hard to see details at that distance. Again she had the impression that the sea seemed further out. The limestone reefs and rock stacks seemed much higher, or had the sea withdrawn? But she would know the worst in a few minutes when they rounded the peninsula and would see the township, or however much of it remained. The limestone wave-cut platforms, testimony of earlier, ancient earthquakes, extending out from the peninsula were also standing higher out of the sea than Tui had ever remembered seeing at the lowest of low tides. The cliffs of the peninsula had obviously taken a battering from the quake as all the way along Tui could see the stark whiteness of freshly exposed limestone.

The wave-cut benches were so much higher that they had to round the peninsula much further out to sea than Tui could recall doing on previous fishing trips. It was very strange and Tui feared what might confront them when they came round the peninsula to its north side.

It was not until now she realised they had not sighted any whales. Normally along the route they had followed they would have sighted at least one whale sounding or blowing. Inati, she thought, a bad omen of what has happened to Kaikoura.

The rocky outcrops on which the seals sunned themselves were high and dry. The seals had now taken up station on rocks that had emerged some 100 metres further seaward.

The old Fyffe House and the wharf came into view. Tui couldn't believe her eyes. The wharf now stood five or six metres higher above sea level than previously and according to Hemi it was now high tide. They were now turning into the northern bay and Tui prepared herself to see the extent of the damage.

The old Fyffe House had lost a wall on the seaward side but Tui was amazed to see any part of the house still there. But incredibly the house, in relation to the sea, was now also five or six metres higher than it had been. Tui turned to Hemi. 'Is the land that much higher or has the sea gone back?' Hemi had spent much of his life at sea but this was something outside his experience.

'Well, it's supposed to be high tide so the land must have come up. I don't know – but I suppose we measure the height of the land as above sea level, so…' he trailed off.

The old slipway where the whalers had dragged up the whales for flensing was now at least 100 metres from the sea.

'Look at the wharf. Oh, my God, there's no water there. We can't land there.' Their keel scraped a rock but they were almost a hundred metres from the wharf alongside which Hemi had many a time tied up.

'This was deep water. The sea can't go down?' Hemi made this more a question than a statement. 'The land must've come up.'

Tui thought, well, the tsunami couldn't have been as bad here as at Lyttelton, thank God. The seaward side of the fishing factory is pushed in. And the old wooden Pier Hotel has every window smashed. It has certainly taken a push sideways. Looks like some of Tangaroa's work. But it's not as bad as I feared.

'Toitu whenua – the land remains!'

Hemi was still shaking his head and looking at the wharf high and dry, and wondering where they could land. He was still trying to work out what had happened.

Tui also was wondering why the tsunami had apparently caused less damage here than when it had roared up Lyttelton Harbour. Kaikoura had been closer to the earthquake epicentre and the tsunami should have been higher here, and therefore more destructive.

They both hit on the answer at the same time.

'That's it,' declared Hemi. 'Simple. A six-metre tidal wave but the land had already been pushed up six metres by the quake. Net result: no contest. There must have still been a pretty big wave but it met a coast that had been uplifted by the same amount.'

'You're right, Hemi. It's just like the big Napier quake. I remember Dad telling me about it. He wasn't born then. Must have been early 1930s but his father had been there and told him about it. Hundreds were killed but that earthquake must have been like this one as the water in the harbour there just receded as the land came up. Thousands of acres of new land came up out of the ocean.'

They were sailing briskly across the northerly breeze parallel with the newly formed beach. Hemi turned the boat inshore and drove it on to the shingle beach. Kaikoura town had always had a narrow strip of steeply shelving beach and boasted a coastal road grandly called 'The Esplanade' but now the beach extended out another 100 metres. Some rocky outcrops which had previously not broken the surface, even at the lowest of tides, now stood high on the new beach.

The great variety of seaweeds, sea anenomes and black mussels exposed by the receding sea, even after only one day in the hot summer sun, had begun to putrefy and gave off a smell that reminded Tui of her school holidays spent at the beach.

Hemi pushed his boat back into the water and ran an anchor up the beach with sufficient slack to allow for the falling tide. He found it hard to believe that the newly created beach would be even more extensive at low tide. He and Tui started up the beach. The sea lettuce and other sea weeds made it slippery under foot.

'Hold on, Tui. Look what we have here.' Large, quite deep pools were contained within the rock outcrops. Hemi had caught a glimpse of a flash of red. He kicked off his gumboots and jumped into the waist-deep pool and within minutes had thrown flapping onto the beach shingle, three small crayfish.

'You little beauties. We haven't had any breakfast, Tui, and there it is. They must have got stranded when the land popped up and the sea receded.'

'You can have your crayfish but I'm going up to the town to see what the damage is. It looks as if our people in the marae on the top of the peninsula should be fine but I'd like to know how Harata and the others on the lower ground made out.' She stumbled on up the beach.

Hemi took a closer look at his crayfish, found one was a female with eggs, held it firmly by the back as it continued to flap frantically, took it down to the sea and released it tail first so that it was able to flap itself into deeper water. 'Well, that's your share, sea, now I'm having mine.'

He pulled his boat in and rummaged around in the stern locker until he found a half drum and his gas cooker. He cleared away some sea lettuce and dug his cooker into the beach shingle. In no time he had the drum filled with salt water and when it was boiling he threw in the crayfish.

Tui had reached The Esplanade and, although shocked by the extent of the damage in the town, thought it could have been worse. She was saddened to see the pile of stone that had been the Anglican church she had attended on most Sundays when her family had lived in Kaikoura. At least, she thought, there would have been no one inside it at that time of the morning.

She flagged down a passing taxi. The roads were fissured, but a grader had obviously been along to push debris, including great heaps of seaweed, to the side of the road and fill in the worst of the cracks. The roads were apparently usable. The taxi-driver had a fare but promised he would return in quarter of an hour to take Tui out to Harata's farm on the flat. He was able to tell her that there had been some loss of life, mainly tourists, who had been struck by the falling walls as they tried to leave their hotel and that there had been some flooding with a larger than normal wave but he considered the residents had suffered worse floods from local rivers. Tui experienced some pangs of guilt at feeling relieved that the local residents had been largely spared the devastation that had struck Lyttelton. She didn't know whether to laugh or cry and ended up doing both.

She returned to Hemi on the beach. He was prodding his crayfish with a piece of driftwood. As he pushed them a grey scum bubbled to the surface. At that time of the morning with the sun just coming out of the sea Tui found the smell nauseating.

'Do you have to do that now?

Hemi hooked the red and steaming crayfish out on to the beach shingle and with much blowing on hands and 'ooing' and 'ouching' broke off some legs and cracked them open for the pink meat inside.

'Best part, you know.'

'You are disgusting, Hemi. You should be showing some respect here. This area of the beach is tapu, this is where Te Rauparaha feasted on our ancestors after he sacked our pa. You can't eat your crayfish here.'

Hemi just grinned. 'Well Tamatea the Pokai Whenua cooked himself a feed here five hundred years ago. If it was okay for him, then I can eat here. Anyway, where we're standing now would have been deep water then.' He dug his gumboot into the beach shingle. 'This has never been coast before.' With a defiant flourish he pulled off a tail, tore off some of the white flesh, thrust it into his mouth with his fingers and, with some exaggeration for Tui's benefit, chewed contentedly and rolled his eyes.

'This is really something, Tui. Do you realise this would cost twenty or thirty bucks in the States?' He patted his stomach. 'You want to change everything, Tui, and put the clock back. You've got to accept what the world is today. You've got to make up your mind whether you're living in the twentieth century or are still clinging to the past of your ancestors. It's one thing or the other, you can't have both.' Hemi continued chewing, warming to his subject. It was not often, he thought, that he got the opportunity to lecture Tui. The boot was usually on the other foot but she was unusually quiet.

'The past and the future don't exist. It's only now that is real and we've got to enjoy what we've got today. If the sea leaves behind a feed of crayfish and all I have to do is pick them up, then I grab the opportunity.'

Tui, during the morning, had run through the full gamut of emotions. She knew she loved Hemi, and had made love with him on the boat. She had been sick with fear imagining the fate of their people living in Kaikoura. This fear had been replaced with joy and thankfulness that through some miracle they had been spared. Now her blood boiled at Hemi's actions and words.

'You are all belly, Hemi. A real pukunui.' When angry, Tui found some Maori words more expressive. 'I'm going back up the beach in a few minutes to go up the hill to the marae to check out our people and then out to see that Harata is okay. I'm sure they're all right but I've come all this way and I want to be certain. The taxi will be back for me in about a quarter of an hour so in that time, before I go, and I may not come back, you and I have some things to sort out. That's if you think we might have a future together.

'You say I've got to choose between the past, the traditions of our ancestors, and the present, the modern world. That's the pakeha way of looking at things. It's the way our politicians carry on. They tell us we've got to choose one extreme or the other. For them it's all one or all the other. My mother encouraged me to look at all possibilities. Not to judge and not to condemn but to challenge the so-called accepted truths, then to move forward with the most useful and fulfilling ideas. If that's a bit of a mouthful, put simply, I think I can take the best of Maori values and the best of pakeha.'

Hemi had stopped chewing his crayfish.

'That might have been all right for your mother, Tui, but women...'

'Don't scoff at our women, Hemi. Maori women have always been at the forefront of initiative and development. You remember the saying, "Without women and land, men will perish"? In Maori society before the pakeha colonists, Maori women had a complementary role alongside men.'

Hemi tossed away the empty crayfish shell. 'Look, I do know something about this, Tui. On the marae women count for damn all, they don't have a say.'

'That's absolute bullshit, Hemi. You Maori men stuffed things up when you bought into a Victorian colonial system. We women spoke, and still speak, on the marae through karanga, tangi and waiata. Your macho image has got in the way of your wairua growing up. But never mind, we're strong enough to take you men along with us.'

'Bloody decent of you, Tui. But Maori men are also contributing something to a Maori revival.' He touched the bone carving at Tui's neck. 'Look at the revival in carving. What about the wood carving they're doing right here in Kaikoura? You've got to admit too that Maori men did a fair whack to win back some of our fishing rights. I'm grateful to them for my fish quota,' he gave a rueful laugh, 'although at the rate we are depleting fish stocks I don't know how long I'll still be fishing.'

'Well, that's the whole point, Hemi. Pakeha society's main objective is in profit, turning your crayfish into dollars. That's what colonialism was all about, along this coast, making a profit, no matter what the real cost. It was the same motive whether hunting whales to extinction or turning our forest and tussock land into sheep and wool and eroded gullies. On the other hand, the Maori sought to sustain resources, such as seafood. But what I am saying, Hemi, is that we can take the best of both the cultures whose blood runs in our veins.'

Tui shook her head, 'But it would be a tragedy if we were left with the worst features of both. We can have modern tourism without damaging the environment and spoiling our still empty places. Look out there,' she pointed beyond the peninsula, 'we've got all that beauty, and the whales, and we can use them for a tourist industry. If we go about it the right way we can make a living and retain our clean, green land. And we can achieve this not by capitalism, which sets people against each other, but by using our Maori way of doing things – owning and doing things together – sharing and taking collective responsibility.'

'Hemi,' she took both his hands in hers. He had given up on his crayfish and was trying to take in with open-mouthed amazement what Tui was saying. This was a side of her he had not seen before, it was certainly a different person from the one who had meekly towed his golf trundler.

It was still too early for many of the people of Kaikoura to be up and about. It must have made a strange sight in the early morning to see Tui and Hemi arguing on an empty beach that had not been there the day before. They would have been seen by some of the townspeople who must have peeped out under their blinds to check if the events of yesterday had really happened. The newly raised beach was still there, the sun brilliantly lighting, like a stage backcloth, the Seaward Kaikoura mountains behind.

Tui felt that for her too, like the recently raised beach on which they stood, it was a new beginning. She had been supported by her whanau to enable her to go to university, although she still had to waitress and take a string of part-time jobs to get herself through her degree and she now felt obliged to take others of her people with her along the path of education. And those 'others' of her iwi certainly included this impressive hunk of manhood who stood facing her now.

And what are we going to do without men, Tui asked herself. She did not have a high regard for a good many Maori men in general. She considered few able to match their women in strength of mind and emotional development. Some of the older Maori men she knew were hypocrites, bashing up women then hiding behind being elders and speaking on the marae about the importance of the house of man – the womb of woman. But Tui felt that now, on this newly born beach, she had been given the opportunity to hold out a hand to Hemi so that they could travel into the future together.

I'll drag him along kicking and yowling after me into the twenty-first century if I have to but I've got to get through to him now, now, on this beach or now, we separate. I stay here in Kaikoura and he returns. Tui glanced at her watch, in less than eight minutes the taxi should be back. I've got to make sure he knows the direction that he and I and our people have to take if we and our children are going to have any sort of future worth having.

'We've got a lot going for us, Hemi. The ancestors of both of us were pakeha and Maori. The differences in the cultures don't matter, we can take the best of both. And we can provide for change, things don't have to be set in concrete. I don't know how to put it but perhaps it's a softer 'water' approach to solving problems I'm looking for. Perhaps it's more a woman's, and a Maori woman's way of thinking. For God's sake look at that ABC of tyranny: Albania, Bosnia, Croatia. There you've got grey-haired, grey-faced men, men of different 'tribes' arguing, using men's logic, about things that happened hundreds of years before. Where is that getting them? In a bloody sight bigger pickle, while women and children suffer and die. If we use something of the mana of our wahine, the strength of our older women, and listen to them, our kuia, we can do better in this part of the world.'

The sun was now well up. The sea sparkled and a gentle northerly breeze ruffled its surface. The limestone cliffs of the peninsula glistened. Hemi looked across the bay to the haze of the dark green bush-clad Puhipuhi valley. The Seaward Kaikoura mountains looked close enough to touch. This coast and this woman are what I want out of life.

Hemi, unlike Tui, thought mainly in English, but now 'tongarewa', a Maori word, the most precious of greenstone, came to mind. What I have here is worth more than that. And while I'm dreaming, this, if it didn't stink so much of fish, is a chief's red-feathered cloak, a kahu kura, and he wrapped his oil-stained yellow boat jacket around Tui. Although the morning was now warmer, Tui made no protest and snuggled into it under his arm. Hemi looked down at her: she's undoubtedly a clever one, a proper wananga. Can't think of the Maori word for 'rebel', but she's a real Bolshie, a loony lefty but with her, life would certainly not be dull.

Tui had been more successful in holding out a hand to Hemi than she had realised.

Hemi would have preferred to continue just holding her without speaking, but almost without meaning to, he spoke his thoughts.

'You say differences don't matter, what of those between man and woman?'

'Yes, my love, they are important. I'll answer your question this way.

'I have always spoken Maori, you have picked up some. You understand English better. But you appreciate that our reo, our language, is the very basis of our being Maori, although it's a damn shame so few of us can speak it. What I was going to say was, you know our word 'tona': it means "him" or "her", there's no sex differentiation. We don't get hung up on the differences in sex, as the French seem to do in their language. With us, male and female are not in conflict although they can strike sparks, hika ahi off each other, as we showed last night on the boat.' Tui giggled as her mood again changed and she snuggled further under Hemi's coat. 'That bunk was pretty hard though.'

Hemi thought of their boat journey the previous night and looked towards the sea. The falling tide had almost stranded his boat and they both, carefully picking their way over what had so recently been the sea floor, returned to it and pushed it out again to float.

He returned Tui to his boat jacket as they watched the fishing boat move out with the tide. She looked at her watch. Five minutes before the taxi returned. Would she stay in Kaikoura or return with Hemi in his boat to Christchurch?

As they looked out to sea the steep-sterned outline of a large fishing trawler broke the horizon, heading north. Hemi shaded his eyes. 'Must have been out there before the earthquake. Probably Russian or Korean. I think it is a terrible mistake, you know, to be selling off our fish to foreign trawlers, even if they are joint enterprise. Only a few big investors and accountants seem to be getting anything out of it.'

'All the people who came to this coast made mistakes, Hemi. They treated the coast badly; our Maori ancestors were not blameless either. The moa hunters, even before the arrival of the Ngai Tahu, burnt, either by accident or design, much of the forest and they were not the great conservationists they've been made out to be. They wiped out all the moas. The whalers in their turn hunted the whales almost to extinction, and the sheepmen further burned and overgrazed the hill and high country so that much of it was so eroded as to be worthless. They all treated the land and sea of this coast badly. The Irish settlers hated the flax swamps that meant so much to our people and drained and cleared them. The English were impatient to turn our forests into grass. The rape of land and sea has continued. Do you see the great shoals of kahawai we used to see when we went out fishing as children? No, they've been rounded up by spotter planes and captured in purse-seine nets to make into fish fingers or garden manure. Would you believe they've come up with a scheme to put barbs into some of our whales at Kaikoura and attach underwater cameras to them? Technology is outstripping our ability to think wisely about how we are going to use our land and sea for the best in the long-term – we should perhaps listen to our old people more.' Hemi bent and kissed her but she was not to be put out of her stride so easily.

'We've made a start by thinking differently about how we can use our environment sensibly and retain it. What we are doing with whale watching is a good example. The whales are still there after we've watched them. Sure, we're using them but in a well-controlled way. We can have a good way of life but not at the expense of the environment. Do you realise, Hemi, that between us, Maori and pakeha, we have brought about the extinction of something like fifty birds in this land of ours? They're gone forever. We've got to stop that. We're doing something to save endangered species. But we've got to do better or we also destroy ourselves. We've got a long way to go.'

Staying within his arms and coat, Tui led him down to the water's edge. The tide was now half-way out, and after each gentle surge the sea fell back from the land. Both were barefooted and the ripples washed over their feet.

'Differences don't matter, in themselves, Hemi, but we must understand them. Their meeting can create something splendid. You as a fisherman see land and sea as opposites and in conflict. But the life of this Kaikoura coast; the swirling kelp, the fish, that crab,' as she nudged one with her toe, 'the seals, the whales, we people of Ngai Tahu, the interaction along this line between land and sea,' she dragged her toe along the beach sand and shingle leaving a groove, 'has given us all life. But in our lives one day more is one day less. Our footprints and this mark here in the sand will last until the next tide and then they'll be gone. So it will be for us – "We disappear but the land remains – Whata ngarongaro he tangata, toitu ha whenua." '

The taxi on the Esplanade tooted its horn.

Tui giggled. 'Back to reality. Getting a bit serious there, eh? The trouble is we work everything out and then emotions get in the way – like greed and love.' She stretched on her toes and kissed Hemi on the black stubble under his chin.

'I'm going now to check on the others but I'm sure they'll be okay.'

She slipped and slithered her way up the newly created beach to the waiting taxi.

Hemi squatted on the beach, picked up a smooth, white, rounded stone that had been formed from life, land and sea some sixty million years before and skipped it across the shallows. Each successive skipping ring spread to touch another, the first had disappeared before the last was formed.

Hemi looked further out to sea where the offshore chasms of the Whale Coast plunged from the light of the day to the blackest depths.

If emotion prevails, he thought, I might be lucky, she could come back.

Fact or fiction?

This is a work of fiction but readers may be interested in how much is factual.

First, for overseas readers who have not visited the 'Whale Coast' and watched the whales there, let me assure them that the township of Kaikoura and this wonderful coast do exist.

The raids of Te Rauparaha from Kapiti Island in the north on the southern Ngai Tahu Maori are factual but Moki and his family are fictional characters. I am indebted to my good friend Harold Thomas, who now lives at Waikanae, opposite the site of Te Rauparaha's pa on Kapiti Island, who is a descendant of both Ngai Tahu Maori and Welsh surveyor Captain Joseph Thomas who surveyed Christchurch and Canterbury, for re-awakening my interest in Te Rauparaha's raids. My earlier interest as a student had first been kindled by Roger Duff, then Director of the Canterbury Museum, striding up and down on the earthwork remains of the sacked Kaiapoi (Kaiapohia) pa, brandishing a greenstone mere, and recounting the story of its sacking. Ngai Tahu people captured earlier at Kaikoura by Te Rauparaha did spend some years as slaves on Kapiti Island and some survivors did return to Kaikoura.

Details of shore whaling along this coast from the late 1830s are based on firsthand accounts by those early whalers.

In the 1860s Irish families did settle the Kaikoura swamp, which became a little Ireland, known locally as 'Donegal Flat'. I am indebted for details of the life of my fictional Irish settlers to a family history of the Boyd family, who did come from Donegal.

Wool was exported from Kaikoura as early as 1849 and I introduce a fictional English family of the 'squattocracy' of that time. In fact, the Bullen family from Somersetshire, for example, in 1875 held a house-warming party at 'The Elms' for their Kaikoura friends, to celebrate the construction of their garden-surrounded, two-storey concrete house of eighteen rooms.

For the picture of sheep station life at this time I am very indebted to the letters of Lady Barker. The great snow storm of 1867 and the great flood of 1868 actually occurred.

As in every district throughout New Zealand, there is a war memorial in Kaikoura. The names I have put on mine are fictitious, but the archways formed by whale bone ribs in the memorial gardens do exist.

The main character of this narrative is the coast but the whale has a supporting role and appears in every chapter.

I was able to draw on accounts remembered from my own parents and grandparents to flesh out some details of the Depression years.

For the chapter on the activities of the local Kaikoura Home Guard during World War Two I was able to source little Kaikoura material. However the New Zealand army orders quoted (under Order No. 261) were actual and I imagined, with some help from my own limited army experience, how the local Home Guardsmen may have responded to these. Major-General Young did command the Home Guard and the story of the elderly soldier is his.

The chapter on whale watching brings us to the present day and I am grateful to Chairman of Directors, Mr Bill Solomon of Whale Watch Kaikoura Limited, the community trust owned by the Maori people of Kaikoura in partnership with their affiliated tribal people, the Ngai Tahu, for providing me with information on their operation. However, as this is a work of fiction, the view of whale watching today is mine.

The final chapter might have returned the Kaikoura coast to where it had begun, beneath the sea, but fiction allows a happier ending. I have taken the realities of a severe earthquake from accounts of the major earthquakes of Napier (1931) and more recently Edgecumbe (1987) and imagining a somewhat greater shock, applied these sometime in the future, to the Kaikoura coast and the cities of Wellington and Christchurch.

My scraper-board illustrations are intended to reinforce the realities on which the fictitious story is based.

In 1948 I wrote a thesis on the geography of the Kaikoura coast as a requirement for a master's degree from the University of Canterbury. The University's motto is 'Ergo tua rura manebunt', and so your lands remain, and this maxim more fittingly in Maori provides the theme for this historical novel of the 'Whale Coast'.

Glossary

aha (flesh saw)
aka (bush vine)
ariki (paramount chief)
aroha (love)
ataahua wahine (elegant woman)
atahu (love charms)
atua (gods)
hapu (subtribe)
hapuku (groper)
hika ahi (make fire)
hopu (catch)
imu tua (front notch or scarf side)
inati (bad omen)
io (God)
iwi (tribe)
ka tahu (light up)
kahu kura (a chief's red-feathered cloak)
kahurangi (blue)
kai moana (food of the sea)
kainga (unfortified villages)
kaitahutahu arikinui (a commander of tribal warriors)
kaitangata (human flesh)
karanga (call)
kaunoti (lower grooved stick in firemaking)
kererereu (pigeon)
ko (digging sticks)
koeaea (butterfish)
kohanga reo (language nest school)
koura (crayfish)
kuia (old people)
kumukumu (a red fish)
kuru (ear ornaments)
mana (prestige)

marae (central meeting area)
moko (tattoo)
mootekoko takahore (immodest naked person)
muka (flax fibre)
ngaru taitoku (tidal wave)
niho manga (barracouta tooth knife)
pa (fortified village)
pa tuwatawata (great fortified stronghold)
pataka (food storehouse)
patu (club)
piioi (song)
poa (bait)
poho (bosom)
pokaiwhenua (pioneer rover)
potiki (runt)
pounamu (greenstone)
pouwhenua (long club
puku (belly)
pukunui (glutton)
Rangi Inu Wai (the water drinking place of Rangi)
raoa (top strakes)
Raukawa (Cook Strait)
raupo (rush)
roimata (tears)
taiaha (spears)
takakau (straw)
tangata whenua (local people)
tangi (lament)
taniwha (water monster)
tapu (forbidden)
Te Ahi Kaikoura (the fireplace for cooking crayfish food)
Te Ika a Maui (the North Island)
Te Wai Pounamu (the South Island)
tikitiki (top knot)
toa (expert)
tohunga (priest)
tohunga ta moko (tattoo priest)
toki pou tangata (the adze that establishes a man in authority)

tongarewa (greenstone treasures)
toto (blood)
Tu (god of war)
tuna (eel)
umu (stone oven)
utu (revenge)
waiata (song)
waiata tangi (lament)
wairua (spirit)
atua toro (visiting god)
waka taua (war canoe)
whakapapa (family tree)
wananga (wise person)
whaiaipo (love)
whanau (family)
Whakaraupo (Lyttelton)
whare (house)
whare tangata (the house of man – the womb of woman)

References

For those readers wanting further information on the 'Whale Coast', some of the main sources consulted by the author are listed here.

Barker, Lady, *Station Life in New Zealand*, McMillan, 1870.
Belich, J., *Making Peoples*, Penguin Press, 1996.
Best, E., *The Pa Maori*, 1927 and others.
Boyd M., *From Donegal to Blackguards Corner*, Boyd, 1992.
Brailsford, B., *The Tattooed Land*, Reed, 1981.
Brown, Amy (ed.), *Mana Wahine*, Reed, 1995.
Buck, Sir Peter, *The Coming of the Maori*, Maori Fund Board, 1949.
Buick, T., *Te Rauparaha*, Capper Press, 1976.
Elvy W., *Kaikoura Coast*, Hundalee Scenic Board, 1949.
Evison, H., *Te Wai Pounamu: the Greenstone Island*, Aoraki Press, 1993.
Harris J., *Tohora, The Story of Fyffe House*, NZHP Trust, 1994
Morton H., *Recollections of Early NZ*, Whitcombe and Tombs, 1925.
NZ Army, *Home Guard Manual*, 1941.
Orbell, M., *The Natural World of the Maori*, 1985.
Rhodes, Capt. W.B., *The Whaling Journal of*, Whitcome & Tombs, 1954.
Sherrard, J.M., *Kaikoura, A History of the District*, Christchurch, Kaikoura County Council, 1966.
Stevens, G., *Prehistoric New Zealand*, Reed, 1995.